To Mom, Dad, and Rach,
who see the world with heart and humor
and mean everything to me

I would be displeased and scared shitless if my little girl started talking about wanting to be a chef. I guess it could be worse. She could talk about wanting to go OUT with a chef.

—*Anthony Bourdain,* Daily Blender, *March 2010*

CONTENTS

Introduction

Let's be honest. I am not one of those food-obsessed people. I *like* food. But I am just as happy with a Pop-Tart from Costco as a tarte tatin from Paris. I don't plan trips around the Tomatina tomato fight or street meat in Sri Lanka. My dreams are without rack of lamb, ramen rituals, or Eric Ripert.

Until recently, I thought truffle shavings had something to do with chocolate, that escarole was escargot, and that sweetbread was, well, sweet bread. My best birthdays involve Carvel, not Bouchon. And even at the world's best steak house, I am most excited by a clean baked potato and a dirty-minded man, not Kobe, Wagyu, or whatever.

My last meal would be a pastrami sandwich followed by an entire jar of Nutella, not a night at the French Laundry washed down with a bottle of Chateau d'Yquem. I can't even pronounce "Chateau d'Yquem"! And speaking of which, I am absolutely fine with crappy, even corked, wine. As long as it doesn't taste like poison and it does make me feel like Penelope Cruz.

Of course I do have some standards—I am not a barbarian or an Olive Garden goer—but I was not, as some might say, *born to eat*. It is not my raison d'être. Gluttony is my least favorite sin. If you were to see me perched on the floor of a bookstore in

Brooklyn, I'd be rolling around in druggie memoirs and prison tales, not Julie, Julia, or Jamie Oliver.

It feels liberating to confess that I once thought "kale" was the name of a rock band, that the Ladurée luxe *macaron* was the same as Passover's canned macaroon, and that a growler involved a kinky bedroom, not a nice, cold beer. Five bucks' worth of Manchego at New York's legendary Murray's Cheese is not my idea of a cheap thrill, nor is an afternoon of foraging, pickling, or preserving. I'm afraid, Alton Brown, that the etymology of cheddar, chard, and chanterelles cannot keep my attention for all the El Bulli–like experiences in the world. Oh, and I'd sooner discuss unwanted hairs than the meaning of umami.

To some people, food can be better than sex. I am categorically not one of them. No food tastes as good as a great kiss, as far as I'm concerned. I'll go even further: no food tastes as good as watching *Little Miss Sunshine* in my sweatpants, getting a Thai massage for ten dollars, reading a juicy book on a long train, finishing a spin class without cheating, listening to "Empire State of Mind" while walking the Brooklyn Bridge, or unhooking my bra after a hard day's work.

Alas, I am sorry to admit that I have had *many* pleasures that far exceeded even the most celestial meal. It's just that those pleasures didn't change my life. Something else did—something sweet, savory, and salty . . . and oftentimes unattractive, overcooked, and underseasoned. The truth is I was accidentally anchored by the apron. It happened "organically," as in childhood dreams and crazy love, not farm-to-table and Alice Waters. But then again, this is my story about all of that.

I.

Raised by Drake's

Every morning of my life, my mother has eaten a packaged Devil Dog for breakfast.

She dunks it into milky tea while skimming the *New York Times,* glancing at *Good Morning America,* and preparing for a day of real estate domination. Her "Devils" have been her mimosas, her morning stretch, her sun salutations, and her beloved first lick-of-the-lips for nearly sixty years. She brings them everywhere, from early morning meetings to trips around the world, stashed in leather briefcases, burlap bags, and woolly blazers. She buys them in bulk, hides them from the family (as if anyone would steal her dry, wannabe whoopie pies), and writes letters to the CEO of Drake's when the taste or texture is "not quite right." She is, after all, a full-blown Virgo.

It's an endearing, yet deranged, quirk of hers. Especially if you know my mother. She doesn't drink alcohol, eat fast food, or engage in anything else that would piss off Michael Pollan. She religiously consumes at least five pieces of fruit, along with a small village of raw vegetables (all locally grown, of course), every single day. It's not unusual to find her walking home from the farmers' market blissfully biting into a glistening red pepper or a fat head of purple cabbage, the way one would a huge frosted cupcake. Lunch for her involves fresh eggs, nice cheese, crispy toast, or some peasantlike variation of such, and dinner is light and often vegetarian. My mother listens so carefully and respectfully to her body and its needs, she's never had any issues with her weight or health. If you can get past her dirty little habit, you might even call her a purist.

Being a locavore with a Devil Dog addiction isn't the only trait that makes my mother, and by extension, my entire family, a bit idiosyncratic. My younger sister, Rachel, and I grew up in Longmeadow, Massachusetts, a bucolic town where do-gooder Irish and wealthy WASP intersect. As funny, touchy-feely, free-thinking Jews, we never quite belonged in either category, but we liked our uniqueness and had a lot of friends. It's not like we were mouth-breathing, worm-collecting weirdos; we were just a little offbeat.

For nursery school, my parents sent me to a New Age program at the Unitarian church, where I ate carob all day and splatter-painted my dreadlocked teacher's Volkswagen Bug. When I was five years old, my mother took us to a production of *Hair,* a mirage of music, revolution, and raw penis; we gave it a standing ovation. By third grade, I wrote screenplays, confessionals, and fan letters to reporters at the *New York Times.* I played Suzuki-method violin and picked up the bassoon because it was so awkward and oafish that I felt bad for it. I acted and danced, atrocious at both, but nonetheless, I was passionate about all my hobbies. I was also wild about shag haircuts, redecorating my room, and winning limbo contests. Naturally, I held several lucrative tag sales, a biannual backyard art installation, and weekly fashion shows of jelly bracelets and bandannas. Everyone loved me or hated me, and so it would go.

But I was prone to trouble, too. At seven years old, I traumatized my parents by disappearing at the mall, only to be found on the lower level, giving an interview about shopping trends to the local TV news. (A few years later, at the same mall, I swiped Chanel No. 5 from Lord & Taylor and got arrested.) At age eight, a rotten friend convinced me to fake my own neighborhood kidnapping . . . which got way out of hand, and I felt bad about it forever. Around fourth grade, a rude boy called some new girl a "fat slut" and I slugged him in the stomach, getting me sent home immediately. Around that time, I practically forced our neighbor's teenage son to whip it out and then pee in a Coke can, which I couldn't *not* tell the world about, branding the poor kid a "sick-perv" to the gossips on the block. And even before I could spell "adolescence," I was obviously caught in some filthy rounds of the game Doctor.

The thing that kept me on the side of sensible, even as a young kid, was that I required an absurd amount of stimulation, followed by an absurd amount of personal space. A writer from the womb, I kept countless journals about life, death, and dreamy boys—all of equal importance. Some thoughts were so dark that I should have been committed; others were so frivolous that I could have been on *The Hills*. But there was always that duality: writer with a heavy heart, and wild child with a stethoscope on her crotch.

I definitely didn't get the badass in my bloodstream from my dad. Edward Shelasky is a gentle, easygoing, law-abiding citizen. He's a simple Red Sox–rooting, Monopoly-playing, Seinfeld-loving "Masshole," and the youngest of three children from the lovely and successful couple Milton and Dorothy Shelasky, my grandparents. The Shelaskys had a third-generation uniform business (which my father eventually took over), and they raised him to be quiet, warm, and understanding. In other words, the perfect father to two dramatic daughters. My sister and I may idolize my mom, but we feel as equally blessed to have the world's most attentive father, who played with us as kids and listens to us as adults. Both Milton and Dorothy passed away before I turned thirteen, but I adored them so, and I can still taste my grandmother's luscious brisket and my grandfather's stash of frozen Snickers. They were wonderful grandparents . . . even if they always suspected my mother to be a crazy, hippie, gypsy freak.

Laurie Temkin Shelasky, my mom, comes from a struggling, salt-of-the-earth family. True survivors. Her loving father, Lazar Temkin, was a good but complicated man. He died when she and her five siblings were children. Along with my wise, beautiful, ever-resilient grandmother, Dorothy Pava, the Temkin children had many hardships and tragedies, but they survived through endless laughter and fierce loyalty to each other. My aunts, uncles, and cousins are always the first to have my back and are fully responsible for the one thing I know to be true in life—that family is everything. They may not be perfect, but there aren't better people than the loud, lawless, rambunctious, rough-around-the-edges Temkins.

The Temkins also have a contagious secret language. "P.T." is shorthand for "poor thing," like people born without faces, or my shy sister who threw up on every school field trip. "O.D.D." stands for "odd," but dangerously so, like the Unabomber or Octomom. "N.G." is "no good," like my friend who made me fake the kidnapping. And my favorite is the family motto, borrowed from *The Big Lebowski:* "Sometimes you eat the bear, and sometimes the bear eats you." This has evolved into any one of us screaming, "I ate the freakin' bear!" or "Bear Stew!" whenever something goes our way. And for the Temkins, *that* isn't every day.

One time, as a kid visiting New York, I was on the bus with my mother when a bloated man in Burberry, complete with croissant in his beard and crust in his eyes, yelled at me for resting my pocketbook on an unused seat. Mind you, the entire bus was empty except us. "Were you raised by wolves, you stupid girl?" he mumbled bitterly. I didn't know if I should laugh or cry until my fearless mother—the same woman who grounded us only if we were rude or remotely unkind to others—came to the rescue with fangs: "Actually, she was raised by *me,* you fat fuck!" My mom and I laughed so hard we had to exit the bus to contain ourselves.

Accordingly, with the fusion of the elegant Shelaskys and the untamable Temkins, my sister and I turned out somewhere between highbrow and hillbilly. We are Bergdorf Goodman *and* Bob's Discount Store; we are Veuve Clicquot *and* watermelon wine coolers; we are JAPs *and* townies. We are . . . who we are.

Our family ate almost every breakfast and dinner together, not that any of us helped Mom with the preparations. We were not spoiled financially, but for some reason, we never lifted a finger when it came to getting fed. My mother's time in the kitchen was her private pleasure. I think that because her childhood was so chaotic, the kitchen gave her a sense of control. She baked before anyone woke up in the morning, or when we were at school, and to be honest, I'm not even sure how or when dinner got done. Even though she'd always rather be near her children than not, we instinctively left her alone when she was at the stove in her apron.

My mother approached ingredients like a European. She'd drive an hour away, toward the Berkshires, for rural, street-side produce stands almost daily. Rarely did she purchase anything canned or processed at the supermarket, and needless to say, she's never "nuked" a thing in her life. (How to work a microwave is still a mystery to all of us.) Mom baked most of her own breads and all of our family's desserts from scratch. With her riffs on *Moosewood* and *Silver Palate* recipes, she made delicious soups, hearty stews, and simple proteins, experimenting with couscous, quinoa, and other rustic dishes that didn't really show up in the suburbs during the 1980s and '90s. When we did have meat, it was nothing fancy, just whatever cut was on sale, proudly served to the family and cooked "extra well done." Fish was infrequent and also baked to a crisp. My mother didn't know or care about the secret rules to fine dining, where steaks are bloody and fish is gently seared, and ironically, it's that disregard for cooking conventions that made her so comfortable in our happy, terra-cotta kitchen. We might have held our utensils in the wrong hand and had inappropriate (yet unthinkably funny) conversations at the dinner table, but we drank sparkling Pellegrino with fresh lemon, sat with excellent posture, and spooned out our sauces and gravies from cherry red ramekins.

We also semi kept kosher—not so stringently, but enough that pig roasts and shrimp cocktail were totally off the menu. And my dad had perilously high cholesterol, so that meant light on the red meat, *treif* or not. For those reasons and the irrefutable fact that my folks were also a bit frugal, we almost never went to restaurants. When we did, it was always Italian. Mom loved a fresh marinara; Dad loved just being out and about with his girls. And we never ordered in either. Besides once with a babysitter and a Domino's pizza, I have no recollection of a delivery guy ever coming to our front door.

For school lunches, I brown-bagged it with hits and misses like cold chicken salad made with grapes and cashews on homemade whole-wheat bread, or leftover veal loaf with ketchup on a fluffy onion roll, or the dreaded splatter of chopped liver atop a wedge of crunchy iceberg lettuce (which resulted in a cafeteria-wide gag reflex). Suffice it to say, sugary soft drinks and fake foods like Slim Jims were foreign concepts to me. While other kids had snacks like Cool Ranch Doritos and rainbow Fruit Roll-Ups, our accoutrements were always two pieces of bruised fruit . . . and a note from Mom. Sometimes she would include a poem. She'd quote Thoreau: "Live the life you've dreamed." Or W.C. Fields: "A rich man is nothing but a poor man with money." And most often, Cora, her hippie shrink: "Balance, form, rhythm, and order." Other times she just said "Hi." No matter what, my mother's words were always signed with "I love you MTLI," which, in case you don't have a parent who holds family meetings from the bathtub, means More Than Life Itself.

If I have one small qualm about food and my upbringing, it has something to do with frog legs, in that frog legs . . . and kimchi . . . and baby octopus . . . and drunken goat are examples of foods that we were never exposed to. There was no emphasis placed on adventurous and exotic eating; no expeditions in the name of new food experiences, unless you count apple picking. Compared to the white bread and mayo around us, we thought we were eccentric eaters, of course, with our ratatouille and butternut squash, but we really were not. Farro salads and toasted pine nuts might have been a sign of subtle sophistication back then, but it's not like Andrew Zimmern would have knocked down our door to tape an episode of *Bizarre Foods*.

At least we grew up with an inherent love of healthy food and a genuine disinterest in Mc-anything. It's just a minor shame. Had Mom encouraged us to be as adventurous, exploratory, and *outside-the-box* in our taste buds as she did in art, travel, literature, and especially love, Rachel and I would have grown to be world-class gourmets. Rather, we approach food the way she does, positively, if somewhat reservedly: eating tons of fruit, raw vegetables, and light, simple meals. Our inherent eating style might not be daring, but it's nice, moderate, and devoid of *most* crap. We are in tune with our bodies (which, if we listen carefully enough, always tell us when we need fat, protein, roughage, etc.) and like Mom, we also have our weaknesses, and welcome them without any guilt or inner anguish.

I wouldn't touch a Devil Dog if it were the last empty calorie on earth, but I sure had my own sugary habits. Growing up, we were technically allowed "one junk per day," which I interpreted as the consumption of an entire pint of Ben & Jerry's Coffee Heath Bar Crunch ice cream. For an entire year, I ate one pint a day. I was long, lanky, and always in good health, and no one blinked at my grotesque ice cream intake, not even my quasi–health nut mom. With a spoon in one hand and a pencil in the other, I would close the doors to the den, pour my heart into my tattered journals, and my *junk* into my bottomless stomach. I went through the same phase with oversize Italian cannolis; "Lynn Papale's cheesecake," named after the recipe from one of my mother's best friends; and gooey banana bread with extra chocolate chips. If the chocolate chip quotient was just right, I'd eat half a loaf per day.

The moment high school started, Ben & Jerry weren't the only boys in my life anymore. I was totally carefree when it came to my sexuality (though I was actually an inexperienced virgin until senior year). The summer I turned fifteen, I went to sleepaway camp, Camp Ramah, as a skinny little runt and came back as Jessica Rabbit. I gained twenty-five pounds in two months, taking me from a training bra to a double D. It was a fascinating turn of events, and everyone back in Longmeadow was entranced by my new assets, especially me. One sip of beer and I'd take off my top and flash an entire room of horny teenagers. Blame my early exposure to the Age of Aquarius, but I didn't see anything wrong with it. This became my shtick.

I liked a reaction. I'd accept any dare, too. (My friend Andy McArthur swears I once humped an Oreo cookie, but I don't even know how that would work.) After a few weeks of this kind of behavior, my group of girlfriends anointed my most protective pal, Anzo, to be my "agent." I could only strip if she supervised and approved. Safety first.

I cherished my girlfriends, who, much like me, were good kids with a splash of the devil inside. Our late-night hangout was the Lil Peach parking lot; Lil Peach being what New Yorkers would call a bodega. There we rolled joints, stole Blow Pops, listened to 10,000 Maniacs, and perfected the art of female bonding. We were obsessed with boys, of course, but no one came before one another. Anzo and my other closest friend, Kates, had colossal appetites. Nothing got them more revved up than a night at Rube's (Ruby Tuesday). I have never seen such pretty girls who were such glorious pigs. I stuck with the salad bar, simply because I barely knew how to approach things like twice-baked potato skins and blue-cheese buffalo chicken wings.

When I wasn't busy with Rube's or my boobs, I was writing for the *Springfield Union-News* (now the *Springfield Republican*). After a few dozen submissions to their youth-oriented section, "Unlisted," they assigned me a weekly column about honest, if clichéd, high-school issues like the temptation to drink and drive, and getting asked to the prom by the last person you'd want to go with. Unsurprisingly, I found it easy to be so open. In real life or in print, there was nothing I was uncomfortable talking about. All my aunts, uncles, and friends' parents clipped my articles and pinned them up on their fridges. They all told me that I would be a famous writer. My mom, dad, and sister were my trusted editors. It all felt so good, and confirmed what

I had known my whole life: I would go to college in New York City and become a professional journalist.

Whether I was writing about it or living it, our kitchen table was the headquarters of boy problems and girl talk. It was the estrogen center of Western Massachusetts as far as my clique was concerned. My less-than-prude core posse, Anzo, Kates, Court, and Jean, loved confiding in my open-minded mother—who was half Joan Baez, half Jewish intellectual—over good cries and comfort food. During our hours and hours of deep thoughts and confessions, my good-natured dad kept himself fake-busy in the yard, and my sister would hide in her room because my funny, filthy friends freaked her out. The girls were fixated on a pasta dish my mother made that we called the Pasta. It's light and clean, with thick spaghetti, fresh tomatoes, a touch of garlic, and a sprinkle of cheese; we would inhale it like wildebeests. At school, the girls pleaded for it through our rampant note-passing, which, among other much more vulgar topics, always included, "Tell Laur to make the Pasta tonight."

Our absolute favorite place to hang, however, was Jean's big, antique house in the center of town. Jean Rogér was the most popular girl at Longmeadow High School. She was the star of the swim team who could out-party anyone, a straight-A student who skipped most of her classes, and a beautiful girl who was way beyond appearances. Every day before the first bell rang, she would perch alone in the cafeteria, with her long legs and short hair, breezily slicing her bagel and buttering it in the same circular motion morning after morning. Jeanie and her bagel were like clockwork. She'd quietly read the paper or pleasantly engage with anyone who excitedly walked her way. Even the teachers were drawn to her dazzling yet totally disarming energy. "Jeanie has it all," my mother would always say.

What made Jean even cooler was her mom. Punky Rogér

was (and still is) a cig-smoking, golf-playing country clubber with a good marriage and a vibrant social life. Our teenage hearts would sing when she stayed home to hang around with us, in her clunky, rose-gold jewels that dangled over her tanned, slender frame. Around the holidays, Punky always made these round, chocolate-covered peanut butter balls called Buckeyes, and when we weren't stealing her Barclay 100's, playing her Jimmy Buffet records, or learning to drive stick on her old BMW, we were pounding dozens of them.

While Jean's family and their social circle, which included most of my other friends' parents, were "old-money chic"—cocktails, nicotine, and khakis—my family was the absolute opposite. My father drinks two beers a year, if that, and my mother never touches the stuff. My friends' families summered in beach houses in places like Hilton Head and Nantucket; we visited old tombstones in New York City. They skied and sailed; we played Scrabble and saw off-Broadway plays.

Needless to say, there wasn't much intermingling between my parents and the Rogérs' crowd, but there *was* a mutual fondness. My mother was Annie Hall to their Ann Taylor. She never cared one bit about fitting in. It was almost like she was empowered by being an outsider. The strong women who were my friends' mothers truly respected that Mom, the only one who had never been to "the club" for gossip, gin 'n' tonics, or golf lessons, marched to her own beat in such a quietly rebellious way. Of course, they also knew how much she adored their daughters.

Five years after graduating from high school, with all of us girls scattered around the East Coast and enjoying our twenties, the events of September 11 happened. My mother called just as I saw the first black suit jacket flapping through the sky, not too many blocks down. Trying to process what the hell was going on and praying that everyone I knew who worked in lower Manhattan was okay, I just couldn't pick up the phone at that moment. It didn't occur to me to worry about anyone not living in the city. Until Mom called again, and I heard her voice.

She could barely say the words: "Jeanie was on that plane."

She loved that girl.

Everyone did.

Following Jean's death, my friends from Longmeadow, including their siblings and parents, became cemented as the most important people in my life, outside my own family. We pulled together that year and have remained tightly interlocked ever since. There is no friendship like the one born in youth and forged in tragedy.

I think back to my childhood all the time, and as most people would say, the memories always take me to the kitchen table—telling secrets to my mother, sipping cauliflower soup with my dad and sister, or scarfing down the Pasta with my lifelong best friends. And sometimes, the memories bring me back to a buttered bagel, too.

The Pasta

SERVES 6

When I was growing up, my mother made this meal at least once a week and I never got tired of it. This simple dish is fresh, healthy, and very much her. It is my happy childhood incarnate. We always ate the pasta al dente, but that's only because we insatiable teenagers were too impatient to wait. Add a salad or crusty bread for a lovely meal.

---

4 tablespoons extra-virgin olive oil
1 clove garlic, minced
4 teaspoons chopped fresh basil
1 teaspoon kosher salt, plus more for salting pasta water
4 medium tomatoes, diced or sliced
1 pound spaghetti, or bucatini if you're being fancy
½ to 1 cup (or less if you'd like) freshly grated mozzarella or Romano cheese
½ cup grated Parmigiano-Reggiano

Place a large pot filled with water over high heat. Bring to a boil.

Meanwhile, heat the oil in a medium skillet over medium heat. Add the garlic and cook until tender. Stir in the basil and salt. Toss in the tomatoes and simmer for 15 minutes, or until they soften.

Throw a generous pinch of salt into the boiling water. Add the pasta, stir, and cook according to the package instructions. Taste a piece of pasta toward the end of the cooking. When it's done, drain it and return it to the pot. Add the grated mozzarella and the tomato mixture to the pot. Stir gently for about 3 minutes, until the cheese melts.

Transfer the pasta into bowls. Sprinkle some Parmigiano over each bowl and serve.

Punky Rogér's Buckeyes

MAKES ABOUT 60 BALLS

There are so many things I remember about Jean Rogér—how she loved to laugh and dance, her aversion to anything catty, and how totally comfortable she was in her own skin. I'll also always remember the chocolate-dipped peanut butter candies I'd devour at her house, with their supernatural aura of "how the other half lives." Her incredible mother, Punky, tells me these sweet treats are supposed to resemble the nuts of a buckeye tree, but all I really know is that they taste like the holidays in Longmeadow, and remind me of the friend I'll never forget.

1½ cups creamy peanut butter
8 tablespoons (1 stick) unsalted butter, at room temperature
½ teaspoon vanilla extract
3 cups confectoners' sugar
4 cups good-quality semisweet chocolate chips
2 teaspoons vegetable shortening

In a large bowl (or the bowl of an electric mixer fitted with the paddle attachment), combine the peanut butter, butter, and vanilla. Gradually add the powdered sugar until it is well mixed.

Prepare a large plate, or a cookie sheet, lined with wax paper. Using your hands, roll the mixture into round balls the size of strawberries and place them on the prepared plate. Stick a toothpick (to be used as a handle) in each of the balls. Place the plate in the freezer and let chill for about 30 minutes, until the balls have set.

When the balls are firm, melt the chocolate chips and shortening in the top of a double boiler, stirring frequently, until smooth. If you don't have a double boiler, fill a small saucepan with water and bring to a boil. Reduce it to a simmer and set a heatproof bowl that fits tightly into the top of the pot. Proceed with melting the chocolate and shortening in the bowl as described above.

Holding a peanut butter ball by the toothpick, dip it in the melted chocolate. Leave a little bit of the peanut butter showing at the top of each ball. Place the finished buckeyes on a cooling rack. (The chocolate may drip, so you might want to protect your counter with paper or foil under the rack for quicker cleanup.) Gently remove the toothpicks and smooth over the holes. Refrigerate for at least 2 hours, or until the balls are set, before serving.

The buckeyes can be stored in the refrigerator or in a tightly sealed tin on the counter. They make beautiful holiday gifts.

2.

Life on Fire

Growing up, some young girls wish for ponies, Prince Charming, or perfectly symmetrical C-cups. Not me. Growing up, I only wanted New York. To be precise: I wanted Greenwich Village. I wanted the subway. I wanted struggle. I wanted culture. I wanted action. Therefore, the only thing I really cared about in picking a college was that it got me there.

Mischievous as always, I found a back door into Columbia University through a joint program with the Jewish Theological Seminary, where I ended up with two bachelor of arts degrees, one from Columbia and another from JTS. Applying to the joint program made it a little easier to get accepted into an Ivy League school because they wanted well-qualified Jewish students who were willing to take the double course load.

Once you got in, it was pretty much all the same. Even the elitists knew that with the killer syllabi, getting by was no picnic, not even a kosher one. Still, my Ivy League friends will now see that I am not exactly one of them. They probably had a hunch. I don't quote Plato or Sylvia Plath. I sleep through foreign films and primary elections. Howard Stern is my NPR. I am sure that to them I sort of smelled like state school.

When my parents dropped me off on the Upper West Side

campus, they managed to keep it together, relatively speaking. I'm pretty sure I heard my mom repeating to herself, "You give your kids roots to grow *and* wings to fly . . . You give your kid roots to grow *and* wings to fly . . . ," as she made up my bed with new flannel sheets and filled my fridge with strawberries and grapefruit. As for my own separation anxiety, I had none. Because I've always been so close to my family emotionally, it was never hard for me to be away from them. I'll admit that it was rough seeing my dad a little frazzled though. And I purposely asked Rach to stay home because that was one good-bye I couldn't bear. Before my parents took off, we played "the trick," which is a Shelasky tool that makes leaving one another a lot easier. We sing "See ya tomorrow!" with as much joy and enthusiasm as we can find under the big, fat lumps in our throats, walk away without looking back, and then sob in a fetal position for a few horrible moments. After that, we're usually fine.

Independence came easy. I was ecstatic about living in New York, but instantly had buyer's remorse about being trapped in the Jewish dorms and kosher cafeterias (which was part of the deal) and spending half my time studying all the theological rigmarole. I've always loved being Jewish—I grew up going to synagogue regularly and had fifteen amazing summers at the *hamisha* Camp Ramah, several pilgrimages to Israel, plus one awful trip to Auschwitz. I can read and speak Hebrew, I don't eat pork, and I even lost my virginity on a kibbutz. Yet I've never been religious. My closest friends from home weren't Jewish, nor were the boys I liked. I believe in God, but never wanted, or needed, to flesh him, or her, out. So the whole thing just felt way too restricting. And to me, well, lame.

On the other hand, down the street at Columbia, where the brainy student body was definitely more eclectic, I dreaded having to reveal my joint-program status to potential new friends, so I kept to myself there as well. I should have been proud to be part of something so rigorous, but I was hung up on being in an academically "inferior" breed. It embarrassed me. If I were more mature, or able to laugh off the insanity of me shuffling back and forth from Sociology of Punk Rock Youth to Yiddish 101, it might have been an okay situation. But I resented everything JTS-affiliated, and felt overwhelmingly "less than" lingering around the Columbia campus.

I had only one close friend: Annie, a high-spirited sweetheart from Akron, Ohio, who called soda "pop" and sneakers "tennies." She was also in the joint program, but much more secure with it than I was. She loved socializing around the dorms, but I was totally disinterested in Shabbat dinners, sing-alongs, and any of that Kumbaya shit. So I spent most of my time alone.

My family visited me every few weeks, lugging pots of frozen chicken soup, totes spilling over with nectarines and peanut butter, and suitcases stuffed with all my favorite junk food. Even while I was in college, Mom took care of my kitchen. Despite the over-the-top food shipments, which I always gladly accepted, my weight dropped to the point where my parents and sister became concerned. They had an underlying fear that I was developing an eating disorder, but I adamantly denied that I was struggling with any deep-rooted body-image issues. The real subtext of my food aversion had to do with tension and nerves. This was the first time in my life I felt unsettled. And it's how my body would function for years to follow: when I'm unhappy, I have no appetite. The first sign I'm a wreck is when my jeans ride low.

It was not the time of my life as college is meant to be, but I channeled my mother, who wouldn't give a summa cum laude about having friends, or the perils of fitting in, and by sophomore year, I joined the one sorority I *knew* I belonged to: the sorority of New York City. I landed an internship at MTV News and hung out at the headquarters as much as possible, even if it meant bringing cappuccinos to Kurt Loder's loft and sucking up to the hot anchor of the moment, Alison Stewart, who refused to remember my first name. It was the unfriendliest working environment, but the egos and attitudes made me feel very cool, and I welcomed it all with pleasure.

I also juggled a hostess job at a gritty Upper West Side nightclub, where I got harassed by the coked-up manager and groped by married patrons. The scene was pretty seedy, but it tickled my attraction to trouble. Riding the subway home at four o'clock in the morning after having to French kiss the boss for a paycheck was demoralizing, dangerous, and so much more exciting than school.

My only significant boyfriend during this time was a guy named Jesse, a handsome and brooding scholar who went to Columbia (by way of Beverly Hills), and who communicated so esoterically that I never knew what he was saying. So, we let our bodies do the talking. This, along with all my time-consuming jobs, got me to graduation (though I didn't go). Jesse and I ultimately broke up because he was on a crazy intellectual binge that I couldn't even pretend to understand, but we remained exceptionally close friends. I didn't want any attachments then anyway. The moment college was over I would be free to be *me*. And by this time, "me" meant a bona fide city chick. Hardened, hot, and bothered.

Unchained from school, my confidence soared as I conquered the city, at least in the wide eyes of a twenty-something wannabe writer. I rented a tiny studio off Central Park, quit my MTV and nightclub jobs, and started freelancing for multiple advertising agencies and PR firms. I wrote whatever they needed on topics ranging from gastric bypass surgery to prison reform. And because I wanted an employee discount, I also created a "publicity manager" job for myself at the stunning home furnishings empire ABC Carpet & Home, absorbing everything I could about design and architecture while browsing cassis-scented candles and pineapple-shaped chandeliers. On weekends, I waitressed at the ebullient, uptown café Sarabeth's. Every hour of my week seemed to be occupied by one job or another, which was totally fine because I didn't have many friends from college, and my true pals—Anzo, Kates, Court, and Jean—were still living in Massachusetts. So the hustle and bustle became my life.

On my twenty-first birthday I splurged on a low-cut leopard-print Diane von Furstenberg wrap dress from Saks Fifth Avenue, and my sister threw a party for me, inviting all my acquaintances from my various workplaces to a groovy tiki lounge. I made her invite a bunch of her friends, too, as space-fillers, just in case. That night, about sixty people showed up; I felt like the star of my own movie. "Sorry, Lys, but you really can't say you have no friends anymore," toasted Rachel. Then, under a plastic palm tree, over a rum punch, Rachel introduced me to Gary, a great-looking guy with big green eyes and a starter job on Wall Street. He reminded me of my dad—not as playful and funny, but similarly good and honest. He was definitely on the square side, but he became my first serious post-college boyfriend.

Speaking of my dad, around this time my mother had threatened to divorce him if he refused to move to New York City so they could be closer to me and my sister, who was attending college upstate. He put up a fight for a full three hours, and then closed his uniform shop and did as she said. Their plan was for her to sell real estate and for him to keep his regular uniform clients via a home office. They swapped our lovely home in New England for an apartment the size of an armoire, and arrived on the Upper West Side with no savings, one subway map, and not a second of regret.

Money became tight in my folks' transition from Longmeadow to Manhattan, so I'd insist on comping meals for them a couple nights a week at Sarabeth's. Like most of my customers, they'd salivate over the famous, velvety tomato soup, slurping up spoonfuls and spoonfuls with pure delight. I finally had an appetite again and drank the yummy soup now and then, but by in large, I remained uninterested in food. I would eat whatever didn't sell from the Sarabeth's bakery, or grilled chicken salads on dull double dates with Gary, or anything that I could find in the mini-fridge at my studio. Food didn't turn me on or off, and it certainly didn't make me moan. But the sexy struggling actor who worked the night shift at Sarabeth's, while my oblivious boyfriend put in banking hours, took care of that.

Life was good, back in early 2001.

And then one morning, I got off the subway downtown on Fourteenth Street and saw a big crowd on the street. It sounds crazy, but my immediate reaction was *Sample sale?* I walked to the corner deli and ordered an egg-and-cheese sandwich, and everyone was acting strange in there, too. When I went outside, already unwrapping my breakfast, a woman had dropped her dry-cleaning bags and collapsed into tears in the middle of the street. And then I looked up. The second plane had just hit, and my mom was calling.

AT TWENTY-FOUR, I began my career as a professional journalist by way of a news editor at *Us Weekly* named Marc Malkin. I befriended Malkin while at ABC Carpet & Home, after I leaked to him a story about Julia Roberts's shopping spree there. After I aggressively insisted that he give his staff the night off on New Year's Eve 2002 and relinquish their red-carpet duties to me, I spent the night running around in the freezing cold, barelegged and beaming, interviewing an unknown named Scarlett Johansson and a little girl named Lindsay Lohan. My sister, who had finally broken out of her shell, tagged along and ended up making out with Mark McGrath. We jacked his yellow puffy vest and gave it to my dad for his birthday. The night was too magnificent to comprehend.

Soon after, in 2003, Malkin offered me a well-paid reporting job, my first real gig in magazines. Forever thankful for the position, I would have done anything to please him. I stalked Britney Spears in Kentwood, Louisiana (where I was warned, with a straight face, not to reveal my religion or ethnic-sounding last name), sat for months on a stoop belonging to the Olsen twins, and shopped for silky corsets beside Angelina Jolie at Saks. I adored Jessica Simpson's then-husband, Nick Lachey, one of the nicest guys I'd ever met. The magazine had me interview him so many times that we couldn't help but feel like real, and completely platonic, friends after a few months. Once, we spent so much time talking off the record at a nightclub that someone took a picture of him whispering into my ear, and days later, he and I were falsely linked together on the cover of *National Enquirer.* The silly, short-lived buzz around the story resulted in paparazzi showing up at my grandmother's house on Thanksgiving because they thought he was there with me, followed by relentless phone calls from publicists, snoops, and lawyers throughout the entire holiday. It was terrible, and gave me a small taste of my own medicine.

But the most stellar part of the job happened when I met my colleague, co-conspirator, and future best friend, Shelley.

Shelley's temperament distressed me a little at first, but not enough to stay away. On the inside, she was a nice Jewish girl from Michigan—good-hearted and hilarious, my two favorite qualities—and at our core, we shared an instant, unspoken familiarity, an easy closeness, like that of first cousins. But on the outside, Shelley was a real flamethrower. Physically incapable of taking no for an answer, professionally or personally, she owned the New York nightlife scene, never having to wait in lines, always getting what she wanted when she wanted it. She could barge into the ultra-exclusive Bungalow 8 without blinking an eye, and torpedo into a Brad Pitt movie premiere guarded by the feds. She was a bull, and sometimes a bully, but I've never had more fun with anyone in my life.

Meeting Shelley, with all her contacts and connections, was like landing on a new planet. She was constantly bellowing into her cell, or banging out e-mails on her Sidekick, demanding to know "Where is *ehhhveryone* tonight? . . . I heard *ehhhveryone* is going to Marquee. . . . Wait, is *ehhhveryone* there, already?" I'd listen to her carry on, slightly stunned by the high-school-ish tone, but totally mesmerized by her sensational fast-track life. Eventually, I had to ask her, "Who is this *ehhhveryone* we're always chasing?" She didn't answer, but I wasn't really that dense. We were playing with *the popular group*.

Shelley was deeply in the cool crowd. Backstage passes to the Kanye West show? Easy. Free haircuts at Frédéric Fekkai? Obviously. Private jets to the Hamptons? Of course. With enough finesse, she could make anything happen. Especially reservations.

We used our corporate cards to eat at New York's most fabulous and flashy restaurants. Nobu, where even fancy people save up for celebratory meals, was our daily cafeteria. The owners of Tao, which was absolutely on fire in 2003, treated Shelley from Detroit like the Queen of Dubai. We *never* got a bill at the booming Dos Caminos, where we'd bounce from table to table like sangria-stained bunny rabbits, because the overgenerous publicist was a pal. I loved going to these restaurants . . . but not for the food. It was the energy, the electricity, the heartbeat, and the buzz. The truth is I knew nothing about the menus, wine lists, or grass-fed whatever, but that didn't make the meals any less luminous.

It was a glamorous time, jetting around from the MTV Video Music Awards in Miami to Hollywood premiere parties at the Chateau Marmont in Los Angeles, feeling all shimmery and self-entitled. I was absolutely enamored with Heath Ledger, whom I'd bump into every now and then on the impossibly guarded third floor of the Spotted Pig. He once touched my shoulder and asked if I wanted to smoke a cigarette together, and for the first time in my life, I fucking froze. We could have been friends.

But we ran with a cutthroat subculture, often dealing with druggies, lies, mean girls, and manipulation, too. Celebrity handlers were always using us to get into the magazine, or abusing us for working there in the first place. (As they say, the only thing worse than being in *Us Weekly* is *not* being in *Us Weekly*.) The rat race—euphoric and evil as it is—can really scrape at your soul. I never would have lasted long without Shellz.

At a Tommy Hilfiger party in Bryant Park, I once spotted a drop-dead-gorgeous guy sitting all by himself. So many people in "the scene" were lonely and hurting—I could never find *any* correlation between fame and happiness. He looked like one of those lost souls. By this point, I was more or less committed to Gary, so I wasn't shy about walking over to meet the tall drink of Fashion Week. (It's always easier talking to cute guys when you genuinely don't care if they like you or not.) I did notice, as I got closer, that this was the most handsome man I'd ever seen.

"Hey, you okay over there? What's your name?"

"Oh, yeah, yeah, I'm fine. Just tired. Thanks for asking. That was nice. I'm Tom." Holy Hilfiger, Tom was hot.

Out of the corner of my eye, I noticed Shelley spontaneously combusting in her platform shoes, trying to send me some sort of telepathic message. Maybe she knew him? Maybe she'd slept with him? I waved her over.

"Shellz," I said with a nudge. "This is my new friend, Tom. . . . Wait, what's your last name, sweetie?"

"Brady."

Oh boy.

I'd find myself in crazy situations like this all time. In the winter of 2004, at the Sundance Film Festival, in Park City, Utah, Shellz and I were dropped off by a taxi at our private rental home on the highest point of a mountain, in the middle of the night, only to realize after the driver sped away that we were completely locked out, with no cell phone reception whatsoever, wearing stupid, skimpy outfits and strappy, open-toed stilettos. It was pitch-black and frigid, without any neighboring homes in sight, and no streetlights or passing cars. We were screwed. Like, dead skanks in Park City screwed.

Then, as we were shaking from fear and frostbite, trying to figure out how far we'd have to walk for help—it felt like miles—Nick Nolte stumbled out of the woods, stinking of whisky, holding a walking stick, and saving the day. He couldn't explain how or why he was up there, but he managed to call a van of angry butch filmmakers (we've never figured out the connection), who barely knew him and deplored the ditzy, decked-out Shelley and me from the start, to drive us to shelter in a baby blue minivan. Nolte, in the meantime, scurried back into the arms of Mother Nature before our teeth could stop chattering, and we could say thanks. Miraculously, all ended well. Except no one believed a word of it.

Shellz and I had so much fun being the Thelma and Louise of the gossip scene. I am sure many people found us obnoxious with our Jimmy Choo shoes, diva-like mood swings, and smudged, morning-after eye makeup, but we had each other and that seemed to be enough. The only other person we took care *never* to offend was Yolandá, the feisty Filipino lady in accounting who signed off on all our expenses for the price of a black 'n' white cookie. Bless her.

At age twenty-six, while I was half paying attention, I got engaged to Gary and moved into a great apartment with him in the Flatiron district. I dismissed my ambivalence about the whole wedding thing with the excuse that I was too busy with work, calling myself an "Indie Bride," which I think translated to "screw this." Following the marriage proposal, I took as many travel assignments as I could, ate most of my meals "on the field," and avoided domesticity as much as possible. At our beautiful new apartment, I never once turned on the stove or attempted to cook. I never bought groceries or so much as made a cup of tea for my hardworking future husband.

Gary was a more imaginative eater than I was, perhaps one of the first foodies I ever knew. He was always on a mission to evolve my palate, so when an acclaimed new Indian restaurant, Tamarind, opened just down the street from our apartment, he dragged me right out the door. I was reluctant—mostly because it meant skipping a night out on the town, and also because I had never even contemplated eating Indian food. But the staff was so warm and gracious, and the decor so tastefully done, that it was hard to keep up my gastronomical guard.

Gary delved into the menu, eager to please me, as always. He ordered us basic but authentic-enough dishes like biryani (a casserole of saffron-scented rice with vegetables and meat), saag paneer (cubes of unaged cheese floating in warm, creamy spinach), lamb samosas (big, fried triangular pockets filled with meat and spices), and chicken tikka masala (chicken in a rich red sauce). When the food came, I threw a napkin on my lap, pulled back my hair, and crammed as much curry down my esophagus as humanly possible. To say that I liked it would be an understatement. "Um, Indian food is everything," I texted Shelley.

Gary was "pumped" to take my taste buds even further, and next planned to sequester me at some hard-core Japanese restaurants. It killed him that I wasted precious opportunities to try the most exotic raw fish night after night at Nobu. But he wouldn't even get the chance to teach me how to hold chopsticks. Before my taste for sake could develop, my relationship with Gary ended. I was not a good fiancée, and he deserved better than what I could bring to the table (or not). For me, real life in New York was just beginning. I was tipsy, untamable, and totally caught up. There were too many mistakes to be made and too many pinch-me moments to be had. Especially when it was guys like Derek Jeter doing the pinching.

Our relationship officially ended on our fifth anniversary, the night Gary planned to take me to Gramercy Tavern, arguably the best restaurant in town. But instead, I was downing margaritas at the Maritime Hotel, flirting with a party-hopping photographer I was in love with for a few seconds, and interviewing Mischa Barton, who was launching a sexy new show called *The O.C.* Meanwhile, Gary was at the apartment, waiting with flowers, continually calling the restaurant to extend the reservation. I never came home that night and we broke up the next morning. Gary might not have been the great love of my life, but I did love him, and I wish he never got hurt. I still can't walk past Gramercy Tavern without hating myself a little.

But that's New York. The streets are filled with neon-lit restaurants that taste like nostalgia, glamour, guilt, and goose-bumps. If you've lived here long enough, every corner booth, deli counter, dive bar, coffee shop, and critic's darling becomes a Polaroid of your life. The meals at Sarabeth's with my parents, or Nobu with Shelley, or Tamarind with Gary—they are seasoned with moments I pray to remember and things I hope to forget. But for me, the food always came second to the snapshot.

~~~

I DON'T know what revolves more in New York, relationships or real estate, but a few weeks later, I was walking up seven flights of stairs, carrying a laundry basket of mud masks, pumpernickel pretzel rods, and Cosabella thongs. I'd moved out of my place with Gary—who let me go gracefully, like the gentleman he always was—and into a shared walk-up on the Upper East Side.

The schlep up the stairs was nothing short of sadistic, but it led to a huge, whimsical furnished triplex, with big bedrooms, a California kitchen, and the most important amenity of all, excellent roommates who were never home. They were a few boho-chic girls I knew peripherally from the magazine world, and, to my benefit, had loaded fiancés with Tribeca lofts and Hamptons weekend homes. This left me with three floors of Moroccan rugs and Barcelona chairs, and a rooftop decorated with lanterns and potted tulips, all to myself. It was like *Last Tango in Paris,* but with a Pick A Bagel on the corner.

Twenty-seven and newly single, I had promised myself that from this point on I would date only men who intensely intrigued me. I don't know why I stayed in such an uninspiring
~~~

relationship for so long. Chalk it up to being young, immature, or the fact that, despite his pin-striped shirts and fantasy football league, Gary was a great guy.

Betrothed to no one, I found that I was happy to just hang out. I had my job, my friends, and, on this particular night, my sister to keep me busy. Rachel, who was working on her master's in education, was visiting my apartment for something that couldn't possibly be less academic: she was making an audition tape for *The Bachelor* and needed my help. After three years of televised weddings, celebrity-endorsed tanning creams, and press releases from Donald Trump's assistant, I was so turned off by reality stars that I was mortified to even be part of such a mission. But hey, anything for my sister. Even a rose ceremony.

To commemorate "the wrap" of her three-minute monologue—which was not her most poised, Natalie Portman moment—I offered to make us some hot cocoa with a few Nestlé packets, which were covered in cobwebs in the cupboard. There was just one problem: I had no idea where to start. Twenty-seven years old, with double degrees, tons of bylines, and the private phone number to every *Queer Eye* and straight guy in New York City, here I was with two polka-dotted mugs, a few stale packets of cocoa powder, and a stupid, blank stare on my face. I considered asking my sister for help, but this was a girl who wanted a flower from a stranger with a man-tan. I decided to handle it myself.

One of my roommates kept a shiny coffeemaker on the slate countertop. I thought I'd just fill the carafe with water and heat it on the stovetop. Simple. I was sure that I'd seen my mother do this before. (In hindsight, *that* was a teakettle.) So I did just that: I turned on the gas stove as high as it would go, and felt quite satisfied with myself. I skipped downstairs with my sister to wash up and get into our pajamas. But as we wiped off the silver glittery makeup from Rachel's big brown eyes, the fire alarm started to screech. I ran to the kitchen.

"Call 911!" I screamed. "The house is on fire!"

The plastic carafe had caught on fire. Disaster. I had flashes of my roommates losing all their fancy family heirlooms and Louis Vuitton luggage, and me going to prison for pyromania. We frantically called my father: "Come over! We need you! We set the kitchen on fire!" He must have been watching a Red Sox game because once we assured him that we weren't in any serious danger, all he really had to say was "Oy vey. You girls." Thanks, Super-Dad. My mother, much more helpful, urged me to grab my tax returns and run. My guess was that they didn't want to walk up those seven flights of stairs to save us. Luckily, the sexy NYFD did.

The firefighters arrived at the scene before any serious damage was done. After they saved the day, and the pretty, pre-war apartment, a few of the firefighters even asked for our numbers. Everything worked out in the end, except *The Bachelor* rejected Rachel, and I became content on giving the kitchen, and all of its compadres, my continued cold shoulder.

Such was life in my late twenties. It was a time of sparks, stories, and self-discovery. It didn't take long after calling off my engagement with Gary for me to start meeting guys everywhere I went. They landed in my life with ease and delight, swinging gently on the hammock that was my heart, until I affectionately released them to their overprotective mothers, ovulating ex-girlfriends, minuscule bank accounts, enormous penises, Bar exams, probation officers, or some combination thereof. I found a certain thrill, a built-in drama, in the lost puppies I liked and who liked me back. They came in all looks and livelihoods, but they usually shared a similar nature: sweet to the core and microscopically unstable. At least I stuck to my guns . . . not one fling was boring.

~~~

MY HEART got wounded only once. It all started when my new dentist, John, a drop-dead-gorgeous Greek, walked into the examining room, as I prayed not to bite, dribble, or drool. For the least sexy profession, he was one of the most attractive men I had ever laid eyes on. But it wasn't just his looks that had me aflutter. I liked *everything* about him: his soft, deep voice; old-fashioned, doctorly masculinity; and especially the way his scrubs fell on his six-foot-two frame. After the requisite doctor-patient small talk, I gathered John was a fine man who happened to be dressed up as George Clooney's younger, fitter brother. And before I could barely spit, he went from being my new dentist to my long-term boyfriend.

On our first date, at a tiny trattoria near my walk-up, John admitted that, ideally, he wanted to date only Greek Orthodox women because he felt strongly about marrying within his religion, and it was a nonnegotiable family rule. He also told me that he still lived at home, and would not feel comfortable telling his family about our first date, and probably any to follow. Being Jewish, I have always understood the concept of "marrying in," though my own hyper-groovy parents would be overjoyed with an interracial, interfaith, same-sex story line inside our already why-be-normal family. I admired, rather than begrudged, his forthrightness. And naturally, it only made me want him more.

Our feelings grew fast and feral, and before I knew it, we found ourselves living in a strange, futureless world for two years, on and off. My heart throbbed harder for him each day,
~~~

yet the circumstances remained exactly the same: John was forbidden from dating a non-Greek, and was petrified to tell his family the truth.

It was 2006, and *Us Weekly* was keeping me busy and paying me well, so I alternated the drama of celebrity gossip with the drama of my own bottomless love. When I wasn't working, all I wanted to do was bask in Greek culture: the music, the customs, and, surprisingly, the food. My family adored John and continued to hope that he and I could overcome "the Jesus thing." Every few weeks, he'd bring them pastries from Astoria, the Greek neighborhood in Queens. He'd present honey-drenched treats like kataifi (a Shredded Wheat look-alike that tastes like baklava), galaktoboureko (a sweet, custardy cake), and loukoumades (round fried balls covered in cinnamon and powdered sugar), and we'd all have a great time getting silly and sticky. They asked John to teach them their Greek names and became avid fans of George Stephanopoulos.

As a couple, John and I would sometimes sit at cafés in Astoria, even though I sensed his anxiety about running into a family member there. It wasn't like anyone could spot us with our heads buried in crazy-caffeinated frappes and flaky, fried spanakopita. Learning about Indian food with Gary was a good time, but nothing compared to exploring Greek cuisine with John, who would put his fork to my lips, as I practically purred. We'd wrestle for the last lamb chop or bite of halloumi cheese. I eventually put a stop to anything involving tzatziki, because it resulted in the world's worst garlic breath, which was the only thing on earth that could keep me from kissing him. I didn't know much about food, but these simple Mediterranean ingredients—olive oil, lemon, and oregano—were the flavors of some of the best nights of my life.

But I was almost thirty, and the issue of my non-Greekness was escalating every day. Approaching our two-year anniversary, with all our breakups and makeups, I found a Greek therapist, Dr. Pappa, who understood our situation, and we both began to see her separately. She told me that John truly loved me and was "working extremely hard" to find the strength to confront his family about us, but still had a *very* long way to go. "It could take months; it could take years," she said bluntly, but kindly. This ripped my heart out. *Years?* I became terribly frustrated, and my family, who began to grasp that we were truly at a stalemate, started to intervene. So, too, did my colleagues at the magazine. Our Shakespearian tragedy wasn't endearing to anyone anymore, least of all me. I loved John like no other, but the ride was making me sick and I wanted off.

In a span of seventy-two hours, I collected as much strength as I could, resigned from my job at *Us Weekly,* sold all my material possessions on Craigslist, walked into John's office, and begged him never to contact me again. He pleaded for more time, but this patient had lost her patience. I kissed my forever-supportive family good-bye, did "the trick," and flew across the country to California to quit John. Through work, I had come to know Los Angeles quite well and knew it was the only city that could energize me almost as much as New York. I wasn't moving there for good, but I didn't buy a return ticket either. I convinced an equally down-in-the-dumps Shelley to move there, too, with the caveat that we couldn't live together . . . I needed my space.

My spirit was broken, but it was hard to stay sullen in sunny California. I accepted a job as a dating blogger for *Glamour* magazine because it seemed like a good gig, and knowing me, there would be plenty of fodder (even though I hadn't looked at another man since my fateful dentist appointment two years ago). Sight unseen and off the Web, I rented the first furnished apartment that seemed like my style, a bungalow at the foot of Runyon Canyon. It came with a porch, a hammock, and a banged-up convertible. The landlord said the neighbors were "a bunch of hilarious gay guys," which sounded really good to me. On move-in day, she was showing me the kitchen already filled with exotic spices and grains when I interrupted by asking, "Great, but where are your take-out menus?"

For the first few weeks in the bungalow, I'd take a half hour to write my *Glamour* entry in the morning, scrambling for compelling stories that I was willing to share about my newly single life. The problem was that my editors and readers wanted to see me single and mingling, but really, I was in no place for miniskirts and martinis. So usually I'd just inflate something true but totally insignificant, hit SEND, and be done.

I'd spend the rest of my day hiking, riding bikes, reading by the beach, and seeing movies, sometimes with Shelley, but usually by myself. I got a cherry blossom tattoo on my ankle just to see what it would feel like. And then I got a lotus on the back of my neck. There was no TV in the bungalow, so I was completely out of touch with pop culture, a cleanse of its own. This would have been a nice time to take up cooking, especially with all the raw beans and funky rice I had inherited in the pantry, but I was just as happy snacking on fruit, nuts, and chocolate all day, or take-out from any of the boho-Californian joints on Sunset Boulevard.

With trail mix in one hand and a California Chardonnay in the other, I'd sit quietly in the dark, spying on the neighbors sitting on the shared lawn. They were usually hand-rolling cigarettes and getting their cocktail on. They looked like young, adorable party animals, and they never stopped. Of course, I didn't mind.

I'd hear them cracking up (or were they cracked-out?) all night long. When I caught a very famous, "straight" actor stumbling down the driveway at six o'clock in the morning, I felt a flick of a switch. Enough with the heartbreak. It was time to have fun.

In half a second, the "nabes" took me in and became my wild, West Coast ride. Not only were they ridiculously spirited, but they were also quirky and nonjudgmental, and they brought out an uninhibited side of me that had been dormant since my childhood in Longmeadow. They were also raging cokeheads. That didn't bother me—I did plenty of partying in New York, but it was usually encased in work, and since I was always scared about appearing strung-out to my family, nothing got too excessive. But in L.A., no one was watching. I made my own rules and did whatever the hell I wanted.

While Shelley was finding her place with the beautiful and successful showbiz types, I was transfixed by my new, screwed-up friends, and my nights with them were becoming a bit corrupt. They were delighted to bring me (and *party supplies*) everywhere they went—to outrageous parties in the Hollywood Hills, unbelievable barbecues in Malibu, and underground art shows in Venice Beach. They were wickedly funny, highly promiscuous, and totally reckless. They didn't wear seat belts, they never needed sleep, and best of all, they didn't let me so much as mumble John's name.

One night, we went to a party at a rock star's glass mansion in the hills. I ended up so messed up from mojitos and more that I did a strip show on the deck while the nabes cheered me on. We found a disposable razor in the pool-house bathroom and I had one of the Guns N' Roses guys shave my entire body. We called it performance art. It was exhilarating to be so out of control. *Fuck John. Fuck the dating blog. Fuck it all.* When the hot tub found me, things got even crazier with an infamous drummer I had grown up listening to. Later on he told me he had a wife. And that she wanted to join us next.

The nabes and I did the same thing the next night, at a different mansion, with a different crowd, breaking different rules, with a different drink and different drug. And then we did it again. *And again*.

I easily could have found my happy place in the risky world of sex, drugs, and rock 'n' roll, especially on this other coast, where nobody knew what I was up to. All that raw inhibition felt way too natural for me. Becoming an artsy, tortured fuckup was so incredibly tempting, and the road was *right there* for me to take. But I didn't. After eight months in Los Angeles, I broke my lease and moved back to New York. The nabes had too many demons and were rubbing off on me in addictive and destructive ways.

Shelley and I would stay best friends, but her life in Los Angeles was too *Hollywood* for me to handle, especially when it wasn't part of my job anymore.

My dating blog for *Glamour* received substantial traffic, but also armies of haters because of its feather-light content and general lack of substance or self-analysis (I never took it seriously and it showed). Suddenly, I was petrified that I'd made a mockery of my professional self and had ruined my writing career for good.

And John? After almost a year away, I still thought of him every day. His incandescent eyes and boyish humor, and how deliriously good it felt to be near him no matter how grim the circumstances were. I made peace with the cruel fact that I'd never be quite the same again, that losing John broke me in a way that couldn't really be rebuilt. But I came to think of heartbreak as an impetus to becoming a wiser woman, sister, friend, and writer, and, in a way, I felt chosen to have had such a healthy dose of it. Strong women don't just happen.

If nothing else, my sad ending with John got me to L.A., which might have been a bit too sublime, but it did my soul some good. As I flew up, up, and away, back to New York, I knew I was moving somewhere in the right direction.

Sarabeth's Velvety Cream of Tomato Soup

SERVES 8

When I waitressed at Sarabeth's, I would watch in amazement as people bowed down to their bowls of creamy tomato soup. All these years later, whenever I mention that I once worked there, what's the first thing I hear? Oh man, that soup . . . *Well, I finally tracked down the original recipe, posted online by Sarabeth herself, after thirty years of secrecy, and this is it, exactly. The soup tastes just as I remember. Which triggers another fond memory: the adorable actor-slash-waiter who would feed it to me after we closed up shop.*

---

6 tablespoons unsalted butter
1 small Vidalia onion, chopped
2 medium shallots, chopped
4 scallions, green parts only, thinly sliced
3 garlic cloves, minced
Two 28-ounce cans crushed tomatoes in puree
4 cups whole milk
4 cups heavy cream
⅓ cup all-purpose flour, sifted
⅓ cup dill fronds, torn into tiny sprigs
Sea salt and freshly ground pepper to taste
1 cup grated white cheddar cheese, for serving

Melt 2 tablespoons of the butter in a skillet over medium-low heat. Add the onion, shallots, scallions, and garlic. Cook, stirring occasionally, until the vegetables are softened and translucent, about 4 minutes. Transfer the mixture to the top of a double boiler over boiling water. If you don't have a double boiler, fill a large saucepan with water and bring to a boil. Set a large heatproof bowl to fit tightly on top of the pan and transfer the mixture to the bowl.

Using a wooden spoon, further crush the tomatoes into small

pieces. Add the crushed tomatoes and puree, milk, and cream to the vegetable mixture and bring to a simmer, stirring often.

Meanwhile, in a small saucepan, melt the remaining 4 tablespoons of butter over low heat. Gradually whisk in the flour. Cook, whisking almost constantly, to make a roux, for about 3 minutes. Be careful not to brown it. Whisk about 1½ cups of the hot tomato mixture into the roux, then pour the roux mixture into the top of the double boiler and stir until blended.

Reduce the heat to low and simmer for about 35 minutes to allow the flavors to blend and thicken the soup. Turn off the heat and then add the dill, salt, and pepper.

Serve hot, topping each serving with about 2 tablespoons of grated cheese.

The soup can be prepared up to 2 days ahead, cooled completely, covered, and refrigerated. It should last for 4 to 5 days. The soup will thicken when chilled; when reheating, thin the heated soup with milk to the desired thickness. Do not freeze the soup.

Reality Bites Banana Bread

MAKES 1 LOAF

My twenties were crazy and I wouldn't have had it any other way. Through it all—college, the celebrity scene, my split with John, and an escape across the country—I would always beg my mother to make me this banana bread. Before my parents moved to New York, my mom once bought a ticket for it on the bus, along with a larger food shipment. I'm extremely fortunate to have a family I can count on for anything, *and that devotion is exactly what I taste when I dig into this.*

---

2 cups all-purpose flour, sifted
1 teaspoon baking powder
1 teaspoon baking soda
½ teaspoon salt
8 tablespoons (1 stick) unsalted butter, plus additional for greasing the pan
½ cup sugar
1 cup (2 medium or 3 small) mashed ripe bananas
3 tablespoons sour cream or low-fat yogurt
1 teaspoon vanilla extract
½ cup chopped walnuts
1 to 1½ cups semisweet chocolate chips (depending on your sweet tooth)

Preheat the oven to 350°F.

In a medium mixing bowl, stir together the flour, baking powder, baking soda, and salt. Set aside.

In a large mixing bowl (or in the bowl of a stand mixer fitted with the paddle attachment), cream together the butter and sugar until light and fluffy. Add the bananas, sour cream, and vanilla. Mix well.

Blend the flour mixture into the banana mixture and stir in the walnuts and chocolate chips.

Pour the batter into a greased 9 × 5-inch baking pan and bake for approximately 45 minutes, or until the top is firm and golden brown and a toothpick or knife inserted in the center comes out clean.

Cool completely in the baking dish or on a rack before slicing and serving. Wrap the leftovers tightly in foil and store at room temperature, and the banana bread should last a good week. It freezes beautifully too.

3.

Oui, Chef

I am standing near City Hall, heading toward my home across the Brooklyn Bridge, and there's a gray-haired millionaire wearing an Hermès tie, dancing to the tunes of a homeless man on the trombone. New York, it's good to be back.

Over the past year, I left the West Coast, disassociated myself from the *Glamour* dating blog, turned thirty, and after six intense interviews, got a full-time job that I'm really proud of. I'm a staff writer at *People* magazine, with a good salary, a private office, and interesting assignments involving film, music, television, health, human interest, and a lot more than celebrity news. My editors all know that I accepted the job under the condition that I won't have to go clubbing, stalking, or slithering into places where I don't belong, and that I'm a *reformed* party girl with an early bedtime.

Living in California completely reset my body. It took the *mani-pedi, buy-the-shoes, blow-the-doorman* right out of me. Ultimately, I had to go all the way across the country just to come back down to earth.

When I'm not reporting, I spend a lot of time with my forever sweet and easy sister, who's working at *Real Simple* magazine, just a few floors down from *People*. Or I'm having long talks over a few drinks with my closest New York girlfriends, Beth and Jill (Shelley, who I talk to ten times a day, and who is gradually mellowing out herself, never came back from L.A.). Beth is from Western Massachusetts like me. She's strikingly pretty and reminds me, in her unpretentiousness, of the girls from home. (When Jean died, Beth and I had just started working together at a PR firm, and I remember feeling like she was the only person who understood how the tragedy rocked my tiny town.) And then there's the smokin' hot Jill, who's as devoted as she is difficult. She works in fashion and dates only fancy men whom I describe as "camera ready." She's the one I count on every time there's a party or a plus-one; I just love her company.

As always, I'm enjoying a lot of alone time, too—hunkering down at poetry readings, jazz clubs, and other weird and wonderful gatherings, befriending singletons with short bangs and Buddhists with perfect posture, and conversing with total strangers on everything from capitalism to colonics. In this city, you can meet more great people while buying a stick of gum than most do in a lifetime elsewhere. Everyone has a story, mind-bending or blood-racing, on this island of provocateurs. On my favorite nights, I just putter around aimlessly, vacillating between culture and curiosity. There's nothing I'd rather do than roam the streets without watching the clock.

Not that life has been uneventful.

After L.A., I invested my life savings in an apartment in an almost-happening neighborhood of Brooklyn called Ditmas Park. I lived there for a few months, but when a meth-head mooned me in the building's elevator, I realized I wasn't as edgy as I thought. Soon thereafter, I rented the place to two librarian pescatarians on a budget, while I waited for the property to appreciate and the neighborhood to become a little less sketchy and a bit more Starbucks.

I then moved in with my parents, who just bought a luxury loft in a more enviable Brooklyn enclave called DUMBO (which stands for Down Under the Manhattan Bridge Overpass). Now, I listlessly inhabit a spare, windowless, prison-white room meant to be an office (the only option besides bunking up in my parents' bedroom, which, disturbingly, they probably would have loved). On one hand, living at home was a smart, economical decision so I could figure out the next steps in my housing situation. On the other hand, I'm about to turn thirty-one, and I feel a little foolish being a single, stay-at-home daughter with all her money tied up in an apartment that other people live in and that most taxi drivers can't find.

I'm still meeting guys everywhere I go—at Citibank, before a Shakespeare in the Park play, while doing crosswords on the subway—and even though many men have that *je ne sais quoi,* no one has been quite right for me. The problem is I *need* to be with an alluring, off-the-grid kind of guy, otherwise I lose interest. But it seems like all the dazzling men have such dark problems: impending divorces, sex addictions, secret debt. I go to art shows and housewarming parties with no shortage of fetching, successful, normal bachelors who just want to love and be loved like the rest of us, yet I end up embarrassed for their unoriginality and unable to bear a conversation with them about work or the weather. So instead, I wind up in the arms of guys like the hot, Hungarian bike messenger who was at a book reading (on a drug deal) and put me in his phone as "Alyssa Sexy Jew." Bad judgment, exceptional hands. Such lousy, lust-driven decisions are why Dr. Pappa, who I'm still seeing, has me committed to a summer of no dating, no drama, and no strings attached.

Then I get a press release. . . .

Bravo's A-List Awards are happening tonight and the lineup

includes *Top Chef*'s current season of cheftestants. While I have zero interest in cooking, something catches my eye. In my wholesome, post-Californian-life, I've started to watch *Top Chef* from time to time because even as a noncook, the show relaxes me. So much so that I've written about a few of the winners and the master chefs who have influenced them. But what really hooked me this season was a crush I developed on the token bestubbled bad boy, who I cleverly nicknamed "Chef." Chef looks like James Dean, says he's Greek *and* Jewish, and totally turns me on. I even forced my family to watch an episode, because as I tell them, "I'm pretty sure the one making blood sausage is my soul mate . . ." Only *they* would see that as a perfectly logical thing to say.

Today, like a paper airplane sent from Aphrodite, Chef is on the tip sheet thrown on top of the *New York Times* and next to yesterday's coffee. Usually I'd go to something like this myself, but I've just sworn off men, I'm living out of boxes in my parents' apartment, and I just don't look or feel my best; I'm even wearing one of my mother's muumuus—which is not as Sienna Miller as it sounds.

So in my place, I send a pretty, blond freelance reporter named Stephanie to the Bravo party with simple instructions: "Do not leave until you find out if Chef has a girlfriend. And ask him what he looks for in a woman. Get specifics!" Professionalism has never been my strength.

I head home, take a sunset jog, eat a few bowls of cereal and an entire carton of strawberries, floss my teeth, put on a nightgown, and crawl into bed feeling slightly pitiful, not that I'd ever say so. Just before midnight, my phone vibrates as I'm tossing and turning. Apparently, professionalism isn't Stephanie's thing either. She's e-mailed me her transcript from the Bravo event, along with a note: "Chef is very nice and very single. Thanks for the assignment!! P.S. I know you're not looking or anything, but here's his phone number. . . . Just in case." Screw journalistic integrity. Give the girl a raise.

While tucked under the covers in fuzzy socks and shea butter cream, I reach for the light on the bedside table and start to read the two-page interview on my BlackBerry. I am prepared for a slight rush, a raise of the brow, and then hopefully, a better night's sleep. But as I read his responses—part juvenile delinquent, part plain ole Joe—my eyes, freshly dotted in cucumber serum, start to widen. He talks about his family's villa in Greece, and how he dreams of taking a girl there and making her a peasant dish called reginatta, which he describes as stale bread sprinkled with ocean water, covered with bright red tomatoes and crumbled fresh feta. As for the girl, she should be funny, down-to-earth, and extremely family-oriented. He says he's been a "kitchen-rat" his whole life and that it's starting to get quite lonely. He's happy to have been on *Top Chef,* but he might just become a marine biologist in Florida or a fisherman in the South of France.

Wow. He's just what I thought he'd be like: creative, carefree, and vulnerable. As I read his answers, I am struck by how unaffected he is. *How can he be lonely?* He's such a rock star in my eyes. *And the perfect woman he described?* She sounds a little familiar. I mostly love that he's a dreamer but doesn't sound totally dysfunctional. That's exactly what I want, exactly what I need. A flash goes off, and suddenly, I know without any hesitation, that Chef is more than just a TV fantasy. He is my next boyfriend.

Let me explain. There are three things I know about my biological self:

1. If I walk into a McDonald's, even just to use the bathroom, I will get a glistening red zit on the left side of my cheek that will terrorize my life for ten days straight.

2. If I combine alcohol with pot, in any quality or quantity, I'll convince myself that I'm paralyzed from the neck down, pee in my pants, and then puke.

3. When the future-boyfriend flash goes off, though it's always primal and *never* practical, the world better buckle up, because we're all in for a ride.

The next day at work, I immediately e-mail the special projects editor at *People,* asking if I can interview Chef for our annual bachelor issue, explaining that a freelancer had revealed his single status and that he's definitely an up-and-coming heartthrob. It honestly doesn't matter if she gives me the green light or not. *I have to meet him.* I then go to my weekly therapy session with Dr. Pappa, who, just one week ago, made me promise to not date this summer. At the time, I was totally on board, but who would have thought Chef would be right around the corner?

"I am going to contact him and who knows what will happen," I say, after quoting verbatim the cute, off-the-cuff answers he gave to Stephanie. I include the reginatta bit, hoping the Greek nostalgia will perhaps soften her.

"Don't do it, Alyssa. Please . . ." says the shrink. "It's not a good idea. . . . You really need to be single."

"Don't worry, Dr. P.," I say, writing a check. "I'll proceed with caution."

Who knows why I'm so self-assured when it comes to pursuing guys, and in this case, an almost-famous guy. Some people might say that I'm a hot girl; others might go with a hot mess.

I think it's somewhere in between. I can be beautiful or I can be busted, but I can't get by on my looks alone, even if I tried. Whether it's my inherited confidence, or an inner cool when it comes to the opposite sex, or some life-less-ordinary-aura, getting guys has always been easy, and getting Chef should be cake.

Despite Dr. Pappa's warnings *and* my editor's impending e-mail saying that Chef isn't famous enough for the magazine, I leave a message on his cell, in my deepest Demi Moore voice possible, that I want to do an in-person interview with him for *People* magazine's bachelor issue. *Screw it.* I can get him on the pages if I really need to. If not, this could be worth getting fired for. He returns my message in a few minutes, sounding dead tired and terribly adorable. He's excited about the interview, which I feel a little guilty about (but not really). We start to e-mail and text, comparing our schedules, warming things up. He says he lives in Brooklyn but is in the process of moving somewhere else. I write him that the sauce he made on last week's episode looked so good that "I wanted to take a bath in it!" He writes back four seconds later: "That could be arranged." *This is my kind of guy.* Eventually, we agree to meet at a corner café in Williamsburg called Fabiane's. Even over the phone, we are on fire.

Hours before our interview, I am searching online for something food-savvy to say. At this point, the only thing I really know about the culinary scene is that white wine goes in the fridge, guacamole makes you fat, and Tom Colicchio is bald. The more I think about how little we could have in common, the more nervous I get, so I leave early and order a tequila shot at DUMBO General Store, my neighborhood hang. I ask to speak with the restaurant's chef, who is "preparing for the dinner rush," not that I understand what that means. "Hey . . . um . . . what's like a hot topic in the chef scene right now?" I ask. He speaks broken English, is sweating his ass off, and tells me he's totally slammed. "No problemo," I say, pounding the shot and heading to the F train.

On the subway, I remind myself that our get-together is a "business meeting," so I put on my reporter's hat and fool myself into forgetting about any romantic anticipation. I brush into Fabiane's with the look of an unflappable journalist, in a very flappable short skirt, who's done this hundreds of times. Chef is there already, waiting for me by the dessert display, now walking toward me to say hello. He's long, ruddy, and crazy cute. Before I can reach out my hand, there's a kiss on the cheek and a tight hug hello. This doesn't happen with Justin Timberlake.

We arrange a table for two outside, while I take out my tape recorder, which I won't be turning on, and my list of fake questions, which I won't be flipping through. I try to stay in character, but the way he looks, the way he speaks, the way he dresses, how our knees touch . . . I'm trembling. I'm not sure what one orders on a bogus interview that's turning into a first date, with a French-trained chef and me, a kitchen-phobe, so I fumble through the menu and somehow come up with chicken curry salad. He gets a tomato and mozzarella tartine. We agree on a round of Stella Artois. When the waitress walks away, we waste no time getting to know each other.

"So, what's your story?" I ask, with a beer bottle to my mouth, half reporter, half temptress.

"I'll tell you about me, if you promise to tell me about you?" He smiles.

"Fair enough." I smirk, locking my eyes onto his for a beat too long.

He swiftly shares fascinating stories about his past, really personal things, and I assure him that everything's off the record. (If he only knew *how* off the record!) We are so instantaneously comfortable around each other that when his Greek and Jewish heritage comes up, I tell him that a Greek man once broke my heart. Our food comes and I make the long story short. My eyes well up when talking about John, as they always do, and he asks if it still hurts. I say that I'm doing fine, that it's all part of my fiber now, and that I've never believed we get only one great love anyway. I realize that I'm committing a faux pas by bringing up old boyfriends, but this is not the kind of guy who plays by the rules. He doesn't even know they exist.

"Go on a date with me," he interrupts.

"Why should I?!" I say teasingly, wanting to kiss him, seduce him, marry him.

"Just be my girl," he says, with a naïveté I have never seen in a man. "I won't hurt you."

I tell him I'll consider it, and we share an excellent piece of lemon cake, taking turns with one fork. It's tangy and light, with a generous rich glaze, the perfect way to end an early summer night. I'm hungry and I hog it because I barely touched my chicken curry, which looked like bad news in school-bus yellow. "Who orders chicken curry from a little French bistro?" he jokes, as we walk away from the restaurant, nudging me playfully on my side. Without a moment of self-consciousness, I confess that I know *nothing* about food. He doesn't so much as flinch. He just wants to know when he can see me again. "Let me think about it." I wink, waving down a cab.

He kisses me good-bye, on the cheek again, but more affectionately this time, brushing back my hair. We play it cool for about two days or two hours. I can't remember. But I do remember not being able to sleep or stop smiling. I also refuse to acknowledge that this is his last week in New York. He is moving to Washington, D.C., to open a casual neighborhood restaurant in Capitol Hill with a few partners. Caught up in the fervor of it all, this strikes me as a minor detail, as if D.C. is just down the street, somewhere in between Westchester and love-comes-first. He seems to share my geographical haze.

We text every few hours, figuring out our next plans, and the following night he calls just to see how I'm doing. Midconversation, I fess up about the bachelor issue hoax: "You really think I'd share you?" I tease, hoping it doesn't come across as too forward. He had totally forgotten about that which predicated our entire interaction, the actual "interview," and replies that he doesn't want to be shared anyway. "You're the one for me," he says without any pretense. I have no idea how to respond, so I say, "Thank you."

There is something so innocent, so coltlike, about him. He still has an old, cracked flip phone; he doesn't have a Facebook account. His favorite restaurants are diners and his dream vacation is fishing on a lake with rolling papers, a transistor radio, and a few cans of cold Coca-Cola. When I tell him a long-winded story about Winona Ryder, which he follows carefully, he says at the end, "I love that. But who is she?" He's a simple guy, who works really hard, rewarding himself by putting his toes in the sand and his hands on a woman, and I'm mesmerized by the authenticity of it all.

Not long after he moves to D.C., Chef takes a train back to New York for a proper first date. He finds his way to DUMBO, where I am counting down the seconds. It's a hot, humid night in late June and just as he rings the bell downstairs in my parents' lobby, a summer thunderstorm hits hard. I take a deep breath, check my outfit, smooth down my frizz, and head to the lobby. My heart pounds as I spot him waiting outside in the rain with ripped jeans and amber eyes. Before I can ask if he wants Italian or Thai, he kisses my lips, wraps his tender arms around my waist, and walks us down the cobblestone street, under the

Manhattan Bridge and the splitting skies. Our bodies are sticky; our hair is wild. We don't care where we're going. It is the love affair I never want to end, the perfect storm.

After that night, which rocked both my body and mind, Chef starts buying me train tickets to visit him every weekend in D.C. He's renting a three-bedroom house with "the Boys," his tireless and tattooed sous-chefs. I like the Boys a lot; they're real teddy bears, but the house is situated in a dangerous neighborhood, and ironically, their kitchen is infested with bugs and beyond. In the morning, before he heads to the restaurant, Chef always manages to make me strong coffee and cheese toast, which is basically cheese melted on bread in the toaster oven, but constructed with such confidence and so perfectly crispy. I eat with my feet elevated, petrified of any critters that may whiz by.

It breaks my heart that in building and launching the restaurant all summer, Chef and his roommates haven't had any time to clean up this run-down Capitol Hill clunker. It also breaks my back—Chef essentially sleeps on a cot. So the first present I ever buy him is a nice and comfortable "W Hotel" mattress, which I purchase with my press discount. It's the least I can do—for both of us. He beams over the bed, saying it's the nicest thing anyone has ever done for him.

We like all things hotel-related. After making such a splash on *Top Chef,* my guy is now invited to do a lot of cooking events around the country. He includes me in everything, as if we're a package deal, and I am tickled pink to tag along. I sit in the audience as he does his food demos, oblivious to his knife skills but obsessed with his aura. When it's time for the Q&A portion of the event, I wait for some smitten soccer mom to ask if he's single, and for him to blush and brag about me. "Actually, that's my girl over there. . . . She's the best writer in the world. . . ." I swoon when he says this, especially because all he's read are my love letters to him.

When we go to a celebrity poker tournament at Foxwoods Resort Casino in Connecticut, we skip most of the festivities and stay in our suite, with the room-service menu and *The Hangover* on demand. No one wins bigger than we do that night.

For a corporate event in Philadelphia, he is paid to make an appetizer and meet some fans. Bored by the crowd, and enamored with each other, we sneak off a little early. Arm in arm, feeling very much like the untucked artist and his slinky muse, we duck away, and I walk right into a glass door. Face first. Bloody nose. He dies laughing. I die laughing even harder.

We have so much fun traveling in our pack of two, checking into hotels, hiding out, watching movie marathons, and tying and untying our terry-cloth robes. He *always* orders a couple club sandwiches for us to share throughout the night. Chef is a club sandwich aficionado. It personifies his style—simple without being bland, layered without being complicated, and ever so slightly retro. The sandwich has two things I've always abhorred, mayonnaise and bacon, but I quickly get over that and fall in love with everything about our toasted, toothpicked ritual, the first of many.

He never has much time to enjoy New York with me now that his restaurant is officially open, but when he comes in for meetings, he tries to make a full day of it. I find us cool things to do, like abstract one-act plays and raunchy underground comedy clubs. Since he's been living behind a stove for most of his life, he's self-admittedly clueless when it comes to most things nonkitchen. We see an outdoor production of *Hair,* just like I did when I was little, and have such a wild time it's as if *we're* the ones hallucinating. Despite his first-class cooking pedigree, fine dining isn't really our thing. After a movie or concert, if we end up somewhere fancy, he does the ordering and I enthusiastically oblige. But normally, we have picnics in Brooklyn's Prospect Park and eat at laid-back bistros. We could both exist on cheese and bread, though he'd definitely prefer prosciutto with his.

One day we visit Jill and Beth, at Alison Brod Public Relations, the glammed-out PR firm where they both now work. The girls shower Chef in swag from their clients—Sephora skincare, Godiva chocolates, Havaianas flip-flops. He's floored by my friends' warmth and generosity, walking out with five bags of freebies, and hugs and kisses from a dozen blushing girls. "Um, your new boyfriend is really hot . . . and has really big feet," Beth, who married her first boyfriend, giggles into the phone later that night. "You're great together, Lys."

On a muggy Tuesday morning, I'm in my office pricing out train tickets for the weekend when Chef calls and says, "Coffee break?" What a surprise! *He's in New York?* I run downstairs, where he's holding a cappuccino from my favorite local bakery, and an important-looking envelope.

"What are you doing next week, and the week after that?"

"Working, visiting you, the usual. Why?"

"Because remember how I said my dream was to take the love of my life to Greece?"

"Yeah?" I squint, slowly slipping into shock.

"Well, Lyssie, that's you. Will you come with me to Greece?"

He has arranged and paid for the whole thing. It's the end of August, our three-month anniversary, and he's taking me to the villa he shares with his family, for fifteen days. I am speechless. We're going to have it all to ourselves. He took the train in just to see my reaction.

When I tell Liz, my boss, that I'll be using up all my vacation days and darting off to Europe to be with my new chef boyfriend, she immediately gives her full approval. Liz loves hearing about my life, and because she grew up in the seventies with five sisters in San Francisco, there's nothing she hasn't seen or heard. "Keeping up with the Kardashians is easier than keeping up with me, right?" I say, twirling out of her office.

My family is also thrilled for me. They've treasured Chef ever since they met him, when he told them a hysterical story about waking up in a hospital room with his frowning mother, a disturbed nurse, and a mysterious case of loud, uncontrollable flatulence. That night at their loft, my mother made everyone extra well done steaks burned down to hockey pucks, and Chef, bless his heart, asked for seconds.

Getting to Greece is a saga of its own. Chef is as disorganized as he is romantic, and there's mayhem involving all things customs, passports, and visas. But after seventy-two hours of smoked almonds, Bourne identities, and broken sleep, we arrive at the port of a village, where a beady-eyed taxi driver takes us to the house. The orange sun is just coming up.

Perched on a cliff at the end of a narrow road and framed in exotic flowers, olive branches, hummingbirds, and clotheslines, the villa is more like a pretty little beach house than a sprawling ancient estate. We find the hidden key nestled in the outdoor wood-burning oven and let ourselves into our private haven. The inside of the house is lovely and understated, and already, I never want to leave. We haven't slept in about two days, but before we crash, Chef finds the keys to the blue truck sitting in the driveway, leads me outside, and buckles me into the passenger seat. Delirious, I don't ask where we're going.

Driving down the steep roads of this gorgeous seaside village, I stare at the views layered in lemon trees, mountaintops, and an aquamarine ocean, while Chef stops at the market down the street that's just opening for its morning business. Then he drives us down the coast. It's astounding that a guy who can't remember to close the front door, and sometimes isn't sure of the month or year, can find his way through these rocky roads like he's never lived anywhere else. He hasn't been back to Greece in years, but he is in his element; he is by the sea.

Chef parks the car at a private cove, and we walk, holding hands, down to the beach. I sit at the edge, where the waves meet the sand, as Chef rolls up his pants and opens his market bag. He takes out a hardened baguette, perhaps a day or two old, breaks it in half, and sprinkles salt water all over the insides. Using his bent knee as his cutting board, he slices some very ripe tomatoes and takes apart a huge hunk of feta. Sitting in the rocks and shells, barefoot, jet-lagged, and awestruck, I realize that he's making me reginatta, the dish he described in his interview. We eat, kiss, and cry. It's almost too much to process that we're both experiencing the phenomenon of a dream coming true. I wanted to be with him before we even met, and he wanted to be on this beach before he knew with whom. *Unbelievable.*

We sleep away the rest of the day and resurface the next morning feeling fresh, swiftly falling into our daily ritual. For the next two weeks, I wake up first and make us a pot of coffee, a vital activity I have cultivated over the past few years. He wakes up two hours later, first calling me back to bed, then boiling eggs to go with toast and homemade apricot marmalade (brought over by a nice, nosy Greek neighbor). Over breakfast on the porch, with bed heads and pajamas, we decide which beach or covelike "crevice of love," as he likes to call them, to explore. I pack our CDs for the car ride, books for me, and diving gear for him, and we get in our bathing suits and go.

Lunch is an ice cream, or a couple of Mythos beers, and when we get too sunburned, hungry, or horny, we head back to the villa by way of the market. The thing about Chef and cooking is that when he's not in his restaurant, he really can't be bothered. This doesn't disappoint me one bit. Our meals are low-key wherever we are, but I'm still careful not to cross the line between adorably foodie-illiterate and downright stupid.

At the tented, outdoor markets, we shop for the glorious food basics I grew up with—fruit, cheese, yogurt, bread, and cakes—with a few delicious diversions. I can't say no to baklava and he's a lamb gyro junkie. One après-beach afternoon, Chef waits in the car while I run outside to buy a few bags of succulent peaches and plums for the house. My selection looks outstanding, but when I feed him a rock-hard peach, he scrunches his face and tells me it's totally not ripe! I'm not sure where I got the idea, but I had always assumed *all* fruit should be hard and crunchy like apples. He delights in calling me out on that one (and I still prefer nectarines hard as tennis balls).

For dinner, we eat casually and compatibly, popping into the local trattoria for Greek salads, a shared order of pasticcio, and maybe a few bites of sweet, giant baked beans. While eating gelato or ice-cream sandwiches, we walk home, watching for shooting stars.

On our last night in Greece, we have to pack up our things and close down the house for the season. I can't seem to fit all my sarongs and straw hats into my suitcase with all the evil-eye charms and jars of honey I've bought for my family. Chef nonchalantly suggests that I leave my beachwear here. "You're going to need everything next year, aren't you?" he says, with no clue how much his suggestion means to me.

Flying home, we review our upcoming schedules, with me in New York and him in D.C., and suddenly the long-distance just seems insane. It takes a two-minute conversation to decide that we should move in together in Washington, and by the time the plane lands, I've already e-mailed my boss, Liz, that we need to talk.

The same day I return to New York, I tell everyone that it's official. I am leaving town and moving to Washington, D.C., to be Chef's writerly girlfriend, who wears off-the-shoulder T-shirts and says provocative things. Yes, me, in the nation's capital, where I have no roots, no friends, no facialist, no freelance work, no favorite homeless guy, no transgendered Starbucks girl, no go-to spin instructor—nothing other than my unbelievable new boyfriend and his uncontaminated, hippielike heart. We'll light up the city, grow Chef's business, make babies, and map out a beach house halfway between his restaurant and my family. Or something like that.

I give *People* as much notice as they need, which most of my colleagues use as precious time to dissuade me from "throwing away my career." They're not trying to be negative. It's just not the kind of culture at the magazine where women leave their promising jobs with full benefits and car service just because they've met scruffy guys with great hair who whoosh them away to the Greek Islands. I can barely look at Liz, who's been like a big sister to me since the day she brought me in for a formal interview, when I couldn't help but blow off all the super-corporate questions and fixate on her translucent skin and uncanny resemblance to Julianne Moore. A seasoned editor with supreme grace, Liz has done her best to keep me on track ever since, and because I respect her so, it's my great pleasure to deliver her good work. But like my mother, my sister, and the other good women in my life, Liz also knows that my mind is made up on moving to D.C. She accepts that I'm three parts love, one part logic.

I have a good-bye lunch with J.D. Heyman, another top

editor at the magazine and a smart, funny, straight-shooting guy that everyone at *People* really respects. Unlike Liz, he's openly apprehensive. "I know you really like this person, Alyssa, but are you sure you want to do this?" he says, looking me directly in the eye. It's not like J.D. to get so personal. "I'm asking you to wait it out. Give it a little more time, will ya?" J.D. recently guided me through my first cover story, a huge profile on the actresses from *Sex & the City,* an enviable assignment that brought me so much joy. He worries I'll feel depleted without New York's incomparable energy and the camaraderie of being around other people like me. While too gentlemanly to say so, I'm sure, J.D. has also noticed my habit of rushing dangerously into romance, further validating his concern. "New York will always be here," I ultimately tell him, with a trusting smile. "And the bus is only twenty bucks."

The few people who are excited for me are mostly friends who are *Top Chef* fans. They think I'll get invited to the best dinner parties, have barbecues with Bobby Flay, fly to France with *Food & Wine.* But I tell them that even though it's what intially drew me to him, the "celebrity-chef shitshow" is the last reason I'm uprooting my life. Turns out, Chef's career is my least favorite thing about him. Owning a restaurant is a grueling, self-vandalizing profession—I can see that already—and his place has been open only a few months. And being on TV, in my very jaded opinion, is overrated. It can be lucrative if you're prepared to play the game, but show-business whoredom is not for the fainthearted. It can make you, and it can break you.

Nonetheless, Chef likes the taste of celebrity; the validation fulfills something inside him. And so, I feed the beast. I help him hire a publicist and an agent, both with major reputations for making chefs super famous. I buy him a BlackBerry for his birthday, and we create a Facebook and Twitter account for him. I even pull a favor with a producer friend to get him on *Good Morning America.* I am totally committed to his burgeoning career, even if mine is on hold. We'll take turns kicking ass.

As my days at *People* wind down, I take the train to D.C. every few days to look at apartments for us. It's fall and Congress is back in session, which means that work is booming for Chef. I worry about adding any stress to his workdays, so I leave him alone at the restaurant and stroll the streets of Capitol Hill solo, checking out the one-bedrooms and bumping into portly politicians who smell like shaving cream and never say "Excuse me." As I explore the neighborhoods, I try to mesh with my new stomping ground. I stop into coffee shops, read the *Washington Post* in the park, browse the stores in Dupont Circle, and do all the things that bring me simple pleasures in New York. I try to stay lighthearted with all the unfamiliar people in their unattractive outfits; I smile but no one smiles back. It's not like we're all so copacetic in New York City either, yet I totally *get,* and appreciate, *those* fuck-my-life dirty looks and broke-and-exhausted blank stares. In Washington, no matter what I do, or where I go, I can't catch a vibe anywhere. But that's okay. Nothing is going to bring me down now.

On my last day at the magazine, I attend a morning staff meeting with more than fifty people, where the editor-in-chief asks everyone to raise their venti skim lattes in honor of my scandalous stories, great sources, and something about an inner sparkle. . . . Truthfully, I have to tune out the words. Otherwise I'll start to cry. *People* was a really nice place to work.

Luckily, the buzz of my BlackBerry distracts me as soon as the meeting shifts back to business. I look down to read that Chef has found us an apartment in Capitol Hill and rented it on the spot! "OMG, LYS. It has a writer's den overlooking a cherry blossom tree, and a big, open kitchen . . . it's soooo us!" he texts. That I trust his taste to sign a lease without me shows just how much I like his style. And it's such a relief.

In our own version of "the trick," Liz and I have decided not to drag out our farewells. She's not the type to get theatrical in the office, and I'm almost embarrassed by my affection for her. So she's purposely going home early today to make things easier on both of us. When I hear a soft knock on my door in the late afternoon, I know it's time. "You take care, chérie," she says kindly and gently, and as our glossy eyes lock, she exits my boxed-up empty office and shuts the door.

I stare at the blank wall, where I once hung a framed copy of a John Updike quote, "The true New Yorker secretly believes that people living anywhere else have to be, in some sense, kidding." And I weep.

I don't know why the experience of parting ways with my boss hits me harder than separating from any of my girlfriends or even my family, but I suspect a small part of me knows that in saying good-bye to Liz, I am leaving behind so much more.

Cheese Toast for Two Kids in Love

SERVES 2

I could become a James Beard Award–winning food writer or a Top Chef Master and I will always believe that the best food in the world is a simple thing called "cheese toast"—which is fancy for cheese melted on toast. Chef has made me cheese toast with Muenster, cheddar, Gruyère, Swiss, smoked mozzarella, Roquefort, and anything else we can find in the fridge. The more options in our cheese drawer, the more he layers. Usually he'll use three slices with interesting flavors on a piece of thick, hearty bread (I like pumpernickel). But to be perfectly honest, a few slices of Kraft Singles on a frozen sesame bagel could make me swoon, too.

2 large slices of bread, approximately 1 inch thick
Dijon mustard (optional)
Unsalted butter (optional)
4 to 6 large slices of cheese
Salt and pepper

On your bread, spread mustard or butter if you so desire. Cover the bread with 2 or 3 slices of cheese. Put the bread on a baking sheet under the broiler or in a toaster oven for about 2 minutes, or until the cheese gets brown, bubbly, and almost burned. Then remove from the heat, sprinkle with salt and pepper, and serve.

Life-Altering Lemon Cake

SERVES 8 TO 10

My life changed forever that night at Fabiane's in Williamsburg, and the lemon cake was the star of the meal, so it deserves a lot of attention. This version is from the original Silver Palate Cookbook *(Workman Publishing, 1982), and it's one of the best. I will never forget sharing dessert that night with Chef.*

For the cake

½ pound (2 sticks) unsalted butter, at room temperature, plus additional for greasing the pan

2 cups granulated sugar

3 large eggs

3 cups unbleached, all-purpose flour

½ teaspoon baking soda

½ teaspoon salt

1 cup buttermilk

2 tightly packed tablespoons grated lemon zest

2 tablespoons fresh lemon juice (about 1 lemon)

For the lemon icing

1 pound confectioners' sugar

8 tablespoons (1 stick) unsalted butter, at room temperature

3 tightly packed tablespoons grated lemon zest

½ cup fresh lemon juice (about 4 lemons)

Place a rack in the middle of the oven. Preheat the oven to 325°F. Grease a 10-inch tube pan.

Make the cake: In a large mixing bowl (or the bowl of a stand mixer fitted with the paddle attachment), cream the butter and sugar until light and fluffy. Beat in the eggs, one at a time, blending well after each addition.

In a medium mixing bowl, sift together the flour, baking soda, and salt. Stir the flour mixture into the egg mixture, alternately with buttermilk, beginning and ending with the dry ingredients. Add the lemon zest and lemon juice.

Pour the batter into the prepared tube pan. Set the pan on the middle rack of the oven and bake for 1 hour and 5 minutes, or until the cake pulls away from the sides of the pan and a tester or knife inserted in the center comes out clean.

Transfer the pan to a rack and let cool for 10 minutes.

Prepare the icing: In a medium mixing bowl, cream the sugar and butter thoroughly. Mix in the lemon zest and lemon juice. Set aside.

Remove the cake from the pan and spread the icing onto the cake while still warm.

Let cool before serving.

4.

Capitol Hell

I have rug burn.

In the first six weeks of living in our unbelievably cool apartment in D.C., which is on the second floor of an enchanted corner brownstone, I have dragged a dozen huge, heavy rugs—shags, sisals, and stripes—from every store imaginable, tethered them to the straggly-gold Jeep I bought us from Craigslist, and hauled them up to our living room, where I lay down the padding, unroll the rug, and mumble to myself, "Close, but not quite—damnit." Then I pull it all up, roll it all together, go down the stairs, into the Jeep, and straight back to the store, where they already think I'm a lunatic with some version of architectural OCD.

The floor coverings aren't the only thorn in my side. The entire apartment, as sun-drenched, bohemian, and beautiful as it is, is a bitch to furnish. The rooms are quirky, curvy, and easily cluttered, and the minimalist in me wants to murder the original contractor.

"Strong as an ox," as my mother would say, I've single-handedly carried a few couches up and down the stairs, too, shuffling heavy objects all day long, until the Crate & Barrel Outlet escorts me out, or my left arm dislocates, or I stub my toe so bad that I tell an oversize credenza to kiss my ass. And then I head home to our love-pad-in-progress, with its misshaped rooms that reject *all* clean lines, and wait for Chef on whatever yellow-velvet or caramel-leather midcentury chair I've decided that I can actually live with that day. I've always needed my home to feel exactly right, but I'm being extra crazy with C Street. The furniture gives me some purpose and helps me temper a certain nervous energy that's crept up from behind.

My life with Chef happens between 11:00 p.m. and 8:00 a.m., except on Sundays. This isn't much time, but if love is measured in quality not quantity, our romance is as rich as ever. The second Chef comes home, he switches from local personality to cozy homebody. Because he's bone-tired, dinner is designated to me. And by dinner, I mean sandwiches. For three months straight, we eat sandwiches every night that we're home. (Sometimes we have cereal.) I stock up on smoked turkey and Swiss cheese, and Chef requests foreign and porky meats like mortadella and sopressata, which I research, find, and buy. I've learned the difference between salumi and salami, and I know that spicy mustard is a must. Mayo makes its appearances, against my will, and sometimes Chef brings home interesting-looking chutneys, which he teaches me to slather on ciabatta, and lay with sharp cheddar. And chips. All kinds of chips. Chef has a potato chip problem.

When I present us with the sandwiches, he's always so appreciative that it makes me feel like the winner of *The Next Food Network Star*. He offers subtle suggestions like taking the time to really toast the bread instead of rushing the process and popping the slices out before the ding, or using fresh basil the next time I opt for Brie. I gladly process his constructive criticism and get a little better with each baguette.

We always eat in front of the tube, in the dark, with as many body parts entangled as possible, every ligament fitting together perfectly. We love our shows—mostly on Showtime and HBO—and we usually watch them (with breaks for fooling around, ice-cream sessions, or making tea) until three o'clock in the morning. We fall asleep feeling like two of the luckiest people in the world.

And then the sun always rises, and our rushed, unruly mornings begin. The alarm goes off, the phones start ringing, or one of Chef's business partners comes knocking on the door to get him somewhere that's not with me. I turn on some music and quickly make us coffee, which he drinks in the shower. When he gets out of the shower, I turn up the volume and he *gets down* in his towel while I roar with laughter. Unlike me, Chef is an awesome dancer. We kiss, as he dresses himself in ripped Dickies and whatever T-shirt smells best; he reads his e-mails, morphing into a crackberry addict; and then he hops on our fluorescent green bike—which I secretly bought at Kmart, but he thinks is vintage—and rides off into a fifteen-hour day in the weeds. Being "in the weeds" is a restaurant term for an insane kitchen situation where a chef is busting his or her ass with no end in sight. It's all I really know about Chef's work: he is always in the weeds.

The second he leaves the apartment, my world is silent. After a few months on C Street, I have nothing to do and nowhere to be, especially now that the decorating is done. There is no in-box to empty, no morning meetings, no breaking news, no tight deadlines, no lunch dates, no après-work appletinis. No one needs to borrow a tampon, tell me a secret, or raid my closet. As much as I adored them, I had no idea how important my girlfriends were until they weren't around.

With hours and hours of time to kill, I Google "Best coffee shops for writers," and find my way to "quirky cafés" that are neither quirky nor cafés. I graze around new neighborhoods, with my laptop and notebooks, but I can't get comfortable anywhere. Either the couches are itchy, the Wi-Fi connection won't work, or the scones taste like sneakers. I ride the Metro—thinking of New York's freestyle rappers, teenage runaways, and impeccably dressed women who all would enwrap me in their world for the short duration of my commute to wherever—but it's dead air in here, dead on arrival, devoid of emotion, a snoozefest of political stiffs and school marms. Dejected, I always come home to C Street, where at least our apartment has style that the city does not.

Halfheartedly, I contact some local magazines, but my stories lack enthusiasm, and I never follow up. Between my savings account and Chef's pathological generosity, I don't feel the need to make serious money, and for the first time in my life, I am utterly unmotivated. The only work I really want to do is on Chef's marketing. It helps me stay connected to him and his career in a way that doesn't involve the kitchen. Plus, any time I've met a successful chef's significant other, they say that working with them—whether it's as their pastry chef, general manager, or marketing director—is the only way to ever see them. I take that advice very seriously. By now, Chef has a publicist, an agent, a manager, and a bunch of partners, but I push myself into all their projects, demanding to be cc'ed on everything, like I'm Chef's CEO. I have a feeling this embarrasses him, but I just really, desperately, want to stay in the loop.

We cherish Sundays, as the restaurant is closed, which means we sleep late and Chef makes us pancakes in any rendition I desire (always with chocolate chips). In the spring, which marks four months on C Street and seven months together, we incorporate gardening into our Sunday ritual. Early in the morning, we drive to the local nursery, discussing which produce we'll want to eat come fall, and what flowers my purple thumb can't kill, since I'll be chief waterer. We load the car with dirt and shovels and spend the day planting our garden, which essentially entails me sipping spiked lemonade on the stoop, and Chef raking, digging, and planting our oregano, basil, arugula, tomatoes, bell peppers, and brussels sprouts. I play music and feed him fresh fruit, and just sit there and love him.

On most Sunday nights, we explore new restaurants in the D.C. food scene, trying to integrate ourselves into the community that has been so kind and generous to Chef. Sometimes he experiments with recipes at home. One night he serves us a Vietnamese-style whole fish but doesn't do a thorough job filleting it because I keep making him lie with me on the couch instead. So he accidentally serves the dish with lots of little bones in it. He tries to save face by saying that's how it's done in Asia, but he's busted and he knows it. In my best Padma impression, I tell him to pack his knives and go, and we both get our kicks. The fun we have on Sundays carries me through those stagnant weekdays.

For one weekend, we make plans to hit a hot spot that's getting glowing reviews for its elegant Italian entrees and ultra-chic interior, and it's only a ten-minute drive away. The best part about these date nights is that I have an excuse to dress up for him. It feels like Chef sees me only in pajamas during the week. So, as he finishes watching an episode of *Planet Earth*—the only TV show we're not equally addicted to—I surface from the bedroom in a short, flowy miniskirt, smoky eyes, and a spritz of Stella McCartney perfume. It's hard to get him out of my bra and into the car after that, but I force him to behave. He drives with one hand and tickles my thigh with another.

The second we walk into the restaurant, I get a really bad vibe, which is strange because I'm not a restaurant snob. The place looks like a hospital cafeteria, and there's a faint smell of fish. Chef nods in agreement, making a funny expression with his gingery eyebrows. But it's late and we're hungry, and quite frankly, we don't know D.C. well enough to escape to some "old faithful" yet.

So we sit down graciously and I try to wipe the sour look off my face. But I'm let down. Our date nights are precious to me and this place is a bummer. I can't seem to laugh it off or let it go. The music in my head has come to a screech. *This is what Washington thinks is cool? Really?*

When our waiter comes to our table, he reaches over me to pour some water and I get a whiff of the world's most pungent body odor. The stinky pit really sets me off. More than anything, it reeks of the disappointment I'm finding *everywhere* I turn in this town. There's not enough Right Guard in the world to fix that.

And then I start to hyperventilate; I am derailed. Chef looks really frightened. I've started to bawl my eyes out. He's never seen me lose my cool like this . . . and over B.O.? He apologizes to the staff, cancels our order, and delicately takes me outside.

By now, I am laughing and crying in unison. I can't believe what a scene I made. Chef is laughing, too, but he's concerned. What is going on with me? We walk back to the car and he insists that I tell him what provoked my outburst. "It just felt so wrong in there," I say, weeping. "That place pushed me over the edge."

As we keep talking, I admit to him, and to myself, that lately I've been feeling a little panicky. It's making me kind of cuckoo being home alone all day, and that as hard as I try, I can't seem to catch a wave *anywhere* in D.C.

Until this stage in my life, I've always sided with Confucius on the "Wherever you go, there you are" philosophy. But *nothing* is clicking in Washington. We recently went to a White House party at a rooftop bar where everyone wore panty hose, no one voted on *Idol,* and I was impossibly invisible. Standing in line at J. Crew, I made a friend who worked for a senator, but the second she found out I had once written for *People,* she demanded I lose her number, stating, "You can't be in politics without being paranoid." Earlier this week, Chef and I went on a midnight stroll, hoping to get a late-night snack, a fresh pastry, or swirly soft-serve, only to come home with hot dogs and Snapple from 7-Eleven. "Wherever you go, you miss New York" is more like it.

"Nothing feels right in this city," I say, my wet face nuzzled into his chest. "The people aren't my type, and I'm not theirs. I mean, look at tonight, this entire city is raving over this ugly, impotent restaurant. This place wouldn't last a second in New York," I say, fully upset again, knowing my frustration is not *really* about the bleak restaurant, and that I'm sounding like a real brat.

"Baby, calm down. Please. You're still adjusting . . ."

"No. Fuck adjusting. A paper clip has more heart than that place." I pout, pointing to the restaurant.

"You're right, Lys, it sucked in there," Chef says. "But what's this really about?"

I look gravely into his eyes and say that I'm just sad for myself because, among other things, I have no life.

My first few months in town, Chef made it a point to extract himself from the restaurant every few days to be near me, take me out, and share the occasional afternoon of doing nothing. We'd roam around the neighborhood, or grab an afternoon matinee, and make nice little memories wherever we went. Now, a mass hysteria has surrounded his restaurant. The lines are always out the door, the press is hot on his success, and D.C.

just wants more, more, more. Throw in a blossoming TV career and a jam-packed schedule of events and appearances, and he is always on the go. He can't just "peace out" when he wants to anymore. Even our Sundays aren't a sure thing.

"It's not your fault, but when you're not around, I have nothing here," I cry. It embarrasses me to swallow my pride and verbalize this, but it just comes out.

"Don't say that."

"Why not? It's true and you know it. I have nothing here."

I'd never begrudge Chef for having an impeccable work ethic, and I'm not trying to make him feel guilty about it. But it feels good to let it go. He listens carefully, and cries when I tell him how rootless I really feel, and how silent my existence is every day. We keep talking, making our way to the car, and eventually to 7-Eleven for some cereal and milk. He says he understands exactly what I'm saying, and together, we sit up all night long figuring out how to make my life in Washington less of a wash.

We decide I'll join a gym for some sense of community and because exercise has always been my best release. And I'll follow up on a few potential new friends that have been recommended to me by trustworthy people from New York and Los Angeles. We contemplate befriending our perky neighbors, but with their freshly trimmed bangs and cutesy toddlers, I doubt they'll give me the spark I need. And lastly, we agree that I'll visit him more often at the restaurant. He wants me to feel like it's as much mine as it is his. "Every hour I put in there is for our future," he says, not for the first time. As far as my writing career, or lack of, he reminds me that I've worked hard my whole life, and not to be so tough on myself; a little break isn't so horrible. He wipes both of our sniffles away (because whenever I cry, he cries, too) and we watch an episode of *Sons of Anarchy*, all curled up.

The next day, I join the local gym. In New York, I was going to a spin lover's candy shop called Soul Cycle, where bikes have the sweat of Brooke Shields, Renée Zellweger, and Kelly Ripa. It's the Rolls-Royce of workouts, way out of my league, but I got to go for free because I wrote a big story about them. I would always leave class feeling fit, refreshed, and unstoppable, not to mention two pounds lighter. Returning to spinning, even at a not-so-glam gym, would be the perfect solution.

Despite my newfound optimism, I fight back tears throughout my first class. The music has no beat (a mix of Shania Twain and show tunes!) and nothing, not even the flabby naked, unwaxed women in the locker room, feel vaguely familiar or okay. Determined to make it work, I offer to teach the damn class myself. I present my credentials to the seventy-something manager and his rusty whistle, explaining that I've had the world's best spin instructors in New York and Los Angeles, that the super-cool DJ Sam Ronson has made me an original workout mix, and that I could maybe even get the editor in chief of *Allure* magazine, Linda Wells, another spinning devotee, to vouch for my riding style, if that's what it takes.

Nobody cares. Condé Nast name-dropping has no place on Capitol Hill. Coach says I'm not experienced enough and coldly dismisses me like I'm some Jehovah's Witness ringing the doorbell at dinnertime. I walk away feeling undignified. No soul. No cycle.

"You would die if you saw me right now," I say on the phone with my sister, driving away with one hand on the steering wheel, one to my ear, talking illegally. "I'm wearing crotch-padded spandex, with like, a big lump in my throat, because I just got dissed by an old man who looks like John McCain in warm-up pants."

"What the hell?" She laughs, muffling her voice at work. "You okay?"

"Yeah. Fine. Ya gotta laugh, right?" I say, hanging up quickly because there's a cop about to pull me over.

I go on a Ferris wheel of "friend dates." The women are either profoundly conservative or profoundly crazy. One covers her ears every time I say a swear word; the next one tells me, like it's nothing, how she (perhaps the whitest girl in America) wears a big, black dildo on her married CEO boyfriend, cordially inviting me to join in. *Check, please.* They're all either painfully boring or on the bad side of weird, and I feel ridiculous having these first-day-of-college-like conversations when, in the real world, I have the most amazing and hilarious friends ever, whether they're ER nurses in Western Massachusetts or man-eaters in Lower Manhattan. Our neighbors also keep trying to chitchat, introducing me to their depressingly adorable kids, and asking if Ryan Reynolds is as dreamy in real life (duh . . .), but I have convinced myself that they're just too ordinary to ever understand me.

"Still no friends?" Shelley says with an evil smirk from Los Angeles, where she's now representing celebrities and seeing Leonardo DiCaprio's life coach.

"Shellz, the last girl I was 'set up with' said she was thinking about leaving her husband . . . which I thought sounded promising . . . but it was because they couldn't agree on health-care reform!"

"Yikes. Come to L.A. It's Oscars season."

In the next few weeks, I try to visit Chef more often at the restaurant. His partners and I don't quite mesh—it seems we're in constant competition for his attention. They think I'm a prima donna, coasting in with my big shades and flowery sundresses. If only they knew that I once worked eighty-hour weeks, too, also all stressed out and exasperated by my job. But no one in D.C. knows that girl. "Just another day at the beach," they say to me. Or, "Must be tough being you." I try not to be oversensitive, but their ridicule is not very pleasant.

Even more belittling, I don't have any friends to bring along when I go there, so I end up eating alone, pretending to catch up on e-mails, trying not to look too pathetic. I once tried to help at the cash register, but I screwed it all up, then hid in the car until closing. Chef thought it was cute, but I felt like an idiot.

One afternoon, I show up at the restaurant wearing a tight white pencil skirt and carrying my black leather portfolio. I tell Chef I have five minutes to kill before a big meeting with *Capitol File* magazine. I make sure his partners overhear this. Of course, I am lying. I have nowhere to be. I never have anywhere to be. All my plans are fake. He kisses me all over, wishes me good luck, and then I leave the restaurant to go to a bar by myself.

Belga Café is the only spot in town I hate a little less than the others, so that's where I go for my faux power lunches and imaginary creative consultations. Really, I'm drinking huge beers for breakfast, reading a four-dollar *New York Post,* and trying to connect with whomever is the least creepy person also hiding from life like me. I'm not proud of lying to Chef, but I'm sick of looking like such a loser. And anyway, part of me thinks that he knows I'm fibbing but is too sweet to say anything.

Another time, I surprise Chef at work for a quick hello and to borrow his computer because our Internet isn't working. He's happy to see me, puts everything on hold, and gets me situated with a salad and Diet Coke downstairs in his office. I am not snooping, but his e-mail happens to be open, and staring me in the face is an X-rated fan letter from a *Playboy* playmate, and a few flirtatious e-mails from prominent women around Washington. I feel like I've been kicked in the stomach. I knew he had admirers (after all, I was once one of them), but I naturally assumed they were obese or incarcerated. Chef hadn't responded to any of these hussies, as far as I could tell, but I still yank him from the kitchen and start crying hysterically in front of all his customers and colleagues.

These days, it seems he spends as much time behind the grill as he does talking me off the ledge. Miraculously, he never loses his patience. The worst he'll say is that my attitude is "unbecoming," which for some reason always cracks me up and snaps me right out of my mood. Such a rigid word from such a rugged guy.

We do still get out of town now and then. We travel to Miami for the South Beach Wine & Food Festival, a promlike weekend for the country's most famous foodie insiders. I am so excited that I buy us shopping bags of clothes, sunglasses, and swimsuits. (If nothing else, I'm definitely Chef's stylist.) It's an intense and intimidating crowd, with cliquey food writers and chefs that he's only observed from afar. We share most of it with our eyes wide open, hand in hand.

At the end of the long weekend, it is announced that Chef has won a big cooking award and I scream at the top of my lungs! *My boyfriend ate the bear.* He makes a short speech, thanking the Boys, his partners, and publicists, but he doesn't mention me. I try to let it roll off my shoulders, but not before mentioning it to him.

"Hey, you forgot to thank me!"

"It's not always about you, Alyssa, jeez. Are you really doing this right now?"

He's never been that sharp with me before, and I assure him that the issue is dropped.

Instead of sulking, I focus on celebrating. After all, I may not know how to patty a burger but I do know how to party. Not long after we arrive at the rooftop gathering in his honor, however, I find myself slouching next to Chef, uncomfortable in my own skin, as everyone bonds over blends of meat, Michelin stars, and the technicalities of deep-fried bubble gum. "That actually sounds yummy," I say, trying to participate. "Ew, babe, really?" shuns Chef, making me feel gauche.

As the alcohol flows, a famously unfiltered female chef says in front of all the jerks who are already pushing me aside for a piece of my guy, "So you're the *People* magazine reporter who stalked him!" Thank God I have a sense a humor, but it was really tested at that moment. I spend the rest of the night nonconversational, afraid to say the wrong thing, and freaked out by the whole environment, including Chef, who's having a grand time.

A few weeks after the festival, one of Chef's partners plants a seed that it's unprofessional to bring one's girlfriend everywhere. He shrugs it off, but in the days to come, there's a shift imperceptible to anyone but me. Sometimes he still includes me . . . other times I feel forgotten about. Deep down, I think I let him down at the food festival because I couldn't hold my own. That weekend turned me into a real drag. No one from my old life would believe it.

He's traveling almost weekly now—from Anaheim to Amsterdam and everywhere in between. It's mental motion sickness, especially with his disorganized ways—uncharged cell phone, expired driver's license, missing house keys, disappearing wallet, unflossed teeth, and untied Vans. I try to see the charm in it all, as I always have in the past (*who wants an uptight guy?*), but for the trips where I'm excluded, or worse, the ones he forgets to tell me about, my tolerance is diminishing. "I am not some 1950s housewife, whose only purpose is to find the fucking passport," I say, dumping his entire dresser on the ground.

I use that same argument to explain why our fridge is always empty, save deli meat and beer, and why, on the counter, there's only a sad butcher block with a few slices of bread, a box of stale granola, and two avocados encircled by fruit flies. Despite a full year of dating a chef, I remain sanctimoniously kitchen-phobic. He comes home exhausted and famished, and I, having done less than nothing all day, have no excuse for our sandwich-only fare. For my own meals during the day, I eat peanut butter on a spoon, cheese and crackers, green olives, rocky road ice cream, or whatever is around. Sometimes I just drink. I don't tell my mom how disenchanted by D.C. I am, but when she says "Why don't you give cooking or baking a shot, hon? It's always been so therapeutic for me," I know she's picked up on my mounting sense of instability. I tell her she sounds crazy, while inhaling dozens of dried apricots for dinner.

I wish I could say that I refrain from my domestic duties out of some *real* sense of feminism or gender equality, and maybe subconsciously I do. But more likely, I'm just depressed. I can barely buy milk without a meltdown. Chef goes easy on me as far as my culinary inadequacies—he's much more worried about my perpetual tears than my prep table. We do have a good laugh when I buy him cheeseburger-flavored Pringles, though, thinking it's some heroic act. "Never buy cheeseburger-flavored anything for someone who makes cheeseburgers allll daaay looong!" he sings, wrestling me to the ground with one of his famous tickle attacks.

He rarely cooks for us at all anymore. There's no time for

such luxuries. In opening a second restaurant, his hours get even worse. He comes home so physically drained that all he wants is a long kiss, a bag of chips, some juice, and for me not to be upset about anything. It kills me to see him so weak and bleary-eyed. The guy has more joie de vivre in his pinky finger than most people in their entire life span, and here he is struggling to stick a straw in a Capri Sun.

"What would you say if I gave you a list of five things I want my wife to cook for me one day?" he says in the middle of the night, over some soggy cereal.

"Um, was that a proposal?" I say, jokingly, deflecting the issue.

"One day, babe, one day." He smiles, mischievously.

"Remember, rubies, not diamonds," I remind him, reiterating my preference for my birthstone, rather than the typical rock.

"Okay, but you remember: roast chicken, not Cheerios!"

WE DON'T have too many Sundays together after he starts working at his second place. And he comes home so late now, after closing the restaurant and getting through his paperwork at the office, that I can barely stay awake for snuggle and TV time.

Nor can he accompany me to *anything* at all. I visit New York about once a month, and unless it's tied to a TV appearance, Chef doesn't come along. So, I go to most family birthdays and friends' weddings alone, leaving some worried that I'm robbing myself of a normal life. You can't truly respect the grind of the restaurant business until you've lived with it. That said, it is rough. If I had my New York life, that would be another story. It would be so much fun finishing up our grueling days around the same ungodly hour, collapsing on top of each other with hot pizza and cold beer, too tired to talk, though not too tired to sleep without sex. Now, I just stare out a window and wait all day.

While helping out with Chef's PR is the only activity that makes me feel ever so slightly relevant, I am also getting the drift that my input is becoming a serious annoyance to everyone involved, even him. By now, he has a well-oiled machine on payroll; they know what they're doing and don't need my input.

"You don't have to include me in everything that's going on with the media anymore, if you don't want to," I say to Chef, a few days before our one-year anniversary. He's just come home from work at 4:00 a.m. and I've forced myself out of bed to fix him a roast beef sandwich.

"Okay, baby, perfect . . ." he says, not looking up from his BlackBerry.

Okay, baby, perfect hurts.

It triggers a catastrophic sense of rejection.

Hello, cruel nothingness.

So I start drinking at noon and logging in and out of his e-mail to read the latest slutty note from some sex-deprived housewife, or the details of his travel itineraries to places I've always wanted to visit yet haven't been invited to. I eat very little, can't sleep at all, and have developed adult acne. I show up at the restaurant tipsy and in tears, unraveling every time one of his partners gives me a disapproving look or a customer pushes me aside for a photo with Chef.

I think about shaking things up the way I would in the old days . . . partying hard, starting an affair, disappearing for a few days, but I love Chef too much to risk it. And I'm older now. I also wouldn't even know how to bum a light in this town.

One afternoon I'm feeling so unsteady and insecure about all his female fans, and the fact that he's usually perceived as single in the press, that I drink screwdrivers like it's my job and send anonymous sightings of us "looking very much in love" into the *Washington Post* from a fake e-mail account. *He's mine, bitches.* Somehow my real name appears along with the alias, and by the time the reporter e-mails back, "Wait, aren't *you* the girlfriend you speak of?" I just want to curl up and die.

I am not myself, not even a knockoff of myself, which is a problem for so many reasons, not the least of which is that my boyfriend fell in love with a lit-from-within writer, with bluebirds on her shoulders, perfectly content with a few strands of licorice, a handful of real friends, and a library book about Mötley Crüe. We need to find her before he bolts or I have a nervous breakdown.

Chef panics at the sight of me so sad, frustrated, and lonely, promising that his hours will calm down soon. He tempers me by hinting at the ruby, but we both know an engagement ring can't give me the closeness I require.

I'm just desperate to feel part of *something.* But who am I to make a peep? I am a nobody now.

Late-Night Turkey BLTs

SERVES 4

It shouldn't come as too much of a surprise that my ideal recipe has only a few basic ingredients. That said, the BLT was my national treasure in the early days of me and Washington, when I was just navigating the culinary waters. Sandwiches like this got me through a lot of long nights, good and bad. I'm not a big bacon eater (Jewish guilt!), so I use turkey bacon, but even Chef agrees that the substitution yields something just as delicious, and healthier, too. It's easy to wing this kind of thing, but this precise recipe was adapted from Gwyneth Paltrow's cookbook, My Father's Daughter.

8 slices turkey bacon (or real bacon)
8 slices potato bread or whole-wheat bread
½ cup mayonnaise or mustard
Coarse salt
Fresh ground black pepper
Handful of fresh basil
2 tablespoons extra-virgin olive oil
2 large beefsteak tomatoes cut into 8 medium slices

Cook the bacon in a large skillet over medium-high heat until crispy on both sides. Drain on a paper towel and cut each slice in half. Meanwhile, toast the bread.

Spread one side of each slice of bread with mayonnaise or mustard. Sprinkle each slice with a tiny pinch of salt and a dash of black pepper.

Evenly distribute the basil on 4 slices of bread already covered with a condiment, drizzle each with ½ tablespoon of olive oil, then sprinkle with a bit more salt and pepper.

Lay 2 tomato slices on top of each heap of basil, so they each cover over half the surface.

Layer 4 pieces of turkey bacon on each sandwich. Top each sandwich with one of the remaining slices of bread, cut in half, and serve.

Sweet Potato Chips

SERVES 2

When I first moved to D.C., I confessed to one of my oldest New York pals, and consummate foodie, Jill Sites, that I had served Chef and myself sandwiches with potato chips for three months straight. "It's not pretty," I wrote in an e-mail. In turn, she sent me a recipe. "These are healthy enough that you can relax a little; I know you don't cook, but come on, live a little, be brave!" I posted the recipe on my fridge and didn't look at it for a long time.

1 large sweet potato, unpeeled
Grapeseed oil (or any other neutral-tasting oil, such as peanut, soy, or vegetable)
Sea salt and black pepper
2 to 4 sprigs fresh thyme, minced
7 sprigs fresh rosemary, minced

Using a mandoline or very sharp knife, slice the sweet potato very thin, about ⅓ to ¼ inch thick. Place the sliced potatoes in a large bowl of water and let sit for 30 minutes to 1 hour, until the water becomes very cloudy. Remove the potatoes with a slotted spoon and dry them completely using a tea towel or paper towels.

Heat enough oil to go about two-thirds of the way up a medium heavy-bottomed pot (or Dutch oven) over medium-high heat. The oil is hot enough when you put the end of a wooden spoon in the oil and it bubbles immediately.

Place the potato slices in the oil, being careful not to crowd the pot. Fry approximately 3 to 6 minutes (the time depends on the thickness of the chips and the heat of the oil). Turn them occasionally so they brown evenly. They will begin to float and turn slightly golden when they're done. Remove the batch of potatoes with a slotted spoon, drain on paper towels, and continue with the next batch.

When all the potatoes are fried, make sure the oil is still on medium-high heat and fry them again for 2 more minutes, or until they are perfectly crispy. Remove the potatoes from the oil, drain again on paper towels, and season the hell out of them with the salt, pepper, thyme, and rosemary.

Serve hot or cold.

5.

Will Cook for Love

"Don't fuck it up, Shelasky," my Emmy Award–winning friend whispers as we walk to his shiny SUV after dinner at a Mexican restaurant, just off Hollywood Boulevard. "Don't fuck it up."

He's referring to my love life. We're in Los Angeles because Chef has a cooking series in Santa Monica to shoot and he knows I need to get away. The trip couldn't have come at a better time. California has always been a special place for me—it's my long, deep breath, my escape from reality. (If New York weren't my environmental soul mate, and we weren't so stuck in D.C., I'd move us out west in a second.) Despite a jam-packed itinerary, Chef has taken the night off to finally meet my old, naughty neighbors, who are still fabulous, but now sober and thriving. Shelley, of course, comes along, and a few other New York transplants, including one who has made it big on a hit TV show and recently won several awards. Over Shirley Temples and corn tortillas, we all have a lot to celebrate, including my one-year anniversary with Chef.

I never want the night to end. To most couples, dinner with friends is known as Tuesday. To those in a "relationchef," as I call our situation, it is known as a blessing. Tonight, Chef is the guy I first met in Williamsburg—sweet, pure, relaxed, and warm. He's not watching the clock or being whisked away. I too am my old spirited self—confident and alive. Shelley and I tell the most dramatic rendition of our Nick Nolte story. Chef spits out an empanada in a fit of laughter, and our other friend falls off his chair. When a young kid comes to the table and nervously asks for a photo, Chef affably agrees, pushing back his seat to stand up, like a good sport. The confused fan says, "Sorry, mister, I wanted one with him," pointing to our actor friend. The gang erupts into more laughter.

The next morning Chef and I hike Runyon Canyon, where I drag his skinny ass all the way up to the sky and back. The crisp air and rigorous exercise feels amazing and we make false promises the whole way down about finding hiking trails back home. "Let's do this every first Sunday of the month," I say. "For sure," he pants.

Then we drive down the Pacific Coast Highway toward Malibu, where we share a delicious avocado and sprout sandwich from the town market, park at the beach, sunbathe topless, and feel a universe away from C Street.

"How do we keep you as happy as you are right now?" he says, standing in the departures line at the airport, his tanned, sandy arms wrapped tightly around my waist. "I've missed you, Lys."

I don't have the answer, but I know it has something to do with keeping this sense of "togetherness" alive. We have to find a way to share more meaningful moments and create our own happy memories, even with his hideous hours. That's how a strong foundation is made; that's what the good life is about. But that's not all. I need to be impassioned. Nothing extreme. Just a little heat, emotion, interaction. I've always had something up my sleeve, a glimmer in my eyes, and a spring in my step. *What specifically can give me that feeling in Washington?*

The second we're home, I try not to fuck it up. I commit to attacking life on the Hill with the same blind faith and determination I'd put forth into everything else I've wanted to conquer in life. I lose interest in my usual "D.C. sucks" soliloquy, and I am bored by my old, bad attitude. In the morning, I send Chef off to work, then shower, blow-dry, and walk to Belga Café to think about my next move. Today, I'm making changes.

On my walk, a great song called "Rise Up" by Ben Lee plays on my iPod. I make it the theme of the day with so much vigor that had I been anywhere near downtown Manhattan, I might have tattooed the words on my wrist. I put my hands through my refreshingly clean hair, lean against a parking meter, watch the cars pass on Pennsylvania Avenue, and beg myself to *rise up*.

Rise up from the sleeplessness, the friendlessness, and the homesickness. Rise up from the restaurant, the hours, and the drama. Rise up from the neighbors who like us but judge us. Rise up from the gym and its unfit women with their untamed pubes. Rise up from the breakouts, breakdowns, and unbecoming bad moods. Please, girl, rise the hell up.

I start by thinking about what I can and cannot change. *What is the truth of the matter?* I know that I cannot change the circumstances of Chef's career, or the opinions of his partners, or the demands of his publicists. Those are simply not malleable things. At least for now, I cannot change that our home is in D.C., and I can't keep blaming it for everything unpleasant in my life. *But what can I change? What can give us that togetherness, considering the reality of our life?*

I pull up a bar stool at Belga and wish for a second I had

someone with me to talk to about this, because I feel a breakthrough coming on.

"How's it going over there?" says a man, practically on cue, with a faded flannel shirt and a great head of silver hair. He's older, husky, and weathered, as if he lived on a houseboat or would be played by Robert Redford in an Oscar-nominated drama. "I've seen you before."

He reminds me of my favorite high-school teacher, Mr. Winseck. "Winnie" made Kates, Anzo, and me scream with laughter because of his wicked sense of humor, suspicious smelling coffee, and hilarious, politically incorrect rants . . . all while teaching us about slavery, the sixties, and human struggle. Simply because of the resemblance, this guy feels safe to talk to. (Winnie recently passed away, and every day I imagine him and Jean playing cards and drinking gin up in heaven.)

"Yeah, I love it here at Belga," I say, exaggerating, but thrilled to chat.

"But you always look so sad."

"Nah, I'm just bored and a little off balance, and not sure what I'm doing here in D.C.," I say, realizing this may be the first, natural, free-flowing conversation I've ever had in this city.

"That's no good," he says without a shred of insincerity. "Let me guess, you're a writer?"

"How'd you know?"

"Both times I've seen you, you were reading, or writing, deep in thought, somewhere else. You were totally oblivious to anybody or anything."

"That sounds about right," I say, laughing. "Lots on my mind."

"Plus, the shirt . . ." he says with a wink.

I look down and I'm wearing a dark gray T-shirt from Urban Outfitters that reads: CAFFEINE. NICOTINE. ALCOHOL.

Finally, someone finds me amusing.

The beer has hit my bladder and I excuse myself to use the ladies' room. There's a person taking her time ahead of me. *Hurry up. I want to go back to my new friend!* When it's my turn, I go fast, wash my hands, and fix my ponytail in the mirror. Returning to the bar, I see that my buddy has left a ten-dollar bill for his half-empty Amstel Light, and a lunch note for me. Just like the ones from my mom, minus the MTLI. "Be well, my friend! Jack. P.S. When life gets confusing, go back to the basics. The rest is noise!"

I fondly take his note and soak in the words as I walk home to C Street. Suddenly, I am walking fast, almost sprinting, motorized by inspiration from this beer-drinking angel sent by my dead history teacher, whom I had never seen before and would never see again.

I close my eyes and lie on our deep brown Danish couch. *Back to the basics . . . back to the basics . . .*

Love.

Truth.

Health.

Sex.

Sleep.

Food.

And like a ton of bricks made of Parmigiano-Reggiano, the answer hits me: I am going to learn how to cook. That's my answer! We never have anything to eat at home; I am tired of being a wallflower at all these food events we attend; and everybody knows there's nothing that fosters togetherness like sharing a meal. *Why not?* It's not like taking up Bikram yoga will feed my hungry boyfriend. Food is the path that will lift me up.

Starting with dinner. Like, tonight! Carrie Bradshaw used her stove for storing sweaters, but I will turn mine on.

As soon as I figure out how.

I spring over to Chef's cookbooks, which are collecting dust on our bookshelf, grab as many piles as my arms can handle, and snatch a few food magazines stacked on his side of the bathroom. I dump out a shopping bag filled with twenty years of disregarded recipes from my mother, which I never had the heart to throw away. And soon, I am sitting Indian-style on the living-room floor, limber and unladylike, surrounded by dilapidated index cards, jagged magazine articles, and coffee-stained cookbooks.

In ruffling through all the food lit, it occurs to me that home cooks can actually create whatever they're craving. That's kind of cool. Feel like pad Thai? No problem. Fried chicken? Fine! It must feel like having magical powers to produce whatever your stomach desires. I edit down my food porn to pastas (which seem easy enough), but that's like editing down my wardrobe to denim; it doesn't make a dent. There's a scrumptious-looking lasagna from an old *Bon Appétit* issue that's giving me bedroom eyes. Lasagna seems like a smart thing to cut my teeth on, but I don't recognize all of the ingredients, which makes me a little apprehensive.

"Isn't Taleggio a DJ from London?" I text Chef, teasing, but not really.

"Cheese, baby, cheese . . ." he writes back two seconds later.

Cluelessly flicking through recipes, I've never felt so unsophisticated in my life. I can't believe I went thirty-something years without knowing the difference between Swiss cheese and Swiss chard, or that "surf and turf" isn't a resort activity. How did I graduate from college, sip wine coquettishly on all those third dates at Babbo and Nobu and Beppe, and manage to interview a couple of Michelin-starred chefs without picking up a single thing about food? *What a dope.*

That I don't recognize anyone's byline in these food magazines also unsettles me. I may not know my cuts of meat, but I do know my New York media. The pages are so unfamiliar—it's like I was airdropped into a foreign country filled with Viking stoves and focaccia bread, and I don't know who to trust. Staring at the pictures of ramekins and radishes, I am disoriented by so many choices—meaty things and leafy things and creamy things (or as the foodies say, "proteins" and "leafs" and "sweets"). They all look equally impossible and over my head. My heart rate is up, but I try to stay focused. I have to thin out the choices of pestos and potpies fast because they might as well be hate mail or hostage notes by the way my hands are starting to shake. I feel like I'm too drunk to see straight, which brings me a moment of clarity: I should get too drunk to see straight.

But first, I call my mother.

"Mom. Help. How do I make a menu?"

It's not the "Mom. Help. I'm pregnant!" call she might have been waiting for. Still, she's tickled pink, even if in utter disbelief. The Shelasky family talks about seasonal boyfriends, not seasonal produce. Our family meetings are a stir-fry of gossip and girl talk. We review love and sex, not restaurants and chefs (unless we're sleeping with one). So, while my mother and I are both in shock over the sheer nature of my call, we go with it. I could have said I was a lesbian or flat broke or moving to Siberia and she would have bought it sooner, but forever my steady rock, she dishes out the best advice she can. "Don't overdo it. Make one great thing and a simple salad with Grandma's dressing. Think about the colors on the plate; make it beautiful."

Searching for the one great thing, I shuffle through pictures of penne and tagliatelle, tossing out intimidating meals that sound better in foreign languages. It's the end of summer, so I avoid stews and soups. Anything too fishy or gamey must go too, because, well, that's just gross. I contemplate a rack of lamb, which is one of Chef's favorite foods. But a Jew making lamb for a Greek is culinary suicide by anybody's standard, and I'd never been to a butcher.

My large pile of edible babble contains a lot of baked, bourgeois macaroni and cheese recipes, so I take it as a sign. It's getting late and I have to commit. I collect them all, close my eyes, and pull just one. Deep inhalation. It's Truffle and Cognac Cream Macaroni and Cheese, a photocopy from . . . oh, fuck my life . . . *Top Chef: The Cookbook*. The originator is a contestant from season one who I think is awesome but Chef finds really annoying. Considering the personality conflict, and that it might be easier to buy crack than truffles, I allow myself a do-over.

First I squeeze out a bit of enthusiasm and further eliminate any mac 'n' cheese recipes involving Velveeta, squirt cheese, or reality TV. I do have *some* standards. When I spot a wrinkled-up *Martha Stewart Living* page featuring a well-tailored Gourmet Macaroni and Cheese with nutmeg and cheddar, I feel good enough to go with it. Like buying the bikini that makes you hate your body a little less than the others, it will do just fine.

The irony of Martha and me existing in the same breath, for even a second, isn't lost on me. Behind bars maybe, but in the kitchen? Hilarious. I also laugh out loud when I realize that I'm making a dish that feeds twelve people. But, right now, the concept of halving the recipe and recalculating the measurements is too much to handle. The only thing I hate more than cooking is doing math.

My mother said to stick to a one-pot meal, but I panic and add a turkey meatloaf by Bobby Flay because I don't yet understand the concept of restraint. Gourmet mac 'n' cheese with turkey meatloaf, plus a simple arugula salad—slightly pedestrian but pretty enough. Demure yellow from the macaroni, rich browns and purples from the meatloaf, and forest green from the arugula . . . I'm okay with it. Especially when I Google "What wine works well with meatloaf?" and learn that it must be red and fruity. *Fine by me.* Last but not least, I decide on a S'mores Brownie recipe for dessert from *Rachael Ray 30-Minute Meals 2.* It's no French *macaron,* but it's not a heart-shaped Jell-O mold either. And I could die happy licking brownie batter, so I'm sold.

I grab a fuchsia Sharpie and neatly craft the perfect grocery list, which includes, well, everything. Even milk and eggs. A bit frazzled but tenacious, I stay in my sweats, slip on ballet flats and Ray-Bans, and walk to the car. I type "Whole Foods" into the GPS, even though I've been there before. Getting lost is the last thing I need today. I've got the list, the tote, and the determination. I want to get everything right.

While driving, I'm white-knuckled and nervous. The deflowering of a kitchen-phobe is no small feat. But inside my fear, there's a beat of excitement. I imagine Chef's sweet smile when he steps through the door and smells a dinner that doesn't include seven-grain bread. I also feel pretty cool pretending to be a home cook, with my important grocery list and MADE IN BROOKLYN bag. The car windows are down, the National is playing, and my long, layered hair is pinned up just right. I look good in foodie.

At the market, I shop like a little old lady, moving gradually and reluctantly through the aisles, giving new meaning to the Slow Food movement. You would think I was cooking for the queen, the way I stoically approach the wine guy. "Hello, sir. . . . I'd like a red wine that would nicely complement a turkey meatloaf, please." After several hours of sneaking carob-covered almonds, and taking pictures of myself in the produce section to text to Chef, I think I have everything I need. Two hundred dollars later, I am carrying the ingredients for my first home-cooked meal.

Back on C Street, I uncork the wine before unloading the groceries. It's 3:00 p.m., and I don't know where to begin. I wrap a high-wasted apron—a tattered old, flowery thing that my mother had snuck in my moving boxes—just under my bra, take a sip of Pinot Noir, and lay out my recipes. I study Martha's mac. She requires many pots and pans, which rubs me the wrong way, but whatever. The first thing the recipe calls for is six slices of bread. Crap. I didn't add this to my grocery list because it seemed like an obvious staple in any human's kitchen, but in our bread basket, I notice a shade of chartreuse on a loaf we've had for some time now. I'm off on the wrong foot. Hastily, I crumble the last of the Kashi crackers from the pantry and throw in some multigrain cereal to make up the difference. I pour some melted butter over the mix, per Martha, and set my alleged "bread crumbs" aside. *All cooks improvise, right?*

For the white sauce (which Chef says on the phone sounds like a béchamel sauce. *Be-sha-who?*), I spastically grate the cheese, all seven wonders of it. The recipe requires a lot of whisking, so I stand at the stove, targeting my upper arm muscles, thinking of Madonna, and texting a video of myself to Chef. He writes back, "You're clenching the spoon like a convict!"

Then I look around the kitchen for the nutmeg, which is up next. Nowhere to be found, despite the fact that I paid nine dollars for it an hour ago. I grab some cinnamon instead. *That's like nutmeg's little sister, isn't it?* My little dash turns into a voluptuous dollop and suddenly my white, creamy sauce turns into Cinnamon City. There's nothing I can do. It's time to boil the water and bathe the macaroni.

So far, no fires, no tears, and no missing fingers. In the seven minutes before the pasta is cooked, I try to tidy up, remembering a tip Chef told me that the first thing you learn in culinary school is to "clean as you go." So banal, yet so brilliant. I don't know why, but it reminds me of the legendary L.A. story where a young actor asked Bette Davis for advice on being successful in Hollywood. She took a long drag of a good cig and said, "Take Fountain." (It's a street with less traffic!)

The amount of mess and dirty dishes for such a low-key meal is absolutely ludicrous. I don't make much money these days, and I don't even have health insurance, but I pay Paula, our weekly housekeeper, without so much as a wince. Needless to say, I have no clue where she keeps things. Nothing resembling a sponge is anywhere near the sink, which can't even hold half the damn dishes, and for a million bucks, I couldn't tell you if we own a mop. *What a crock of shit. Not only am I learning to cook, but now I have to learn to clean, too?* I didn't sign up for this. I'd have more fun shaving my head than cleaning my house. Now cheese and crumbs and scraps are flung everywhere and I start panicking about getting mice. I definitely take after the Temkin women, who are more afraid of mice than Bin Laden or Bernie Madoff.

I drain the macaroni, transfer the slippery suckers into the cheese sauce, and stir. I then pour the pasta mixture into two casserole dishes, one large and one small, assuming the small one can be my tester batch. Thick, beige liquid splatters everywhere, including on my eyelashes. All I can do is throw everything in the oven and pray.

The next thirty minutes is a cyclone of cleaning, scrubbing, texting Chef, and stalking the stove. I am hyper and tipsy, replaying the last hour of my life in the apron, thinking how it was nothing to be afraid of, and maybe it was even a little fun. It's like the feeling you get after a big drop on a dreaded roller coaster, when you scream to your friends, "Let's do it again!"

And then, there's a whiff of smoke.

The casseroles are ready, but they've spilled over, leaving a creamy puddle on the bottom of the stove, with a small fire ablaze. I speed-dial Chef. He tells me to take out the mac 'n' cheese and quickly put the fire out with salt. Because he doesn't realize that I'm half in the bag, he neglects to remind me to use a pot holder. I hurriedly grab the overflowing Le Creuset with my bare left hand and *OUCH*. I let go fast, but I burned myself bad. I scream and swear and curse Martha Stewart to hell. My hand is throbbing, but I somehow find a mitt, save the food, and pour our most expensive sea salt all over the bottom of the oven. Chef can clean it.

As I run my blistering hand under cold water, I can't help but think: *My first kitchen wound. Cool.*

Wrapped in an ice-cold washcloth, my hand will be okay but my stomach is growling with hunger. I let the mac 'n' cheese cool for five minutes, excited to dive in and taste my hard work. Despite the spillage, or maybe even because of it, the presentation looks rustic and hearty. I'm a little shocked by its unassuming beauty, and when the time is right, I take a spoon to the sampler dish with delight. The top is crunchy, the inside is gooey, and all modesty aside, it tastes really damn good. My first meal ever is accidentally amazing.

But there's no time to revel in my *macaroni 'n' glee*. It's 5:00 p.m. I leave the casseroles on the stove top and cover them with foil. Maybe they'll magically stay hot—I'm not sure how that works. I top off my vino and bring on the Bobby Flay. His turkey meatloaf recipe looks easy and impressive. I have premonitions of something smoky and savory, thinking countrysides and Clint Eastwood. This would not be cafeteria meatloaf.

I gather some multicolored peppers and chop away with my knife skills, which are certainly no better than my math and cleaning skills, but I try my best to disco dance with the cutting board. I add zucchini, not sure if I should peel it, so I don't. And in the end, my vegetables are chunky and vibrant, like cocktail rings and Marimekko bags. As far as the meat mixture, it seems pretty hard to screw up. I debate running the disturbingly pink and raw ground turkey under water, because I'm not sure which foods you rinse before cooking or not, but I have the wherewithal not to. Combining the off-putting meat with the awkward vegetables makes me a little queasy. Either I'm a closet vegetarian or I've seen too much *Dexter,* but I decide that I don't like this dish. I throw the ominous meatloaf in the oven and shut the door revulsed.

In the ninety minutes the meatloaf has to cook, I set the dinner table with some Mason jar lanterns, a few soft votives, and three stray daisies inside a petite crystal vase. Despite my aversion to cooking, I've always collected cool, eclectic dishware (which really elevated all those fluffernutters), and I choose two mismatched plates I found in some flea market in Park Slope. I toss all my utensils into a rustic, paint-splattered, wooden box—something I remember the artsy visual team doing at ABC Carpet & Home—and leave it unedited in the center of the table. I roll up two frayed dishtowels to use as napkins and scatter around short, pearl-inlaid tumblers—one for red wine, one for sparkling water. I dim the lights, just enough.

The meatloaf has been in the oven for almost two hours, yet it's still hot pink and wet, and looks too unappetizing to set on the table. I loathe this loaf. So I remove it from the oven, let it cool for ten minutes, bury it alive with aluminum foil, and stick it in the back of the freezer, all slimy and frosted-lipstick-like. It is now 9:00 p.m.

Chef calls. "The anticipation is killing me! I'm coming home early! How's my little apprentice?" I try to sound poised, but as I've just decided not to serve the meatloaf, all I have left is a wussy salad and some mainstream macaroni 'n' cheese. "I'm good, love," I say apprehensively. "Don't get too excited for dinner, okay? Low expectations. Promise?"

My guy will be home soon and I look like something in between a Chassid and a hooker. I warm up the macaroni 'n' cheese, throw my arugula in a Scandinavian salad bowl, and quickly make my grandmother's foolproof dressing. I turn on some Natalie Merchant and dunk myself in the bath. I hold a piping hot towel over my tired skin and stinging eyes, and take a deep breath.

Out of the tub, I put on a long, off-the-shoulder T-shirt and lacey black underpinnings. I lotion my legs with Chocolate Truffle Soufflé Body Cream, which reminds me of something. I forgot to bake dessert.

Martha's Mac 'n' Cheese

SERVES 12

Call it beginner's luck, but this dish was the first meal I ever made and remains one of my best. On the side of sinful, it may be too rich to eat often, but it's perfect for a crowd (and it's a confidence booster). The original recipe is from Martha Stewart Living, *and I stick to it religiously, except for sometimes ad-libbing the bread crumbs with whatever crunchy cracker is in my pantry.*

8 tablespoons (1 stick) unsalted butter, plus more for greasing the dish

6 slices good white bread, crusts removed, torn into ¼- to ½-inch pieces

5½ cups whole milk

½ cup all-purpose flour

2 teaspoons salt, plus more for the pasta water

¼ teaspoon freshly grated nutmeg

¼ teaspoon freshly ground black pepper

¼ teaspoon cayenne pepper, or to taste

4½ cups grated sharp white cheddar cheese (about 8 ounces)

2 cups grated Gruyère cheese (about 8 ounces) or 1¼ cups grated Pecorino Romano cheese (about 5 ounces)

1 pound elbow macaroni

Preheat the oven to 375°F. Grease a 3-quart casserole dish or two 1½-quart dishes.

Put the bread in a medium bowl. In a small saucepan over medium heat, melt 2 tablespoons of the butter. Pour the melted butter into the bowl with the bread and toss. Set aside.

In a medium saucepan over medium heat, heat the milk. Meanwhile, in another medium saucepan over medium heat, melt the remaining 6 tablespoons of butter. When the butter bubbles, add the flour and whisk for 1 minute. Continue whisking as you slowly pour in the hot milk. Continue whisking constantly, until the mixture bubbles and becomes thick.

Remove the pan from the heat. Stir in the 2 teaspoons salt, the nutmeg, black pepper, cayenne pepper, 3 cups of the cheddar cheese, and 1½ cups of the Gruyère or 1 cup of the Pecorino Romano, if using. Set the cheese sauce aside.

Fill a large pot with water, bring to a boil, and throw in a generous dash of salt. Add the macaroni; cook 2 to 3 minutes less than the package instructions, until the outside of the pasta is cooked and the inside is underdone.

Transfer the macaroni to a colander, rinse under cold running water, and drain well. Stir the macaroni into the reserved cheese sauce.

Pour the macaroni mixture into the prepared dish or dishes. Sprinkle the remaining 1½ cups cheddar cheese and either ½ cup Gruyère or ¼ cup Pecorino Romano, and top with bread crumbs. Bake until browned, about 30 minutes. Transfer to a wire rack and cool for 5 minutes. Serve hot.

Ma's Salad Dressing

SERVES 8 TO 12

This recipe originated with my grandmother, Dorothy Pava, but my mother's three sisters (the loving and devoted "aunties": Ellen Wright, Susan Lucia, and Barbara Spiro), and now my sister and I, use this dressing on every single salad we serve. Like these women, it never fails me. Adjust the measurements to make as much as you need for the night, or prepare a jarful to store for the week.

⅓ cup extra-virgin olive oil
⅓ cup white vinegar
⅓ cup sugar

Combine the olive oil, vinegar, and sugar in a small bowl. Stir well. Serve immediately or store at room temperature.

6.

Feeding Friends and Neighbors

It's been two months since I learned that béarnaise isn't the name of a senior citizen and that the act of trussing relates to roast chicken, not eighties hair. And because of my new enthrallment with the kitchen, life has been significantly better on C Street, for Chef and me both.

He *loved* the macaroni and cheese, not only because it was dark and golden on the outside and rich and creamy on the inside, but because the entire experience seemed to enliven me like nothing else has been able to. Since that meal, I've been on such a culinary kick: I've attempted something sweet (peanut butter cookies, hazelnut biscotti) or savory (spaghetti and meatballs, chicken cacciatore) every afternoon to serve us at night.

My tastes and textures rank somewhere between pretty shitty and almost good. And just as I predicted, I possess nothing of feminine grace or refinement in the kitchen. Yet a delicious mood has spread throughout the house. The tension in the air has been gently lifted by the sweet smell of cranberry muffins and cardamom coffee, and what originated as a "quick fix" has become my happy place. I am a busy bee in a dirty dishrag, running around town, searching for celery root, cilantro, fennel seed, and other exotic things creeping into my new vernacular. There is music in my head again; the kitchen windows are cracked open. I run up and down our stairs, plucking fresh herbs from the garden, refilling our kitschy watering can, and watching our livelihood grow.

My homemade meals haven't changed Chef's hours (though he's been sneaking home for lunch almost every day for leftovers, and pedaling full speed to C Street immediately after closing shop each night). He is so excited to hear about my culinary adventures that you'd think I was Anthony Bourdain with boobs.

His delight has nothing to do with my mediocre honey mustard chicken though—he simply loves seeing me so lucid and lighthearted. An infamous, skirt-chasing chef once said to me, "The only way to keep a chef happy is to keep his cock happy." Maybe so, but taco night with a twinkle in your eye works well, too.

As the days peacefully pass, my lemon-thyme lamb chops and grilled portobellos are proving to be much more than a relationship narcotic. Just weeks ago, I felt so insignificant, but my victorious (or even edible) meals now infuse me with pride. And I feel like I'm actually developing a small talent in the kitchen! You can't teach someone to paint like Picasso or bounce like Beyoncé, but cooking is an art that really can be learned. It's basically turning on an Arcade Fire record and following directions. What I love the most is that, unlike the world itself, in the kitchen you get what you give. If I find a solid recipe, gather nice ingredients, and follow the instructions, I will produce something good to eat. Life may be unpredictable, but pasta puttanesca is not.

Of course, without my recipes, I'd be a wreck in the kitchen, and I realize that it takes time and experience to develop a real cooking rhythm. But for now, I am pleased to be a whimsy, flimsy amateur. I find comfort in not needing to be the best.

My cupboards now have all figmentations of dry pasta, plus rice, beans, and lentils; my fridge is stocked with potatoes, carrots, and onions at all times; and my freezer has chicken stock stored in ice-cube trays and vodka infused with pineapple. I try to live by certain rules of thumb. Like how a pinch of salt can transform an entire dish; if you don't have good olive oil, you better just order in; always keep a layer of foil on the bottom of your stove for spillage; Pinot Noir is a "bridging wine," it can go well with fish or steak; cooking with seasonal ingredients is the ultimate secret; and most important, always have a backup plan.

Last week, which was Labor Day weekend, my two best friends from New York, Jill and Beth, took a break from their fashion shoots and kick-boxing classes to experience my new, wholesome life of pretty pinafores and fresh berries. The morning the girls were set to arrive, I baked my mother's famous banana bread, adding a compulsory amount of chocolate chips, and just for fun, a few handfuls of butterscotch morsels. As I let the double loaves cool on the rack, I walked down the street for a coffee, feeling earthy and self-satisfied. As I skipped my way back into the kitchen, with a smile and café au lait, I saw that itsy-bitsy ants were attacking my loaves. Those little bastards! One loaf was so infested that I chucked it as far as I could throw it. The second loaf I saved just in time, with only a dozen or so creepy crawlers to reconcile with. In the end, I served that mildly buggy loaf to my most beautiful, powerful, and refined friends. And they inhaled it.

This weekend, my equally undomesticated sister is here. I get so excited to pick her up and feed her the homemade challah

I've packed in the car, I ram our rusty Jeep directly into the Bolt Bus she traveled on. No one gets hurt, and as luck would have it, the bus driver takes the blame. I'll forever be a subway girl. Rachel cannot comprehend how the hell I baked what she's eating. And I surprise her even more by saying we're going shopping. *For kitchen stuff.* "Wait. Seriously?" she says, in disbelief over my new idea of an awesome shopping spree. I tell her to relax and eat.

We drive to Friendship Heights, where parking is a bitch but the Bloomingdale's housewares department is having a great sale. I browse the clearance section for Le Creuset cast-iron pots and All-Clad copper pans. My wish lists, previously reserved for Helmut Lang blazers and Lanvin flats, now include things like double boilers, pizza stones, "spoontulas," and cleavers. I have flashbacks of my mother dragging me to Macy's Cellar to start a bridal registry after I got engaged to Gary. I remember crying hysterically in front of the Cuisinart section, experiencing my first real panic attack. Back then, life with a food processor meant life without thrills. Now, I'd sell my soul for a slow cooker.

The last time Rachel was here I wasn't feeling like myself, anxiously clocking Chef's hours and bitter that he didn't take the entire weekend off to spend time with her. These days, hopping from supermarkets to specialty shops, I don't have the time or interest in playing the boyfriend police, and I'm embarrassed that I ever was. I've accepted his hours and travel schedule, telling myself that we're just a cool, unconventional couple.

Presently, my only concern is finding a good chocolate chip cookie recipe because I read somewhere that every home cook should have a killer go-to, and the few batches I've made have come out too hard or too flat. So in the spirit of shopping, I decide that Rachel and I should embark on one more try: the

Neiman Marcus Chocolate Chip Cookie. I've heard that they're to die for and that the store, which is conveniently down the street, gives out recipe cards. We stop inside, where I grab the cookie instructions, tear Rachel away from the Marc Jacobs rack, and hit the road.

Back home, I wrap her in one of my aprons and tie one on myself.

"You look just like Mom!" she gasps.

For some reason, I get choked up when she says that. I miss my parents.

"Think about it, when Ma was my age, I was already ten years old," I say to Rach, as I prep our ingredients.

"Life is so weird," we say at the same time.

We turn on some music and stand in position. I preside over the mixer, calling out ingredients and measurements like a drill sergeant ("Flour. . . . Sugar. . . . Eggs. . . ."). Rachel obeys while I beat and blend. Then I scoop oversize balls of batter onto our baking sheet, and like the little girls we once were, we lick the mixing bowl clean. The cookies come out like absolute beauties. A hint of espresso offers the perfect snob appeal, and I know Chef will be impressed—if we don't eat them all before he comes home. We inhale a couple each, and take a picture of the gooey goods as proof of our halfway-legit domesticity for our parents.

As I naturally dive deeper into baking—including so many riffs off that recipe, adding pecans, dried cherries, and white chocolate—it decidedly becomes my preference to cooking. Some say that cooking verses baking reflects a personality difference, that cooks are free-spirited and bakers are by the books, but that doesn't apply to me. It's much simpler: I love sweets. I love cakes, candies, cookies, and pastries. I love them so much that I start worrying about my own muffin top.

Based on the better-your-hips-than-mine theory, I start bringing trays of my homemade treats to our next-door neighbors, whom I've diligently kept my distance from, fearing the obligatory schmoozing and small talk. But because I don't want to gain weight, and because I'm feeling like the happy-go-lucky girl I once was, I finally start to sniff them out. Allison the executive, Laura the intellectual, and Kathe the athlete all live in the brownstones surrounding our house with their handsome husbands and happy children. Most nights, they sit on their stoops like good Samaritans, chatting away with vino and baby monitors in hand, waving me over to join. I always say, "Oh, another time!" And then think . . . *as in never!*

What I quickly learn, after sharing a few sugar cookies and a botched batch of blondies, is that of all the stupid mistakes I've made in my messy, misguided, romantic comedy of a life, dismissing these women without giving them a chance was the dumbest move of all. It turns out, after all those friend dates with debutantes and dominatrixes, and all those spin classes with economists and environmentalists, all I had to do was walk over and say, "What's up?" I had an entire block of inspiring, ass-kicking women, just as worship-worthy as anyone in SoHo or on Sunset Boulevard, waiting to be the support system I so desperately needed. And because they are actually cooler chicks than I'll ever be, the second I open my door with a basket of scones and a shrug of the shoulders, they welcome me onto their stoops and into their circle and everyone laughs it off. "I *knew* you weren't a total bitch," jokes Allison, the blunt one, who I instantly love, and who lives directly next door. "Yeah, well, keep that between us," I say, over the moon.

And just like that, I have a village.

AS A long, Indian summer serenades C Street, I start poking my head out from our bay window, calling down, "Who's got eggs?" and "Anyone allergic to nuts?" It's a seamless transition from cordial neighbors to very close friends, and because of the proximity of the brownstones, our lives seem to gracefully intertwine. Soon, I'm "stooping" every night, bringing down pitchers of minty mojitos and whatever sinful treats I baked that day. The simple act of borrowing sugar and breaking bread turns into bonding over cellulite, sex, fertility, finances, adultery, mortality, and everything else we need to say and hear, as girlfriends do.

Because I am the only one without kids, I take pleasure in playing with their little ones, who are amazing children, and who really make me want to have kids of my own. I text Chef photos of me with Maeve, Ronan, and Libsy, who range in age from three to six. They help me rake the autumn leaves from our sidewalk, water Mister Chef's tomato plants, and frost lopsided carrot cakes in my kitchen. My block keeps me very busy with barbecues, potluck picnics, and backyard pizza parties, with the girls' cute and easygoing husbands tagging along when we let them. It's an unspoken fact that I will come to everything alone. I am the stray who C Street has taken in.

They probably feel bad for me, but what no one ever sees is what happens when Chef walks in the door, right around midnight. Besides cooking for him, I've also started a private food blog about my journey from noncook to good cook, to (hopefully one day) great cook, for his eyes only. I've designed it with a messy, scribbled font, as if the background is slightly ripped, tattered, and stained with coffee and wine; I curate it with whimsy photography and tear sheets of wacky fashion, with silly, random posts entitled, "The Devil Wears Burrata" and "Fucking and Shucking."

No matter how tired he is—and with two restaurants, a major expansion plan, and a couple of regular TV gigs, he is close to comatose—Chef loves watching my cooking education unfold. He longs to hear my latest blog entry; he insists it's his favorite way to unwind. So, while the rest of the street is sleeping, I slip off his shoes, slide him onto the couch, and share my latest confessions about putting brisket under the broiler and throwing away the expensive stinky blue cheese he brought home because, well, it stunk and I assumed it had gone bad. We laugh our way through the reading, and then I feed us dinner.

We have a very specific eating routine once he finally lands at home every night. "Positions!" one of us declares. Then he gets on the couch, prepares whatever show takes precedence on our DVR queue, and freezes it at the exact start of the program. Meanwhile, I plate dinner in the kitchen. Next, we usually share one big plate, or one large bowl, with a can of Coke for him and a glass of sparkling water for me, and eat all cuddled-up and blissed-out in front of the tube. We *live* for our favorite shows, analyzing the cast like they're real characters and plotlines in our lives. In a way, they are the only people we have to share.

During commercials, we talk about the meal and how I could advance it for the next time, like continuously basting my roast chicken or letting the meat "rest." I remember all his advice, word for word. No matter how tired he is, he's never too tired to thank me for cooking. After we make tea and finish our shows, we fall asleep tightly in each other's arms, in the same glorious position every single night, the dirty dishes waiting for me in the morning.

"I met the coolest mother and daughter ever today," he says, half asleep, me wrapped around him from behind, the right side of my face on his warm back like it is every night.

"Yeah? Who?"

"This super-groovy art collector woman named Mera and her daughter, Jennifer Rubell; they want me to promote parties at one of their hotels, the Capitol Skyline," he says, pausing for my reaction.

"Name sounds familiar, go on. . . ." I say, rolling my tired eyes. *Just what I need—more female fans. Rich and artsy ones, no less.*

"Babe, you'd totally love Jennifer; she's beautiful, and she's a famous food artist or something. She reminds me of you, except she's got this, like, rock-star style and went to Harvard."

"Awesome," I groan, grabbing the covers and going to sleep.

I am able to begrudge Jennifer for one full day. And then I meet her. She has only a few more nights in Washington, so Chef insists she and I hang out. The mother of all friend dates, she makes us a reservation at José Andrés's Minibar, a pricey, six-seat, laboratory-like haunt, where they serve things like foie-gras cotton candy and chicken skin served with a scalpel. The restaurant is a gastronome's wet dream and a nonfoodie's worst nightmare.

Experiencing two dozen courses of *crazy* can throw anyone out of their element, but sharing watermelon air and nitrous guns with Jennifer, the "it" girl of foodies, could have been outright *traumatizing*. Luckily, she's incredible. Sure, she has impeccable taste in all things art, fashion, and food, but forget that; she's warm. A few years older than I am, she also has that been-there-done-that mentality that makes her wise. I thank her for being so nice to me, explaining that the people I meet through Chef usually don't *get* me like she does. "No one in the food scene likes me," I confess, thinking of all the events where I still feel discarded. But she doesn't cut me any slack. "Oh, Alyssa, who gives a shit?" *I love her.*

"You were wrong," I say to Chef, late night on the couch, smitten with Jennifer after our heart-to-heart and dragon-breathing popcorn kernels. "She's not like me at all. She's on another stratosphere of awesome."

Now, every time I take my monthly New York trips, I make sure to attend one of Jennifer's famous dinner parties. Her style is so casual, yet so chic, that I watch her every move and then duck into the bathroom to frantically jot down notes. She invites fifteen to twenty people to her place—a mix of mercurial artists, reclusive writers, sexy stylists, and random wanderers—like it's absolutely nothing. She hits the Union Square farmers' market in Manhattan a few hours before dinnertime, conceptualizing understated meals like leg of lamb and London broil.

Over a hunk of Gouda cheese and Turkish pistachios, Jennifer welcomes everyone to her home, with her sharp black eyeliner and razor-straight bangs. While bringing together friends of friends and making sure everyone's glass is refilled with some enchanted cocktail of elderflower or açai, she asks everyone to be seated, spooning out meals of magenta carrots and midnight blue asparagus, and proteins swimming in secretly exquisite sauces. Without a flicker of fuss, we all feast on amazing food and unforgettable conversation until suddenly I'm sucking down stewed peaches and getting seduced. And so I invite myself over as often as she'll allow.

When the winter of 2010 hits, major blizzard alerts shut down everything in town. Chef closes his restaurants for almost a week. For the first time since we moved in together, already a year and a half ago, we are lovebirds around the clock, wearing matching sweat suits and taking turns making meals. As the snow hits hard, Allison, Laura, Kathe, and their husbands pop upstairs with their kids, whom I nibble on like they're my own nieces and nephews. Chef is astonished by how tight I've become with our neighbors while he's been off in the weeds.

Unlike anyone who's visited from New York and even our families, the C Streeters are the only ones who, day after day, truly see how hard our situation is. And they're rooting for us.

The Boys from the restaurant spend several snowy afternoons at our place, too. Being overworked, undersexed, and thoroughly exhausted New York transplants, they're ecstatic over the free days off, and all they want is hard-core chill-out time. They're always serving, but never served, and I'm thrilled to provide them with food, drink, and the foreign concept of not lifting a finger. But this is not as selfless as it sounds. I am well aware that the Boys are apprehensive about me. In the last year, they have seen Chef's bloodshot eyes, heard our fights, and watched me storm into the restaurant with venom. Though they would never say it, I have no doubt in my mind that the Boys think I'm a bitch, if not a total horror. This blizzard gives me an opportunity to reframe myself.

Between their monstrous appetites and culinary school degrees, my cooking is really put to the test. Before the latest storm lowers, with the streets being cleared just enough to drive, I sail into Whole Foods, where the checkout line has a two-hour wait. Without my usual scribbled grocery lists, I buy whatever looks nice and fresh. The concept of snow days brings me right back to Longmeadow, and I dream about soups my mom would make us, and the salads she'd serve with them, and I hunt and gather for those flavor memories.

Shopping from the gut makes me feel womanly. I also have a craving for the shepherd's pie we'd have as kids on cold, snowy days, and I collect what I think the recipe might call for. Then I zigzag around the fruits and vegetables, adding bushels of mandarin oranges, purple cauliflower, and Jerusalem artichokes to my cart, all the produce I know are in season because the *New York Times* told me so. I get packets of hot cocoa—high-quality

Ghirardelli, *this time*—and can't help but laugh. In my puffy ski jacket and pom-pom hat, whizzing through the market, I am truly a home cook.

Back on C Street, where the Boys are boozing and the snow descends, I loosen my shoulders, take a shot of their whisky, and cook up every no-fuss wintry crowd-pleaser I'm capable of: meat lasagna, chicken drumsticks, cauliflower cheese soup, warm rosemary walnut bread, and the memorable shepherd's pie. Every now and then, I catch Chef watching me from a distance, as I measure flour, add salt to the soup, or taste a sauce. He mouths, "I love you," and then says to the Boys, "She's turned into an amazing cook, no?" I blush and check the oven. And then he teases, "But she still holds a spoon like a convict!"

The Boys genuinely appreciate the hard work, inhaling everything I serve them, offering constructive criticism only when I ask. They suggest that my lasagna could use more tomato sauce because the meat will always suck it up; the drumsticks were delicious but needed just a dash of salt and pepper; the shepherd's pie would have been perfect had I doubled the creamed corn; and the beef stew is solid, but could have been better had I used homemade stock instead of the bouillon cubes. Out of the oven come oatmeal cookies, chocolate cakes, and even some humbling half-burned brownies. We're all well fed and in blissful hibernation. Chef is the happiest I've ever seen him.

As soon as spring comes, Chef and I take a break from our respective culinary duties and go on our now annual vacation to Greece. I'm nothing short of flabbergasted that he's making the time to get away, and even more taken aback when he vows to leave his BlackBerry in the glove compartment of the blue truck. We've been together almost two years, and because of my new basil-leafed lease on life, we are feeling like the stable, sexy couple we were the last time we landed in this village. It took about six months and sixty recipes, but I'm back to being me.

On our first night of vacation, overlooking the Acropolis, Chef asks me to marry him. He gives me the most magical ruby ring, and I say yes immediately, not because I have complete faith that we can endure the ups and downs of real life, but because I know how deeply I love him. The ring is unbelievably stunning; I've never had a piece of jewelry that speaks to my heart so. Because I've been engaged before, and Chef's plate is already full, we agree to keep any festivities casual and low-key, and loosely discuss having a tiny, intimate ceremony sometime within the year. I'd be most content eloping—as would my parents, who think weddings are a ridiculous waste of money and far too conventional for our DNA. (The one time I tried on a bridal gown, back in the Gary days, my rebel mom showed up to the all-white boutique eating a family-size bag of fluorescent orange Cheetos, a food I'd never seen her eat before in my life, and didn't even know was in her vocabulary. The salesgirl made her stand in a corner while my sister and I cracked up in our corsets.) But the Greeks on Chef's side would never accept my city hall fantasy, and we say we'll deal with logistics later. Then we get some souvlaki and sit in the center of town.

The nature of this trip is completely different, not because we're newly engaged, but because we can experience the heavenly life of cooking together in Europe. This is the ultimate engagement present. While Chef grills octopus, sausages, goat, and whatever else the big, sweaty village butcher proudly hands off to him, I am the devoted sous-chef, sipping ouzo, pocketing techniques, and organizing our prep table. Together, we putter around the kitchen every morning and night, leaving only for a few hours by the sea and a couple trips to olive oileries and honey beekeepers. On a couple mornings before he wakes, I fail at a few lemon loaves and pound cakes, but that's likely because the ingredient labels are in Greek, and I'm probably using cups of baking soda instead of sugar. Those get tossed, but nothing can keep me from trying again.

Every day at the beach, while devouring Giulia Melucci's *I Loved, I Lost, I Made Spaghetti* and Gael Greene's *Insatiable,* I gather more recipes and inspiration. I feverishly wolf down my food memoirs and more, as if authors like Ruth Reichl were Ralph Waldo Emerson. Over a lunch of grilled octopus and Greek salad at Samos Beach, where paradise herself would be jealous, I finally come up with the name for my blog that describes my own messy journey into the kitchen: "Apron Anxiety: My burning desire to cook, without burning down the house." Chef screams, "Yes, Lys, that's it!" We toast our Mythos beers, link our sandy toes, and I kiss my ruby ring.

One day, the forecast says it's going to rain all day and night. I'm happy to hear this because I've been wanting to slow-cook my first tomato sauce, the old-school way. The recipe comes from Giulia Melucci. It calls for a couple of eggplants, which we don't have at home, so I take the truck and drive down the long, narrow, cliff-top road while Chef is still asleep. As soon as I pull out of the driveway, I turn on Bob Marley, the best, and the only CD we haven't scratched up yet in Greece. After getting a little lost, I find my way to our favorite market, a few towns away. I am wearing a weird outfit, pajama pants and a vintage lace top, and taking nonstop pictures of the excursion on my camera phone. I don't blend in, and I don't care.

Back at the villa, Chef has taken position on the couch with some late-morning coffee and apricot jam on toast. The wraparound windows are open, and with the dark skies and pitter-patter of the rain, it's a gloriously lazy day. I tell him to stay there all day, and he says, "Perfect." In the kitchen, I stir with patience, tasting frequently, slow dancing with seasoning, flattering myself over the developing flavors. I glance at Chef every so often watching the BBC or reading his book about saving the whales; his body is quiet, his limbs are long. He calls "Lyssssie" for me to come cuddle, but I just can't leave the kitchen yet. This level of relaxation, which most couples experience on weekends or days off, is nearly nonexistent for us. Moments like this, with my sweet boy eating olives, catching up on current affairs, and singing my name from his well-slept, sun-kissed frame, seem to come once in a lifetime.

By the time the crescent moon and shooting stars surface, we sit on the porch in our slippers and sweatpants, ready to inhale what will be my first great meal. We lick our plates to the sound of raindrops, hummingbirds, and "Redemption Song." We name the dish Rainy Day Rigatoni.

The Perfect Shepherd's Pie

SERVES 12 (FOR MOST PEOPLE, BUT ONLY 6 FOR THE BOYS)

Kates, one of my best friends from Longmeadow, comes from a huge, amazing Irish family. I adore them all, but especially her handsome, gentle-hearted dad, a world-renowned doctor. How I love to tell him my crazy stories and make him laugh. In the dead of the winter, I called Kates in Boston for a good shepherd's pie recipe, assuming she'd have one. She conferenced in her fabulous mom, who sure has the gift of the gab, and we figured out a very basic recipe that turned out to be absolutely delicious. And yes, I know, this isn't really how the Irish do it, but it's all good.

1 bag Idaho or Russet potatoes, peeled
Salt and pepper
1 tablespoon extra-virgin olive oil
1 medium onion, chopped
2 pounds ground lamb (or a mixture with another ground meat)
½ cup whole milk
2 tablespoons unsalted butter, melted
Two 16-ounce cans creamed corn
Pinch of paprika

Boil the potatoes in a large pot with salted water until they are tender, about 12 minutes.

While the potatoes are boiling, heat a large skillet over medium-high heat. Add the oil to the hot pan, then add the onion and sauté until translucent, about 10 minutes. Season the meat, then add it to the pan. Work a large spoon through the meat as it cooks, so it crumbles. Cook for 3 to 4 minutes, or until brown.

Preheat the oven to 350°F. Drain the potatoes and transfer to a large bowl. Combine the milk and butter in a small bowl and set aside. Mash the potatoes to your desired consistency. Stir the milk mixture into the potatoes.

Fill a 9 × 12-inch deep casserole dish with all of the meat

mixture, using a slotted spoon to drain and discard the fat. Layer with the creamed corn. Then spoon the potatoes over the dish and sprinkle with the paprika. Bake for 30 minutes and then broil for 5 minutes to brown the top.

Serve hot.

Neiman Marcus Chocolate Chip Cookies

MAKES 12 TO 15 LARGE COOKIES

For anyone looking for recognition, validation, honor, and valor, bake these cookies and call me later. They are perfect for sisters, boyfriends, neighbors, and naughty nights alone. Make them grand and generous, and if you're baking for a party, be sure to prepare more than one batch. These bad boys fly. This is the original recipe for the famous Neiman Marcus Chocolate Chip Cookie.

8 tablespoons (1 stick) unsalted butter, at room temperature, plus more for greasing the cookie sheets
1 cup packed light brown sugar
3 tablespoons granulated sugar
1 large egg
2 teaspoons vanilla extract
½ teaspoon baking soda
½ teaspoon baking powder
½ teaspoon salt
1¾ cups all-purpose flour
1½ teaspoons instant espresso powder, slightly crushed
8 ounces semisweet chocolate chips

Preheat the oven to 375°F. Grease two cookie sheets with butter and set aside.

In a large mixing bowl (or in the bowl of a stand mixer fitted with the paddle attachment), cream the butter with the light brown and granulated sugars until fluffy. Beat in the egg and vanilla.

In a medium mixing bowl, combine the baking soda, baking powder, salt, flour, and espresso powder. Beat the flour mixture into the butter mixture. Stir in the chocolate chips.

Drop the dough by large spoonfuls onto the cookie sheets. Bake for 8 to 10 minutes, or 10 to 12 minutes for a crispier cookie.

Eat one cookie while still hot. Then let the others cool before serving.

7.

Unsavory

Apparently I am not the only one who ever wondered if *lemon chiffon* was a dessert or a porn star, because people are reading my blog. In fact, so many people are reading it that I've been asked to do a food demo at a popular event space in D.C., on a big stage, in front of a hundred people for a springtime soiree. Human beings are paying real money to see me make food. It's almost implausible.

The event organizers and I agree on a simple, straightforward cheesecake, so I choose the recipe I grew up with, Lynn Papale's Cheesecake, which I ate every day my freshman year of high school. I ask my mother to fax the recipe to me, to her elation, but I also implore the family not to come to Washington for the demo because it's too much pressure, and I'd actually rather pretend it's just not happening.

I'm on the side of incapacitated for several reasons, not the least of which is that I *just* learned what a springform pan is, and worse, I am petrified of public speaking. It's a horrible hang-up that I have. My voice quivers, my hands shake, and I seem to forget to breathe. Leading up to the big night, I'm so nervous about baking and talking (at the same time!) in front of all those people that I can barely sleep, and I'm tempted to call the whole thing off. But I have to do it. I wanted a voice in this city, and here's my chance . . . poured swiftly into a graham-cracker crust.

Hours before the event, I am in the green room, pacing. I'm pretty sure Chef won't make it, so I've asked my new friend Bella, another New Yorker who moved to D.C. for her fiancé's career, to come along for moral support. Bella is the only friend date in two years that stuck (my sister set us up), and between her and C Street, I finally feel like I'm surrounded by strong, funny, and wise women—the fuel to my fire for as long as I can remember.

The staff gives me a five-minute warning, and I beg Bella to come onstage with me. She's says I'm talking like a lunatic and tries to psych me up. I thank her for being my stand-in fiancé, and reluctantly head backstage. As the hostess of the evening introduces me to the crowd, "One of our favorite food bloggers, who's not afraid to take chances and make mistakes . . . ," I pat down my Anthropologie apron, gather some semblance of cool, and walk toward the mock kitchen in the center of the stage. I look at the crowd, confrontationally, filled with kitchen-phobes and camera crews. There's the celebrated food writer, Carol Blymire, waving at me! And then I see Chef. He's in the front row with a handheld video camera. I can't believe he came.

"I'm Alyssa, and I'm going to try not to pass out or poison you," I begin.

Like a real train wreck, I stumble through the crust preparation, spilling the walnuts on the floor because my hands are shaking so wickedly. Then I add one stick of butter to the graham-cracker crumbs, instead of half a stick. The recipe is right in front of me, but I keep flubbing the measurements, awkwardly laughing at myself. "I guess if I were some domestic goddess, I'd have nothing to write about, right?"

My demo is definitely comical. Chef is beaming.

"Next you add, like, a shitload of cream cheese," I say crassly, because my vision is actually now blurry from my nerves and I can't make out the proper quantity (it's two pounds).

Miraculously I get the mixer working, add the rest of the ingredients, and stick the clumsy cheesecake into a fake oven. I end the presentation by saying, "Don't worry, the cheesecake you're getting was made by real bakers, not me." And then I remember that I wasn't supposed to tell them that.

Following the demo, the floor is opened for questions about cooking and blogging. I offer a lot of nonsensical advice, defer to Chef for the hard-core foodie questions ("Do you guys all know my sexy and famous chef-fiancé over there?" I say, realizing a second too late how tacky it sounds), and thank the crowd for making me feel so welcomed. Everyone cheers loudly at the end and reflexively, my body curtsies. I guess my flawed presentation was kind of the point. At least no one asked for their money back.

As I soak it all in and pack up my things, Bella tells me it was a big hit. I think she's exaggerating, but I thank her for being by my side and give her cheesecake to bring home to her man. Chef covers me in hugs and kisses, asks for my autograph, and mentions taking me out to dinner to celebrate the big debut. It's 10:00 p.m. and I haven't eaten anything substantial all day; I'm overjoyed by the idea. It makes me think of when my parents would take me to Friendly's Ice Cream after violin recitals and school plays as a child.

But by the time we load the car with all my equipment, Chef's already been called back to work. He's leaving tomorrow for a week on an ostrich farm and he has a lot of loose ends to tie up before he goes. So I go home alone with my cream cheese–stained apron and dirty wooden spoons, shutting the door to his car without a kiss good-bye. I take a bath, clean my ruby ring, eat a couple of bites of cold leftovers and crawl into bed.

We've been engaged just a few months, and have been in a relationship for over two years. I've learned to cook great food, bake our favorite things, and feed everyone who's entered our life. I've made just enough true friends in Capitol Hill, bonded with the Boys, and reinvigorated my writing career. I'm feeling creative and inspired, and I'm even enjoying a little preliminary wedding planning. Everything is right with me, and for that, I largely thank the kitchen.

But things with Chef have changed dramatically since getting back from Greece. I learned long ago to expect very little, but these days, I expect nothing at all. Sometimes he still does sweet things like showing up for the food demo, but he *is* my fiancé . . . should that be so extraordinary? Usually, he's MIA, making promises he can't keep, or taking on so many projects that he comes home for only a few hours to sleep. We never have any time to communicate, and he's constantly letting me down. After enough slugs of disappointment, the shine of being with Chef is wearing off.

It hurts me most when he discards my family. My parents and sister know by now that he'll *never* stop by to say hello if he's in New York for business, but a few weeks ago, I did get him to agree to come to Massachusetts so that my mother's side, the Temkins—who have always rooted for us, even though Chef hasn't made it to a big family function the entire time we've been together—could throw us a small engagement party. We'd sleep over at one of my aunts' houses and make a weekend of it.

Over silver-glittered banners and cases of Bud Light, I was wildly happy watching Chef bond with my cousin "Little

Lori," as she's the oldest and has always been the leader of us "kids," and I couldn't wait for him to connect with the rest. But as the restaurant gods would have it, after two hours of fun and relaxation, Chef was summoned back to Washington for a work "emergency." It wasn't an easy decision, and he couldn't have been more gracious with my relatives in his good-byes, but he booked a trip home at the closest airport before even meeting my grandmother.

"It's usually not like this. . . . Don't worry. . . . I smell Dunkin' Donuts French Vanilla coffee!" I said, deflecting the reality of my relationship to Little Lori and the cousins as my dad sped off, helping Chef make his flight. I've become accustomed to such cover-ups. The only thing worse than feeling mistreated by your fiancé is feeling pitied by everyone else.

"You make too many excuses for him," said my sister, feeding me a piece of my engagement cake at the end of the night.

"Rach, don't go there, okay?"

I'm protective of us in public, but back home it's another story. We fight, we kick, we scream, we spiral into severe warfare. And then he does something wonderful and delicious to exonerate himself, like honking the horn outside the house, in a rented red Vespa, and driving us to the Washington Monument for a midnight picnic of pink lemonade and homemade pie. Then we both feel better, the air is lighter, and we can, at the very least, breathe. He always admits he was sorely wrong, that he's struggling with his own issues. And when all is confessed and forgiven, we curl up with our TV shows, sleep in our favorite position, and he swears he'll never be so vile again.

"I'm a good person," he repeats, in my arms. "I know you are," I whisper, praying we'll be okay. "But show me, don't tell me."

Jennifer is throwing the year's most exclusive and imaginative New York City event, a celebration of both food and art, and she's gone out of her way to give us two free tickets. She's also sitting us next to Mario Batali and his wife, Susi—which no doubt, is for our benefit, not theirs. I go to the city a few days before Chef to scout restaurants and rooftop gardens for our wedding, which we've barely talked about, but I think could be something positive to look forward to, in lieu of all the fighting. I'm considering our big day to be more like a lovely cocktail party, with no more than thirty people, where I'll wear yellow and he'll wear scruff, and at some point we'll say, "Let's do it."

I find a breathtaking landmark town house downtown, drenched in famously outrageous works of photography and whimsical decor, and known for its excellent food, no less, so I think it's meant to be. I e-mail Chef several pictures and concepts, and he writes back several hours later, "Awesome, boo. See you tonight!" The only opening for a wedding in the next year is four months away, in October, which is just over a year since our engagement. I take joy in the immediacy of this, knowing that too much wedding planning can kill a couple, and I write a personal check for the down payment. "I booked it!" I text Chef, with a follow-up note to absolutely, positively keep that weekend open.

Later that night, I'm on my way to Jennifer's event, immaculately stuffed into my first Herve Leger "bandage" dress, which I bought on a whim at Bergdorf while in the best mood after booking the town house. I call Chef to make sure he knows how to find the party from Penn Station. I'm so ready for a fun night out with him. But he doesn't pick up my call. I dial again and again, and go straight to voice mail each time. "WHERE ARE YOU?" I text him, in front of the venue, pacing in circles, buckled into my strappy metallic shoes, with perspiration rings under my million-dollar pits.

He calls and predicates the conversation by saying, "Don't yell at me, okay?"

"Just tell me you're close, sweetie, please?" I say, begging.

"Things got crazy here. . . . I lost track of time . . . and missed my train."

I am disgusted by his behavior. Jennifer went out of her way for us, and could have asked *anyone* to come as her guests. She's been so good me, taught me about the kitchen, and helped me break into food writing. Walking in alone, I'm blistering with anger, and I'm also getting nervous about mingling with such fancy-minded people by myself. Fortunately, I suppose, I missed most of the free-roaming cocktail hour by waiting for him, pathetically, outside, and by the time I check my coat, it's dinnertime with arranged seating. In a room filled with five hundred people, the chair to my right is the only one empty.

"He bailed?" asks Jennifer, looking a little hurt, perhaps on my behalf, while warmly making the rounds, hugging her guests.

"I'm so sorry we didn't give you more notice," I say, ashamed.

Everyone sitting at my table, including Mario Batali and his wife, tries to gloss over it. They're all successful people, primarily in the restaurant business, who know more than anyone what I've signed up for. But nothing can console me. Instead of enjoying the masterful creation—one ton of ribs with honey dripping from the ceiling above, playful watercoolers filled with fine red wine, and sparse and cynical table settings of huge steel pots and loose utensils—I excuse myself to call him and lose my shit in the stairwell.

"All you do is disappoint me, my family, and my friends," I wail into the phone. "I can't take this anymore!" He cries back that he's exhausted, overextended, and dealing with his own inner demons. "No, you're just a selfish asshole!" I scream. I cannot control my thick tears, so I hang up and leave the most eye-opening party I've ever been to, just as Jennifer is handing out hammers for her guests to demolish an edible installation of enormous, chocolate bunnies, an homage to the artist Jeff Koons.

And the beat goes on. He waits a few days for me to forgive him, working my heartstrings hard. And of course, I do. It's our year of erratic behavior, our constant benders of love and hate. I push and he pulls, and then we wait for it to pass.

Chef knows I've reserved the town house for our wedding, but we still have all the rest of the planning left. "It's your thing, Lys!" is the longest conversation we've had about it. I suspect that I'm rushing things and that getting married when we aren't in the best place is probably exacerbating whatever defects we might have. But he put the ring on my finger—isn't this what happens next? We obviously have our issues, but I'm trying to soldier on.

I send out an informal save-the-date and hire a duo of amazing folk singers that I once heard on the subway. I start to look for dresses—nothing from stuffy bridal departments, but exquisite gowns because . . . why not? My relationchef is stressing me out so much that even the smallest sizes are falling off my 5'6", suddenly 104-pound frame. It's like my body is waging war on something, but I don't know exactly what. Bella asks if I've ever been this skinny before, and I tell her once, in college.

We find a private little dress boutique in a carriage house in Georgetown. The owner has peacock feathers in her hair and Chanel lipstick on her teeth and she's determined to get me undressed and into some seriously stunning couture. Bella and I have such a wild afternoon modeling boustiers and dancing in boas. We clamp and pin me into many magnificent dresses . . . vintage Prada, elegant YSL, and gorgeous Gucci. Everything is secondhand, with sensational stories to go along with them. We strike all sorts of poses and text glamour-puss shots to our respective fiancés. Bella's guy writes back, "Oh la la!" I get radio silence. "Must be the lunch rush," I lie affirmatively. (Several hours later, he writes back, "No offense, Lys, but you look scary.")

It's hard to keep my spirits up when Chef is being so coldhearted, but I keep telling myself that it's just an ugly phase and it will end soon. I try to talk to him about what's going on beneath the surface. He says he's under an exorbitant amount of pressure with work, and how sometimes he feels like he might actually crack, but that it has nothing to do with us.

"Are you sure?" I ask cautiously.

"Yeah, I mean, if we moved the wedding back, I'd definitely have more time to enjoy the planning with you," he says, testing the waters.

"But October was the only day they had free. I told you this," I retort, instantly annoyed.

"No, I know. Just saying."

"If we waited until your life calmed down, we'd be dead before married," I bark, ending the conversation.

He is obviously in a low place, but I turn a blind eye. I'm drained and just want the chef who made me reginatta by the sea to come back. But then again, he is waiting for the old me to resurface, too. The girl who walked into a glass wall in her willowy silhouette and spent her nights waiting up for him in next to nothing with rice pudding and the remote control. Now, here I am, impulsively planning a wedding that we don't necessarily want, nagging him about red velvet cupcakes and handwritten vows, instead of nurturing our nearly broken love.

Careful not to pick at each other's wounds, we have a few good early-summer days grilling chicken skewers and working on the garden. But there are still some important wedding decisions that I simply cannot make without him, and we're running out of time. So I schedule a "nonnegotiable" twenty-minute meeting with him at the restaurant. As a preemptive strike, I come bearing gifts: strawberry shortcake for the Boys, rhubarb pie for the partners, and a random tie-dyed clipboard, which I found in a freebie box on someone's stoop, for Chef to store his wedding notes on. I rehearse the conversation all morning long, while baking nonstop, and dealing with the nervous stomach that's turned me into a sickly looking twig. *This shouldn't be so difficult.*

I find Chef at the restaurant, dripping in sweat, laboriously unloading boxes in the attic. He doesn't look too well himself today. It's July and hot, and I think he slept for three hours at most last night. When I show him everything I baked and brought over, his eyes brighten, but only ephemerally.

"Shall we get down to business?" I smile, praying he's going to play nice.

"Fine," he says, fast and sharp.

We go downstairs to a private corner table. Chef is looking sicker and sicker. He is trying to say something but he's shaking. I take both his hands in mine. "Hey, you can say *anything* to me, okay?"

And then the worst happens.

Chef says he's agreed to host a cook-off, somewhere in Pennsylvania, on the weekend of our wedding. And that it's probably better if we postpone our big day.

"Postpone it?" I say, crushed.

"Yeah, till spring or something?" he says, afraid to look in my eyes.

"Fuck you!" I scream, throwing the clipboard across the room.

I storm away from the table, falling down half the flight of stairs. My knees are bloody and Chef is chasing me, but I get away as fast as I can. How dare he.

In the days that follow, Chef frantically takes back his words, a hundred times over, says that he's canceled his event and that he's back to being his old self, *a good person*. He says he wants babies, and to be a good son-in-law, and will even move us back to Manhattan. But quite frankly, I'm done with our drama. I call the landmarked town house, the subway musicians, the crazy couture lady, all my girlfriends, and everyone in my family, and tell them that Chef chose a barbecue instead of his bride, and that there will be no wedding.

With childlike desperation, he begs me not to go, but one week later, I flee C Street for a six-week escape to Los Angeles.

I can't marry him and I can't leave him. So I pronounce we're on a long, hard break.

Lynn Papale's Cheesecake

SERVES 12

The thought of combining public speaking with anything is almost enough to give me a heart attack. But because this is a recipe from my childhood, and originally from my mom's dear friend Lynn Papale, it somehow brought me comfort and confidence on such a scary night when I had to cook and talk (and be somewhat charming) at the same time. People have contacted me since the event, saying they've incorporated this recipe into their family's repertoire, so I'm very happy to have spread the love . . . and the cream cheese.

1 cup graham cracker crumbs (about 8 to 10 graham crackers)
½ cup chopped walnuts
4 tablespoons unsalted butter, at room temperature
2¼ pounds plain cream cheese, at room temperature
1 cup sour cream
1½ cups sugar
5 large eggs
½ cup light cream
1 teaspoon vanilla extract

Preheat the oven to 350°F.

In a medium size bowl, combine the graham cracker crumbs and walnuts with the butter. Mix well.

Press the mixture into the bottom of a 10-inch springform pan.

Place the cream cheese and sour cream in a large mixing bowl (or the bowl of a stand mixer fitted with the paddle attachment) and blend well. Add the sugar and combine. Stir in the eggs and beat until smooth. Beat in the light cream and vanilla.

Pour the batter into the springform pan and bake for 1½ hours, or until the top of the cake is golden brown. After 1 hour, start checking the cake for doneness.

Cool completely on a wire rack. Refrigerate for several hours, or at least until the cake is cold to the touch, before serving.

Supernatural Brownies for Breakups and Breakdowns

MAKES 15 (BIG ONES)

When I close my eyes and eat a brownie, many emotional flavor memories come to mind. As a kid, I'd long for the annual Temkin pool party at my uncle David's house, where all my cousins—Little Lori, Sara, Jessica, Andrew, Emily, Zach, Sammy, Jodi, and Eddie—would go absolutely ballistic over the huge plates of double-fudge bliss. Also, Addie Friedlander, a dear family friend who was like another grandmother to Rachel and me, would often visit our home in Longmeadow. She'd come with a box of homemade brownies, packaged in a formal pastry box, properly tied with a silky ribbon, elegant just like her. I never got Addie's recipe, but these brownies make me think of her, too. I used this recipe from the New York Times, *adapted from Nick Malgieri's book* Chocolate.

2 sticks unsalted butter, plus more for the pan and parchment paper
8 ounces bittersweet chocolate
4 eggs
½ teaspoon salt
1 cup packed dark brown sugar
1 cup granulated sugar
2 teaspoons vanilla extract
1 cup flour
½ cup chopped walnuts or ¾ cup whole walnuts, optional

Preheat the oven to 350°F. Butter a 9 × 13-inch baking pan and line it with buttered parchment paper. In the top of a double boiler set over barely simmering water, or on low in a microwave, melt the butter and the chocolate together. Cool slightly. In a large bowl or mixer, whisk the eggs. Then whisk in the salt, brown sugar, granulated sugar, and vanilla.

Whisk in the chocolate mixture. Fold in the flour until

just combined. If using chopped walnuts, stir them in. Pour the batter into the prepared pan. If using whole walnuts, arrange them on top of the batter. Bake for 35 to 40 minutes, or until shiny and beginning to crack on top. Let cool in the pan on a wire rack.

8.

An Interlude in Los Angeles

Strapped to my shoulder is a mustard yellow, corduroy duffel bag filled with sundresses, shades, sweatpants, music, memoirs, and spin shoes: my emotional CPR kit. With swollen eyes and a skinny body, I have no dependable income, no organized plan, and just enough in my savings account to scrape by. For six weeks, I am relying on the kindness of my friends, Mitchell Gold sleeper sofas, and California dreams.

Sadly enough, I am in the same psychological place I was when I flew from heartbreak to LAX three years ago—injured by love, betrayed by happily-ever-after, and utterly exasperated by a handsome, magnetic man who drove me away, then begged me to stay. But I now possess a secret weapon for finding strength through pain: the kitchen. My *French Laundry Cookbook* has replaced French-kissing strangers. And I have a popular blog filled with adventures in food, not first dates. I have no idea what to do about Chef and me, but until there's some revelation, all I want to do is hike Runyon Canyon, reconnect with old friends, touch my toes to the ocean, and above all else, rock the fucking apron.

"Take me to Ralphs" is the first thing I say to Shelley when she picks me up from the airport in her new Audi convertible with her fluffy puppy, Phoebe, on her lap. Otherwise known as Rock 'n' Roll Ralphs, because of the freaky crowd there, it's the only grocery store I remember being open this late.

"Hi . . . love you and missed you right back," she says, smiling.

It's 11:00 p.m., but I need to get into her kitchen. The last few days have been so dramatic—I'm exhausted, anxious, and shaky. Shelley wants to know why she can't just give me a Xanax. "Because cooking works better," I say sincerely.

She's already eaten dinner and uncharacteristically not hungry, so she impatiently waits in the car while I run into Ralphs. The aisles are filled with outrageous drag queens and juvenile delinquents. *Hello, Hollyweird.* The produce has been picked over and the butcher has gone home, so I choose the best-looking vegetables, a box of couscous, and some crumbled feta cheese with a nice, healthy Mediterranean dish in mind. I've made it many times for Chef and me as a fallback.

Back at Shelley's tiny, chic West Hollywood apartment, I unload my groceries before unpacking my suitcase. I can see that she's tired and confused as to why I'm more interested in finding a cutting board than catching up on our lives. After all, I've just left my fiancé and she *is* my best friend. "Just go to sleep, Shellz," I say. "We have six weeks."

Alone in the kitchen, preparing to roast my vegetables, Chef is in my head reminding me to chop gracefully, moving the knife in circular motions, rather than sawing back and forth, and to make sure all my cuts are even—because when I first started making this dish, some of the eggplant would wind up undercooked. It's hard to prepare my meal without sending him pictures as I go—which has been our tradition; it's a learned behavior, as is keeping my prep area clean.

But tonight I'm in the kitchen for myself. I lay the perfect slices of symmetrical eggplant, peppers, and zucchini on a baking sheet, drizzle them with olive oil and sea salt, and put the tray in the hot oven. As the vegetables roast, I prepare the couscous. While everything cooks, I stretch my body, lifting my arms as far up as they can go, then bending over, pressing my fists against the floor; I extend my vertebrae, slowly twisting my waist to the right and then the left, and feeling my blood circulate. I breathe deeply and look out the window for the moon. Cooking takes the edge off in a way that nothing else can.

I wake up early the next day to several heart-wrenching texts from Chef. He accuses me of running away instead of fighting for us, that this *stupid break* is not what he wanted, and that he's dying inside. But he can't be too beat up. While I'm gone, he's going away for about six weeks (almost the entire duration of my trip) to shoot another cooking reality show, something I knew was in the pipeline, but we never really discussed. He makes me promise to come back home when he's done. I coolly respond that I'll be there, but deep down, I'm not sure what will happen past that point. "Let's just take it day by day," I respond.

I pull myself together and prepare to make my first breakfast for Shelley. I contemplate making a broccoli quiche with a homemade crust, or a "sunchoke" frittata, just because I like the word, but my show-off food will be wasted on Shelley, whose password to everything from her e-mail to her bank account is "Big Mac." As such, her fridge is stocked with the following staples: Chanel nail polish in the shade of Vendetta, the same two bottles of Veuve Clicquot she's had for seven years, a tub of I Can't Believe It's Not Butter, dozens of half-drunk water bottles, and last night's leftovers.

I'll keep it simple, but I still need a few things, so I throw on a bra, snag Shelley's aviator shades, and open the front door to a big *buenos dias* from the California sun. I walk to a ridiculously overpriced grocery store just a few blocks away, and there I sparingly shop for fruit, eggs, cheese, butter, and a baguette. If I've learned anything about cooking, it's the fortitude of a few nice ingredients. With one filled bag, I can nourish us beautifully. As I walk home, I am feeling more free-spirited than I should. My relationship is on its deathbed, and all I can think about is the best way to hull a strawberry.

As soon as I hear Shelley rumbling around her bedroom, turning on *Regis* and playing with Phoebe, I get to work on some scrambled eggs. I crack open four eggs the way I was taught—with one quick tap against the counter—and add salt, pepper, and a little cream. Ten minutes later, I serve them onto our two plates, each with a hearty piece of buttered baguette. I set out washed, mixed berries on a damp paper towel and pour two cups of orange blossom tea. I holler to Shelley, ecstatic to present our petit déjeuner. She's taken me in, offered me her car, her clothes, and her unconditional support . . . this is one way I can give back.

When she sees our homemade breakfast for two, it's like she's witnessed a miracle. She marvels again and again, "Wait, no way—you made this? Are you serious? Oh my God!" But then she gets down to business, becoming one with her breakfast, inhaling every last bite. Observing my best friend nourished by my food is a pleasure. And I know we will have many more moments like this.

On my third day in L.A., Shelley goes to Malibu with a client and leaves me with her new car. As soon as she leaves, I scurry off to the Grove, a huge outdoor shopping mall that also hosts lots of food stands and a fabulous farmers' market.

Touristy as it may be, it's one of my favorite places. The second I park, I grab a soy latte at the Coffee Bean and duck into Sur La Table. With summer berries in season, I am dying to make Shelley my whole-wheat berry muffins. It's the easiest recipe, healthy too, and it will fill the apartment with a heavenly smell for when she comes home.

To make that happen though, I need to buy a few tools—measuring cups, wooden spoons, and muffin tins. These small culinary projects placate me. I silence my phone and shut down my thoughts. My body slows in the presence of cooling racks and coffee frothers, as I bond with other home cooks searching for their own essentials. Sometimes I tell them about my blog; once, someone even bashfully asked if I was "Apron Anxiety." She recognized me from the one picture I posted of myself frowning over a frying pan of burned rice. She told me that I made her feel so much better about her own epicurean inadequacies. I almost passed out. My whole life I thought the food scene was for food snobs, and here I am, making an impact just by being *me.*

With a few shopping bags of basics, I pull into Shelley's detached garage, top down and Eminem up. I am so excited by my purchases that I recklessly undershoot the distance between the Audi and the wooden wall, and slam the right side of her car into the structure. "No! No!! No!!!" I scream. This cannot be happening. Half the car is severely dented and all the paint has been ripped off. Dread overcomes me. Shelley loves her car and has a real temper about things like this. In less than three days in Los Angeles, I have de-pimped her ride. With no freelance work or savings to spare, and already on the brink of a breakdown, this is the last thing I need.

All I can do is make it up to Shelley with her favorite thing besides me and Phoebe: food. So I dig out my cookbooks that I had packed in my aprons and frantically bake all day long, crossing my fingers that my self-taught pastry skills are good enough to save my ass. When she comes home predictably "starrrving," I sit her down with an oversize muffin, glinting with mixed berries, and a coffee with frothed milk on top. I contemplate stirring in that Xanax she mentioned, but instead, I fess up. I wait for her to digest the news and lose her cool, but she barely looks up. The girl doesn't want to stop eating. I *could* be off the hook.

We go outside to assess the damage. The car runs just fine, but looks like it has been in a bad accident, and is totally reprehensible for the crowd Shelley runs with. We calmly decide that if insurance won't cover it, I'll compensate her for the cost in small increments at a time. "There's just one more thing," she suddenly says in a serious tone, standing by her busted automobile. "Can I have another muffin?"

Around sunset, I go hiking alone in Runyon Canyon to shake off some stress. I've probably marched up that steep mountain hundreds of times in my life, and I always come down stronger and more poised than when I started. I am totally confused about Chef and me—in fact no one, not even my mother, or any of the sage women in my life, can find the right answer—but I know that on one of these cathartic walks, wisdom will find me. It always does.

When I walk in the door after a two-hour trek, legs tight, cheeks flushed, Shelley is wrapped in a cashmere throw, looking up at me like the cat that killed the canary. As I stare closer into her face, I can see that she's covered in crumbs. There's a blueberry in her tooth, and I know what's coming next. "Alyssa," she says with gravitas. "I. Ate. Them. All."

My need to cook for others quickly extends past Shelley, who devours my dishes but genuinely doesn't know or care (yet) about the difference between *Iron Chef* and Chef Boyardee. Even though I'm trying to keep to myself in L.A.—searching for signs and answers amid the avocados and azaleas—word spreads fast that I'm in town, taking a break from Chef, and growing my food repertoire. Everyone wants to know the scoop on my engagement, but I politely explain that I have no interest in talking about it. It's not because of privacy; I just can't explain what's going on between us. He and I were so damn good at comfort and pleasure, but when real life crashed our domain, we totally self-destructed. All day long, my mind plays hopscotch between "love is all you need" and "love is not enough."

About a week into my L.A. trip, I get a text message from my friend Dara, a type-A TV writer who used to be a buzzed-about editrix in New York. Whip-smart, staggeringly confident, with surfergirl dirty blond hair that she's never even touched, Dara is "a real winner," as my mother would say, unsarcastically. She's also the kind of friend who I can see once a year and pick up right where we left off, which is usually when she's starting a dream job and I'm ending a relationship. In times of despair, Dara is the ultimate, no-nonsense problem solver. She won't lick your wounds or take you for an ice-cream cone, but she'll give you the cold, hard truth like you've never heard it before.

Her text message reads as follows: "this fri, u cook dinner here for us and like ten other fab pple, k? showrunners, v. cute nabes, pple u need to know. will leave door open. take my mini-cooper for groceries. low carbs. kk?"

I roll my eyes but crack a smile—an expression that has always accompanied our friendship. "Done," I write back. Because of the blog, she thinks I'm the Barefoot Contessa. But hardly! This will be the first big dinner party I've hosted. I've cooked for the Boys, made cheesecake onstage, and brought lots of food to the stoops of C Street, but a large sit-down dinner is a challenge I've yet to tackle. Part of me thinks I'm not ready for it, but another part knows that preparing a dinner for a bunch of Hollywood hotshots is exactly the distraction I need. After all, the hardest thing about not being with Chef is filling the time and space previously reserved for loving him.

Back on Shelley's couch, thinking about Friday night's dinner, which is only three days away, I obsess over the menu. I flip through *French Women Don't Get Fat,* Jennifer Rubell's *Real Life Entertaining,* and Mark Bittman's *How to Make Everything.* I've also started to accumulate old columns by *LA Weekly*'s food writer extraordinaire, Jonathan Gold, which are stacked alongside farmers' market maps, restaurant menus, and stolen paper placemats from Mario Batali's Mozza, printed with silly Italian proverbs like "To avoid baldness, cut your hair during a full moon."

Conceptualizing a meal really turns me on. It's one of the rare moments in life where anything is possible. Should we drink tequila, eat empanadas, and get sloppy drunk? Maybe it's a fine-wine-and-grilled-fish kind of civilized soiree? Will deep-fried Southern food help the killer crowd loosen up? While Shelley and Phoebe doze off, I linger in the living room in my pajamas, flipping through recipes, drinking peppermint tea, and eventually deciding on an easy, elegant meal, completely within my comfort zone—herb-crusted baked chicken breasts served with mustardy, multicolored potatoes and a fun frisée salad.

Thursday night, twenty-four hours before the dinner party, I bake a sour-cream coffee cake while wearing nothing but a towel. It's hot these days to begin with, and I'm sweaty and jumpy about tomorrow. I take a chance with the recipe by adding an avalanche of dark chocolate chips—to me, dessert without chocolate is like sex without an orgasm. And I forbid Shelley from coming near the kitchen, which is quite cruel, considering the unbelievable smell escaping from the oven (and it is her kitchen). But she can see that I'm wound up and so she watches TV without a word.

When the cake is cooling, I take her to the Grove to my newfound favorite restaurant, not just because it's cheap, but because it's phenomenally fresh and authentic: a Brazilian churrascaria buffet. "Who needs Nobu?" I say, midplantain, as she gets up for seconds.

I'm too broke to rent a car and too scared to touch Shelley's, so the day of the dinner party, I take the bus to the farmers' market at the Grove. I hit it off with some Mexican housekeepers who warn me not to talk to anyone who takes public transportation in L.A., besides them, of course. I think of how my mother would rather be on that bus with the honest, hardworking people (and even the incoherent crazy folk) than anywhere else in Beverly Hills, and I miss her. The ladies made me laugh, and as I hop off at my stop and skip across the street to the butcher, I'm a little less nervous. I order twenty chicken breasts, the most meat I've ever purchased in my life, and pirouette over to the produce stand for some electric purple potatoes, as well as onions, lettuce, and a few other ingredients that look exciting.

My BlackBerry starts to buzz incessantly, so after crossing everything off my list, I duck into Sur La Table to put down my bags and stand in the air-conditioning while reading my messages. There's an e-mail from an old friend with a big job at *New York* magazine. I had included him in a mass mailing to friends and colleagues, letting them know I was on the West Coast in case they had assignments for me out here. I quickly open his note, which says, "We need you for the Emmy Awards in a few weeks. You around to talk?"

New York magazine. Finally. The number one publication I've always wanted to work for. And the Emmys? Incredible. I've covered major award shows before, but not for such a respected outlet. This is a no-brainer assignment that I can kill. I'm jumping up and down in the utensil aisle, beaming in front of the pastry brushes.

Then I realized the complication. The Emmys are two weeks after I'm supposed to fly back to Washington. Our six weeks apart would be up, and Chef would be coming back from his show. I've promised him that I'd be there waiting. Extending my trip would mean extending our separation *and* letting him down. But how many times has *he* let *me* down? How many times has *he* put work first? "I'll do it," I write back immediately.

Before I rebundle myself with my poultry and produce, I call my sister and friends screaming, "Guess who's reporting for *New York* magazine?!" Rach wants to FedEx me my favorite backless dress. Shelley texts me one "OMFG" after another. Even the security guard at Sur La Table congratulates me. I consider calling Chef, but I don't want to ruin this happy moment with drama. The assignment is not the story of a lifetime or the cure for cancer; it's not even going to pay for tonight's food and flowers. But it's nice to catch a break.

High on life and because the bus *is* a real bummer, I splurge for a taxi to the El Royale, the fabulous, fabled building in Hancock Park, where Dara lives with her boyfriend. I let myself into their apartment and connect my iPod to their speakers to listen to a song called "Start a War" by the National. I've been listening to it nonstop. The lyrics remind me so much of Chef; how we once expected such an extraordinary life together, and now we're barely hanging on.

We expected something, something better than before, we expected something more. I crack open the windows and pull back my hair. I lay out the recipes for my herb-crusted chicken and mustardy potatoes. I pour a glass of wine. *Do you really think you can just put it in a safe, behind a painting, lock it up, and leave?* I decide that I'll improvise the salad. I smell the parsley and rosemary, close my eyes, and think of our garden. *Walk away now and you're gonna start a war.*

By the time Dara comes home, I've done most of the prep work, cleaned my dishes, and am able to display some level of composure. The hard part is over, but I'm still sort of scared. She comments on how amazing the apartment smells, which gives me a small boost of confidence, especially coming from her. We have an hour before the guests arrive. Together, we set the table with a blue-and-white-toile tablecloth and a large vase of sprouting sunflowers. We light a few unscented candles and talk about what's been going on. As overexteneded as her own life is, Dara is the first person to help her straggler-artsy friends find apartments, land jobs, and get laid. She hands me a set of all her keys—to the house, Mini Cooper, and bike lock, as well as the membership card to the studio where she practices yoga, which she advocates that I use whenever I want. She also wants to fix me up. This is Dara's way of showing love, and as always, I am touched.

I tell her I don't want to meet guys while I'm in town, and please not to push it. This is not a matter of morality; in theory, I am not above a little indiscretion (a hot kiss from a dark stranger, some meaningless sex) while Chef and I are summering in the gray. What's wrong with a steamy one-night stand after all the hell I've been through? In fact, I would feel very cool acting all Parisian and polyamorous, lifting my flowery frocks high up above my head. I'm just not in the mood. Orgies of avocados, cherry tomatoes, and toasted pine nuts are all I want to fantasize about for now.

As we chill the Prosecco and anticipate the doorbell, I change the subject by asking Dara for a rundown of who's coming to dinner. "Basically, *ehhhveryone,*" she says, deadpan. I have a flashback of Shelley dragging me to New York nightclubs to take tequila shots in our Bordeaux nail polish and cushioned Dior handbags, with her idea of "everyone," too. In all fairness, Dara's illustrious guest list, the so-called literati of Los Angeles, is a discriminating crowd. They're sophisticated, well traveled, and for the most part, dedicated gourmands. What's more, Dara tells me that Christopher Wagner, the head writer for my all-time favorite TV show, will be stopping by for dessert because he lives down the hall. To meet the mind behind the dark, dysfunctional, sexually devious show, in honor of which I've joined chat rooms and fan clubs, and talked at length about with Chef (also a die-hard fan), is a big deal. When the doorbell rings, I dash into the guest bedroom to change out of my apron and into a long, strapless sundress.

Dara's friends stroll in with their huge screenplays and deep sighs and it is evident that this no-bullshit crowd is ready for dinner. They situate themselves around the dining-room table. After quick introductions, I take my position at the stove. It's interesting to meet all these smart, successful, overly ambitious types, but besides Christopher, who's coming late, I don't really care about their credentials. At this point in my life, I've learned that everybody hurts and everybody is hungry. When Shelley arrives with the coffee cake, I kiss both her and the Bundt pan, and feel more at ease having them there. My pseudo-baker instinct tells me this dessert is stupendous, which comforts me, just in case dinner is not.

My baked chicken is almost ready and the purple potatoes are in the pot. Once they're cooked, I'll mash them with caramelized onions, Dijon mustard, white wine vinegar, olive oil, pepper, and capers. The frisée and endive salad is crisp and self-assured, ready to be served with my grandmother's dressing on the side. For a split second, I get really sad that Chef can't see me in action. It's been a few days since I've told him to stop calling, insisting it's "counterproductive" to the clearing of our heads. But at this moment I miss him terribly. Dara's boyfriend walks into the kitchen, sees me tearing up, and asks if I'm okay. I blame the onions and carry on.

The rock-hard potatoes are holding back the show. I've immersed them in too much water, which is not yet boiling, and the suckers won't soften. I'm screwed. There's good wine, green grapes, and soft cheese on the table, but I sense some displeasure from the dining room. They're hungry! Just as I start to really panic, Dara smoothly walks into the kitchen, covers the pot with a lid, and returns to her guests like she never left. This speeds things up tremendously. *Damn, why didn't I think of that?*

With no time to dwell, I swiftly finish up. I assemble the crispy chicken breasts on a beautiful silver platter, next to a white ceramic plate with the smashed purple potatoes and an etched-glass bowl filled with whimsical leafy greens. We're going to eat family-style. With all my dishes out of the kitchen, I pull up a chair and join the table. As everyone digs in, I watch how my colors and textures really come together. The presentation is unfussy but elegant, and the vibe is great. We eat, drink, gossip, talk showbiz, and eat and drink more. The chicken might be slightly overcooked, but no one seems to notice. I try not to eye who is taking seconds and what's being pushed to the side, because all that really matters is that the room feels just right. Anyway, Dara would have told me if something fell short.

As I start to clear the plates and prepare for dessert, Christopher Wagner makes his entrance. He's my height, but burly and handsome, with a presence so strong and silent that it's almost mystical. A shiver runs down my spine as I clumsily wipe my hands to shake his. We conspicuously check each other out and then I duck into the guest bathroom to inspect myself. I look in the mirror and it occurs to me that I just cooked for twelve strangers without breaking a sweat. *I did it.* My hair comes down and I dot my cheeks with pink blush. As I look at my reflection, I notice a little glow. For the first time in months, I feel pretty.

Back in the living room, the group has gathered to eat my vintage ivory coffee cake and smoke some jungle green marijuana. I'm already a little drunk, so I quietly decline. The room is collectively joyful from the combination of weed and sweets, and since no one is really listening, now seems like a good time to tell Dara and gang that I'm staying two weeks longer than planned to cover the Emmys. No one responds—which is to be expected from a bunch of stoned, self-obsessed showbiz types—and I don't take it personally.

Christopher, who's not even that high, then says, "Maybe you should stay another two months and rent out my place? I'm heading to New York till mid-October for work." While I'm stunned at the prospect of sharing *anything* with someone so connected to my favorite series, and thoroughly enticed by the prospect of shacking up at the exquisite El Royale, I'll never be able to afford some famous screenwriter's apartment. Predicated by the acknowledgment that it's definitely out of my price range, I say I'd love to see it. And just like that, Christopher kills the rest of his cake and quickly jumps to his feet.

As we walk to his apartment at the opposite end of the hall, he stops in his steps and takes a long look at me. "I hope you don't mind me saying this, but I'm very attracted to you. . . ." *Ah, shit! He's just trying to shag me?* This is not exactly the *hard* sell that I had in mind. I point to my engagement ring, shrug my shoulders, and suck back any sexual energy that I might have put out into the air. *No chance.*

He gets the point, and welcomes me into his big, beautiful two-bedroom apartment like nothing ever happened. It's dreamy inside—arty and vast with Juliet balconies, high ceilings, crown moldings, and an eternity of rare books and black-and-white photography. It's the apartment of a rich bohemian and a legit bon vivant. From his endless windows you can see a posh golf course, rows of charming bungalows, far past the canyons, and beyond the famous Hollywood sign.

And the kitchen! Pristine slate tiles, rows of copper pots, and a six-burner Viking stove. He has all the tools I'd ever need to advance as a cook. Watching me delight in his ramekins of Maldon salt and Italian olive oils, he calls from across the room, "So, you're into cooking?" I tell him about my blog, and how, ironically, a chaotic life with a chef led me to a peaceful one in the kitchen. "I like that," he says. "I'm a budding foodie, too." Then we both agree we can't stand that word.

As I relish every inch of the apartment, not just the stainless-steel skillets and saucers, he apologizes for a few scattered things that belonged to the last guy, "Paul," whom he shared the apartment with. He says the first and last name and my ears tweak. I fix my posture, raise an eyebrow, and flip my hair to one side. Wait. No. Is he talking about the star of the show he wrote, and easily my favorite actor? He is. Apparently, they had been roommates while Paul's house in the Hills was being built. If I were to rent the place, I'd actually be sleeping in Paul's bed. All I can think is that life is one big, amazing mindfuck.

"By the way, who's your favorite food writer?" Christopher says with intensity, after the tour.

"Hmm, good question. Maybe Gael Greene? Did you know she slept with . . ."

"Okay, if I give you my apartment till fall, will you read some M. F. K. Fisher for me?"

"Yes," I say, confused. "But I don't think you realize just how broke I am."

He seems too savvy to be one of those rich people who thinks everyone around them is cash happy, too, so I'm not sure what's going on here.

"Well, what can you afford?"

"Like seven hundred dollars per month, at the most. And I'm sure this place is *much* more than that," I say.

"Why don't we sleep on it?"

"Okay."

"Together?" he asks with a wink.

"No."

By the time I get back to Dara's, most of the guests are gone, including Shelley, who snuck off to a movie premeire after-party. Dara's boyfriend is doing the dishes and convinces me to crash in the guest room. I'm now definitely drunk from a few glasses of dinner wine and a sherry at Christopher's, and very tired, with no cash left for a cab back to Shelley's anyway. I hate to be an imposition, but I hate leaving the El Royale even more, so I comply.

As I draw a bath in the guest bathroom, I reflect on everything that happened tonight. I can't believe how easy and breezy my first dinner party was. Maybe I do have a little bit of Jennifer in me after all. But now, I have some serious decisions to make. Subletting at the El Royale would mean extending my trip to three months. That's a long time to be away from my life back in D.C. I'm already getting e-mails from my neighbors on C Street saying that since Chef has been away filming, our car has begun to drown in parking tickets and our garden is starting to rot. A depressing thought, but what can I do?

I haven't even told Chef about the Emmys, and now our separation could last even longer. But I've made no progress in deciding what to do about my future with him. I want answers, but my mind won't go there. It's so difficult for me to compute that I'm in love him, yet I've lost faith in our future together. How can those two truths fight each other? All I know is that I still don't know. I have so much to think about that the system has crashed.

Soaking in the tub, I close my eyes. *What is going on here? Dinner for twelve?* New York *magazine? Christopher Wagner? A six-burner Viking? My head on actor Paul's king-size plush pillows?* I go straight from the bubble bath to the bed. My hair is wet, my skin smells like citrus, and after just two weeks in L.A., my body feels rounder, healthier, and more womanly. If there is anywhere in Hancock Park where one should sleep in the nude, pressed deep into bed, it's at the El Royale.

When I wake up, the house is empty. Dara is off doing early-morning downward dogs; her wonderful boyfriend has left for the office. The house is once again spotless. On the dining-room table sits the *Los Angeles Times, New York Times,* a pot of tea, my leftover coffee cake, a couple of crumbs, and an envelope addressed to me from Christopher Wagner. "The apartment is yours for the next few months. Cook a lot. Bake like crazy. Freeze me some! Pay whatever."

And just like that, the script is written.

Forgive-Me Berry Muffins

SERVES 12

If your best friend loves carbs, and carbs are best delivered by way of blueberry muffins, and the blueberry muffins are made by you, then by the associative property, your best friend will love you—even after you've wrecked her brand-new Audi while she's in Malibu—if you feed her these delicious muffins.

Unsalted butter, at room temperature, for greasing the muffin pan
2 cups whole-wheat flour
½ cup sugar
2 teaspoons baking powder
1 teaspoon cinnamon
1 teaspoon nutmeg
8 tablespoons (1 stick) unsalted butter, melted
1 large egg, beaten
1 cup whole milk
2 cups fresh (or frozen) blueberries, raspberries, or strawberries, in any combination

Preheat the oven to 400°F. Grease a 12-cup muffin pan with butter.

In a large bowl, mix together the flour, sugar, baking powder, cinnamon, and nutmeg.

In a second large bowl, mix together the melted butter, the egg, and the milk. Add the flour mixture to the milk mixture and mix until just combined. Carefully fold in the berries. Spoon the batter into the muffin cups, leaving a half inch at the top for the muffins to rise. Bake for 20 minutes or until a knife or tester comes out clean.

Cool in the pan for 10 minutes before removing the muffins to a cooling rack.

Serve warm, especially when in trouble.

Herb-Crusted Chicken for Hungry and Important People

SERVES 6

This light and flavorful entrée can be prepared a few hours in advance and is easily doubled for a large group, so it's perfect for a dinner party. Each time I've made this dish, I've used various types of herbs, depending on what's available. It's now my signature chicken dish. After all, it charmed even the most arrogant Angelenos.

- 6 skinless, boneless chicken breast halves
- 6 tablespoons fresh lemon juice (about 3 lemons)
- 2 tablespoons unsalted butter
- 2 tablespoons extra-virgin olive oil
- 1½ cups plain dry bread crumbs
- 6 tablespoons chopped fresh basil
- 3 tablespoons chopped fresh parsley
- 1½ tablespoons chopped fresh rosemary
- 1½ teaspoons salt
- ½ teaspoon ground black pepper
- 2 lemons cut into wedges, for garnish

Using a meat mallet, pound the chicken breasts between sheets of plastic wrap to ½- to ¾-inch thickness (or ask the butcher to do this for you).

Arrange the chicken in a 15 × 10 × 2-inch glass baking dish. Pour the lemon juice over the chicken, cover, and refrigerate for 1 hour.

Remove the chicken from the dish and pat it dry with paper towels. Preheat the oven to 450°F.

Melt the butter and oil in a small saucepan over medium heat. Set aside to let cool slightly. Then mix the bread crumbs, basil, parsley, rosemary, salt, and pepper in a medium bowl.

Brush the chicken breasts on both sides with the melted butter and oil mixture. Then coat the breasts on both sides with the bread-crumb mixture. Place the chicken on a baking sheet and bake until the bread crumbs are golden and the chicken is cooked through, about 20 minutes.

Transfer to plates or serve family-style on a single platter. Garnish with the lemon wedges and serve.

Jennifer's Warm Potatoes with Mustard

SERVES 8 AND DOUBLES WELL

A very wise woman once told me, "Success is the best revenge." Well, these potatoes spell success in the most scrumptious way. And they're good in any season. Just remember, if the potatoes are taking a while to boil, cover the pot. Otherwise, my friend Dara will find you and remind you how little you actually know. And trust me, you don't want that.

4 pounds (20 to 30) purple potatoes, or a combination of other fun colors
Salt
2 tablespoons Dijon mustard
2 tablespoons white-wine vinegar
1 cup extra-virgin olive oil
2 tablespoons drained capers
½ teaspoon freshly ground black pepper

Place the potatoes in a large pot and add enough cold water to cover them by an inch. Add a handful of salt to the water and bring to a boil. Boil until the potatoes are tender when pierced with a fork, 15 to 20 minutes.

In a large bowl, combine the mustard and vinegar. Slowly drizzle in the olive oil a little at a time, stirring vigorously and adding more only after the previously added oil has been completely incorporated. The mixture should maintain a thick consistency throughout. Add the capers and season with the black pepper.

Drain the potatoes and toss them in the bowl with the dressing, smashing them roughly into thirds with a spoon while mixing them thoroughly with the dressing. The dish should look chunky and colorful.

Serve immediately.

9.

The El Royale

There's a bittersweet moment when I tell Shelley that I will be relocating to the El Royale at the end of the week and staying there for a few months until the middle of October. She's sad that I'm upgrading from her living room earlier than planned, but happy that I'm staying longer in Los Angeles. I refuse to endorse any melodrama about my moving ten minutes away, and she's over it by the time we finish the beef kabobs with pineapple that I improvise for our dinner.

My family swallows any disappointment over me missing the Jewish high holidays in New York and encourages me to stay in California for as long as I need. My father asks if I've been balancing my checkbook (the same question he's asked, and I've lied about, since high school). My mother says she'll mail me her favorite Rosh Hashanah recipes—honey cake, noodle kugel, and brisket—even though she still can't believe that I'm seriously cooking. It kills me that I've been tooling around in the kitchen for over a year but haven't had a chance to cook for them yet! They had planned to visit me in Washington, where I was going to wow them with some meals, but then things got bad with Chef . . . and that trip went down the drain.

I finally get Chef on the line to tell him everything that's going on (besides our self-imposed ban on talking, his cell was confiscated while filming the reality show). I first tell him about the *New York* magazine assignment, and then that I'm staying an extra two months. It's not the most copacetic conversation, and he reiterates the fact that he never wanted this break and still doesn't like it, but the news doesn't detonate like I would have thought. He might have reacted differently had his next two months not entailed nonstop work and travel. We both know that even if I came home, he'd be gone most of the time. Returning in the middle of such a frantic schedule would be setting us up for failure.

After I assure him I didn't sleep with Christopher Wagner to score the apartment, he concedes that I sound happy, which makes him happy. And he's right. Not only do I have the Emmys coming up, but also a few more exciting assignments have surfaced. I'm covering *Food & Wine*'s Taste of Beverly Hills festival for one publication and researching the popularity of pupusas for another. They're small assignments, but compared to the nothingness that was D.C., all the action has me generally euphoric. If I'm a West Hollywood cliché in my racerback tank tops and baggy, frayed jean shorts, drinking soy lattes and reading Patti Smith, so be it. Even though I've left behind Chef and our home, I feel closer to complete in California.

Shelley drives me to the El Royale the moment Christopher leaves for New York. The place is waiting for me in the most pristine condition—other than half a vanilla cupcake perfectly sanctioned on the kitchen counter. It must be his way of welcoming me to his kitchen. *This is his gift to help me find myself through cooking.* Shelley eats it and makes herself comfortable on a long, leather daybed, while I scour the kitchen. He has all the best basics—Tuscan olive oils, upscale dry pasta, jars of uncooked cannellini beans, homemade chicken stock in the freezer, slow-roasted tomatoes in the fridge, and Valrhona dark chocolate staring into my soul. I don't remember him having so many things in his pantry, and I wonder if he's stocked his shelves just for me.

I'm dying to cook something, so I have Shelley drop me off at the supermarket down the street on her way back home. I pick up a whole chicken, some lemons, onions, and fresh herbs. Roast chicken, with some steamed summer asparagus, will be the perfect first meal at his apartment. Because I'll have to walk a few long blocks home, I try to limit my purchases, but I can't just breeze past the peaches and plums. It's summertime in California, after all. I throw in some Greek yogurt, smoked almonds, a vat of Red Vines, a six-pack of beer, and some sparkling Pellegrino. This is an inventory well worth the back break.

In the long checkout line, a pang of sadness hits me, one that sneaks up on me every few hours since leaving Chef. It's a fast and ugly earthquake that carries so much psychological weight: Chef and I have fallen apart; my career is a joke; my life is nothing; I am totally, pathetically, horrifically, atrociously, and unbearably alone. *Roast chicken for fucking one.*

A tear runs down my cheek and someone taps me on the shoulder. I am startled. A young Latino guy wearing construction clothes is standing there, extending a package of Keebler Fudge Stripes my way. I tell him, "I haven't had one of those since I was a little girl!" He answers, "For you, miss." We wait in the line together, smiling and eating cookies, until my eyes have dried and it's my turn at the cash register. Licking the chocolate off my fingertips, I pay for my groceries and begin to walk away. But I stop and turn around to give the stranger a quick hug first. When things like that happen, you have to believe everything is going to be okay.

Later at home, I don't make the roast chicken. It's the first time since landing in Los Angeles three weeks ago that I've had dinner alone, with no one watching, no one worrying, and I just want to sit in front of the TV with a Swiss cheese sandwich. So I cut a lime, crack open a Corona, and do just that.

Emmy weekend comes and I work my ass off. I hit all the major parties and interview television's biggest stars. There's a whole new level of access when you work for a magazine with such a good reputation, and I revel in the champagne toasts, swag bags, and Cinderella moments. I see so many actors from the shows that Chef and I would obsess over. If he were with me, we would have been literally holding each other up.

After a few days of around-the-clock red carpets, my feet are blistered, my head is exploding, and *New York* magazine is pleased with my reporting. They assign me more work immediately. *I'm in.* But first, I crawl into Paul-the-actor's bathrobe, order in Chinese food, and crash. My body is bone tired, my brain is burnt, and my heart is in purgatory. Let there be pupu platters.

For seventy-two hours straight, I hibernate—catching up on sleep, sodium, laundry, and basic life skills like flossing my teeth and paying my phone bill. When I'm ready to resurface, I call "Auntie Lizzie," my only family member living in Los Angeles, and I invite her over. My mother's first cousin, she's a real Temkin in her good-heartedness. When she moved to L.A. twenty years ago to become an actress, conquering California in a red Mustang convertible, I thought she was the coolest person on the planet. When she'd have cameos on *General Hospital* and *ER,* Rachel and I would make popcorn and scream, rewinding the VCR over and over again. Even though her acting career never reached superstardom, she's forever my idol. She is the consummate "liver of life," and I know she'll understand the nature of an overly emotional couple like Chef and me.

Auntie Lizzie also *loves* food. She signs every e-mail, "Death by Chocolate, Lizzie." So I go straight from bed to baking, determined to make something every bit as vibrant as she is. There's a huge bag of cherries in the fridge, so I find myself a gorgeous-looking pie recipe in an Amish cookbook on a bookshelf. The proverbial cherry pie, I smirk to myself. She'll love it. (She has a dirty mind like me!) The clock is ticking and I contemplate buying the crust . . . who's going to know? But Auntie Lizzie is worthy of more than Sara Lee.

Alas, the homemade piecrust doesn't come out quite right. Either I've overworked or underworked the dough, but there's definitely not enough to cover the top. So I layer the bottom crust, cover it with the fruit filling, and then sprinkle whatever doughy scraps I can manage to find over the entire thing, hoping it will magically create a top crust and that my cherry pie will be less scantily clad. When it comes out of the oven, it looks amateur and sloppy. There're random patches of top crust, but the fruit is oozing all over it. Calling it "rustic" would be extremely generous. So I think fast, work with what I've got, and turn my cherry pie into a cherry crumble by taking a spoon and gently mixing all the gooey fruit and cooked dough (from the top and bottom crust) together. *Crumble.* I have to laugh.

I dash out for some fresh peonies, and when I return to the apartment, I realize how amazing the place smells. I open the windows and French doors and play some James Taylor. The natural light is so stunning that it feels like a religious experience. This is the perfect scene for my Auntie Lizzie. When she walks in the door, I jump into her magnificently big boobs and warm embrace. I make coffee and serve us heaping plates of the still-hot crumble, topped with scoops of vanilla ice cream.

She digs in vigorously, only pausing to call my mom: "She can really bake, Lulu. I'm tellin' ya!"

Because she's family, Auntie Lizzie is the only person in L.A. I feel totally comfortable opening up to about my uncertain future with Chef. I explain to her that I have no strand of doubt that I genuinely love him, but that he hurt me tremendously by choosing work over the relationship and the wedding, and putting me through those many months of neglect toward the end.

Never short on words, she doesn't have the answer. Does anyone? But she helps me release some mental toxins, and because of her visit I even learned how to turn a lousy pie into a luminous crumble. Hours of conversation later, I walk her to the door. We hug each other long and tight.

"You will never be his number one, Lyssa-la."

"You're probably right," I say.

"But maybe a close second ain't bad?"

She said exactly what I had been feeling but didn't know how to express all these months, maybe even years. If being *the first* to safe guys like Gary didn't do anything for me, could I be *the second* to someone with whom I'm so charged? I have one month left before I am scheduled to go back to D.C., and I still don't know the answer to that.

Chef and I begin talking about once a day, briefly. We mostly share neutral news about my blog and his filming, but he continually communicates that our troubles are draining him. His performance has been subpar on the show, and says it's because of us. Our unresolved life together *is* starting to feel stale. One morning, Christopher calls to check up on things while I'm making a batch of hazelnut biscotti to freeze for his return. He wants to know if I've had any revelations. I feel lame telling him that everything is status quo. "It's still in the gray," I say, ashamed of my sedentary story line. I'm sure he'd kill off my character for being so anemic. He suggests that people don't leave a relationship because they're unhappy, but that people leave when the unhappiness gets too boring to bear. "You'll wake up one day and know what to do."

The answers are evading me. I've hiked until my legs are strong and scraped; I've read every memoir on love and loss that I can find; I've cooked with a vengeance, baked with pure bliss, and avoided almost any interaction with men that could possibly make my life any more complicated. Still, I'm as stunted as ever. And then the doorbell rings.

A tiny, rather stunning Eurasian woman with a pixie haircut and an indeterminate posh accent is standing there with a suitcase. She introduces herself as Paisley (as in the ties and tablecloths) and tells me that she will be staying in Christopher's bedroom for an indefinite amount of time. *What in the world is this?*

"Yeah, I'm not sure what you're talking about," I say, overtly annoyed.

I then have a vague flashback of the night I met Christopher, when he showed me his apartment post–Bundt cake. A few things come back to me. *Shit*. He *had* mentioned something about some chick who was going through tough times—he wouldn't say what—and who might need to crash for a few nights. He made it sound so nonchalant, but based on Paisley's suitcases, which outsize her fragile frame, this is clearly not a weekend escape.

On one hand, I am extremely pissed about an imposition that I never *really* signed off on, not soberly at least. This is meant to be a transformative time for me. Christopher left me the cupcake so that I would find myself in the kitchen, didn't he? Not find myself with a roommate. And the kitchen! I don't want to share the kitchen! *What if she's a slob? Or worse, a neat freak?*

On the other hand, here I am living almost for free, in a stunning, sprawling apartment, out of the kindness of some stranger's heart, and I have no right to feel so entitled. Crashers can't be choosers, not even at the El Royale. But it doesn't matter what I think. Paisley drags her bags inside, straight past my incensed expression, without wanting or needing anybody's help or approval. Before I can pinpoint her age, accent, or sexual orientation, I can see she's a lioness. A survivor. A force.

I skulk over to my computer, which is sitting on the dining-room table, and try to focus on my blog instead of staring her down. Emotionally, we stand in our own corners of the boxing ring. She prowls around the place like a Persian cat, as I hate-type on my laptop like it's a steel drum. Maybe this is the sign that I should quit while I'm ahead and go home to C Street. She might look like a Benetton model, but she's bringing me down.

She cuts the silence by blurting out that she, too, was blindsided by the roommate situation. Apparently, Christopher also told her she'd "basically" have the place to herself. I confess that he had mentioned her, but only once, and that it was so offhanded. We try to figure out if he sprang us on each other for a greater reason, or if he was just too overwhelmed in New York to communicate the plans. But after about an hour in the apartment, we actually start to bond over the fact that neither of us wants the other around.

I close my computer, put on some sandals, and ask if she wants to sit with me somewhere in the neighborhood, maybe a few blocks away on the quaint, café-lit Larchmont Street. By now I've established two facts: we're both in transition and we both need a drink.

As we walk down the sun-drenched, picture-perfect streets of Hancock Park, past the bungalows and beautiful people, we go through the basics. She's in her midthirties, born in Hawaii, raised in California, and schooled in Singapore. She just moved back to the West Coast after many years in New York, where she juggled odd jobs in art and fashion. None of these credentials really help me understand her better though. She's wearing a belted T-shirt as a dress and is cute as a button, with a remarkable, folkloric face.

But there's a serious darkness to Paisley, a hard shell. When she talks, she's tentative and terse. It's like she's scared to say too much about herself, and I can't figure out why. All I really know by the time we reach Larchmont Street is that I think we're going to be friends.

We grab a table at a dodgy little bar. She's not giving up too much, so I explain the real reason I'm hiding out in Hancock Park: a strange brew of hard love. When she asks if I know what I'm going to do, considering I have to go home to D.C. eventually, I say, "Yeah, I'm going to make him leave his restaurants and TV dreams and move to Europe with me to make babies and sell pissaladière." We both know I'm kidding, but it feels damn good to say it out loud. She wants to know when the wedding was supposed to be. "October third, a few weeks away," I say. "Good," she says, and nods definitively. "We'll do something that makes you happy that day."

While Paisley is an incredible listener, there's a reticence behind her eyes telling me that her problems far outweigh mine. "Your turn," I say, shutting up. Her first glass of wine sits on the bar empty, and I haven't even sipped mine. "Come on, girlfriend," I say, because something about her first name feels ridiculous to say out loud. "There's nothing I haven't seen or heard." The reporter in me is dying for the scoop.

She orders a second glass of sauvignon blanc, runs her thin fingers through her thick hair, and looks me straight in the face.

"One year ago I had a baby girl." She closes her eyes and clears her throat. "And three months ago she died."

I have no idea what to say, how to hold my face, or if it's okay that there are streams of tears pouring from my eyelids. *Don't make this about you, Alyssa.* Paisley reaches for my hand and holds it tightly, continuing the story of her daughter's sickness, with all the reveal I thought I had wanted fifteen seconds ago. She tells me everything about her baby's battle, and her now-estranged ex, and courageously explains that she's here in California on a quest to conceive another child, someway, somehow. She wants her motherhood back. We sit at the bar for hours, drinking, crying, and even laughing a little. She's been in mourning for only three months, but she has such a sharp sense of humor that I can only imagine the firecracker she once was.

As we walk back to our apartment slowly, somewhat wobbly, I tell her how ashamed I am for whining about my utterly pathetic bubblegum bullshit. She urges me not to minimize my own issues, insisting that it's healthy for her to think about other things besides sickness and death. I know she genuinely means it, but from that day on, I want nothing to do with my own nonsense. I just want to make Paisley's life better.

In the next few weeks, we do everything together. Paisley cooks us glorious, gingery whole fish; I bake her favorite dessert, flourless chocolate cake. We are on the exact same level in the kitchen—dedicated, with a long way to go. She brews our morning coffee; I buy our cases of wine. She names us the LoLaRoos—short for the Lost Ladies of the El Royale. We make plans to socialize with our own friends but always end up bailing. We stay pretty reclusive and generally drunk.

At night, we go through episodes upon episodes of Christopher's show, which she loved as much as I did. We smoke his pot and boil his pasta. Sometimes she locks herself in her room and plays little lullabies while curled up on the floor. On those nights, I read my M.F.K. Fisher in bed, and knock on her door every few hours, just in case she wants some peppermint tea or a little fresh air.

I love taking care of her, and I'm good at it. It makes me think that without having Chef physically around to nurture, a big part of me was stifled. Feeding him certainly filled that void, for a while, but a decent meal at midnight is just not enough.

My instantaneous friendship with Paisley frustrates Shelley, who's always been a little territorial, and who thinks my interest in her and her loss is a little morbid. I become so mad when she insinuates this that I tell my family, and anyone else who will listen, that as far as I'm concerned, my friendship with Shelley is over. I am floored when my mother, father, and sister, the most compassionate people on earth, delicately imply that Shelley—who *they love like family*—might have a point. They very gently suggest that I'm avoiding my own problems by burying myself in Paisley's. I'm offended by their words, but don't want any drama, not with only one week left in L.A. So I let it be, firmly instructing everyone to never go there again, and resuming life like nothing had happened.

Paisley is adamant that I invite Shelley, Dara, and Auntie Lizzie over for a very special rooftop brunch to celebrate . . . my wedding day. It feels a little weird to draw attention to something so unpleasant, and somehow reeditorialize the cursed day, but I *do* want to see everyone before I go. Plus, Paisley is insisting, and I get the feeling she wants to step outside her head a little, or as much as possible. After some mild kicking and screaming, I comply.

Forty-eight hours before the big day, we LoLaRoos start to cook and bake compulsively. It's only going to be a few of us, but our unspoken theme is survival, and that should come in abundance. We make tarte tatin, lemon meringue pie, and chocolate chip cookies. I find a mayo-free chicken salad recipe—my secret tribute to that fateful chicken curry salad at Fabiane's—and roast glorious autumn produce made sweet and sticky with pecans and prunes; I bake whole-wheat bread to serve with farmers' market butter and Camembert cheese.

It's a spellbindingly beautiful day on the roof of the El Royale in early October. Everyone arrives with flowers and champagne. I wear a pale pink shift dress and borrow my favorite necklace of Shelley's (that I've tried to steal over the past ten years). With luscious plates of food and free-flowing drinks, all my L.A. saviors sit for hours where the sun and breeze meet, sharing stories of love and loss, and refilling Christopher's white china with food that Paisley and I made. She excuses herself every so often to regroup, as she tends to do.

I toast each and every one of them for taking such good care of me. They were each, individually, my godsends over this summer of resuscitation, and I am doing so much better than when I came. What an interesting summer. I had the privilege of feeding my best friend an entire tin of blueberry muffins, throwing a lavish dinner party for perfect strangers, serving cherry "crumble" pie to my supercool actress-auntie, and making the saddest soul crack a smile, even just once a day. "To the El Royale," I say, once Paisley returns to the table, looking each one of them in the eye. Shelley tells me to keep the necklace, and everyone clears the table and loads the dishwasher for the bride.

My friends put me in such a good mood, I spend the rest of the afternoon convinced that if I can just hold on to this joy, the rest will follow. Maybe the happiness onus is really on me?

Maybe, if I can remain absolutely impermeable, then I'll be the rock for the relationship to rest on? Late that night in bed, I start thinking I should go back to Chef with that strategy: *Be happy, stay happy, and don't let anyone or anything interfere.* It is the first time the pendulum has swung in either direction and I take it as a sign. I even contemplate leaving Los Angeles a few days early and flying to New York to attend the New York Wine & Food Festival where Chef will be featured at a big event down the street from my parents' place. I'll go, and be radiant and confident, and it will be a great "welcome home" weekend for me! Plus, on my turf!

When I suggest this to Chef, in my most chipper tone, he is less than enthusiastic. It's an extremely rigorous weekend for him, and he explains that he needs to concentrate on winning his competition, not on an intense, emotional reunion with his fiancée. "Just meet me back at home in Washington . . . like we planned," he says wearily. "Please, Lyssie?"

While his reaction is valid, and I suppose I *am* being too cavalier about the whole thing, the rejection stings. It's a sting I know well, one that all the homemade crust in the world can't cure. He promises to keep me posted on all the good parties, and will obviously let me know how he fares at the event. "You better!" I say, hoping he can't hear the ugly in my voice.

And there it is.

Disappointment.

Again.

Forgoing the festival, I stay cooped up at the El Royale with Paisley and a bottle of Scotch, refreshing blogs covering the celebrity chef parties all weekend long. These are my last days in Los Angeles; I should be eating sprout sandwiches at Malibu Country Market or packing picnics for Griffith Park, but I won't leave my computer and I'm too flustered to think about food. *Hello, derailment. It's been a while.* On the eve of the festival's Burger Bash, I stare at photos of Chef enwrapped in bikini models, whom he's hired to promote his brand. Through a website, I hear he's lost the competition. Around two o'clock in the morning, I find a sighting of him at a private after-party and then an after-after-party. But I get no calls, e-mails, or texts.

How silly of me to forget the rules of being second. (And on these weekends, of being third or fourth.) It's been a while since I felt that sense of insignificance, and I almost forgot how hideous it is. When I do hear from him, on his way back to D.C. at the end of the long weekend, he tries to explain something about a dead phone battery, a bad cold, and sheer mental agony as a result of missing me so much. *Right.* None of it makes a difference. Based on my behavior more than his, I finally know what to do.

When it's time to "check out" of the El Royale and fly to Washington, I wake up early to buy Paisley a chocolate-covered doughnut with rainbow sprinkles. I leave it outside her bedroom door with a tulip and a note to open only after we say good-bye. She's driving me to the airport in six hours. I grab Dara's bike and ride a few miles to Runyon Canyon, locking it at the foot of the mountain. On my way up, I listen to my music, working up a good sweat, and when I reach the highest point, I sit on a rock quietly, surrounded by just a couple of little birds and the bluest sky.

I think of life and death, and heaven and earth, and the lightness of Shelley against the darkness of Paisley, and how I suppose I'm somewhere in between. But no matter how enlightened, or accepting, or attuned to life's peaks and valleys I think I might be, I can't be with someone who hurts me. I won't be with someone who hurts me.

On the way to the airport, along the Pacific Coast Highway, Paisley and I come back to our favorite conversation: Did Christopher Wagner stick us together as some sort of mutual awakening? Did he want me to step away from my boo-hoo breakup and get a glimpse of life's real sorrow? Did he hope that Paisley could be ever so slightly distracted from her terrible pain with a walking, talking, and cooking episode of *Sex and the City*? As we get closer to the airport, I tell her about "the trick." She likes it. So when she pulls up to my stop, I kiss her cheek for as long as possible and whisper in her ear, "See ya tomorrow."

Under normal circumstances, I would have cried my eyes out the minute Paisley drove away. But today, my focus is on putting one foot in front of the other. After I go through security, I drift into a gift shop to buy a straw hat. My face is broken out again from the sleeplessness and stress of the past few nights. I buy a coffee and drink it black because I can't find the inspiration to add milk and sugar. I fly the five hours across the country, staring out the window the whole time.

He is waiting for me outside the airport looking every bit the man I dreamed I'd raise a family, grow old, and die with. We kiss long and hard and it has never been so unnatural to keep my heart so cold. Driving home, he says that he's cleaned the house, rented us movies, and stocked the fridge; that he wants to make me chocolate chip pancakes while I take my bath. My head pounds as I fight against all the waves of chemistry and connection. When we are good, transient as it is, there is no broken glass.

In all of our fighting and screaming, Chef swore that he'd never break up with me; that if we parted ways, it would only be because I gave up. And by the end of the night, he will have been right.

I will announce that I'm leaving for good. He will get sick all over the bathroom floor. And the next morning, I will pack the car, drive to New York, and move in with my parents.

But first, he prepares the pancake batter, while I slowly remove my ring in the tub.

Easy, Asian-Inspired Fish

SERVES 4

When Paisley entered my life, she didn't have much of an appetite. We drank many of our meals, but we loved cooking for each other, too. One day I told her that even though I loved eating fish, I didn't have much practice cooking it, and even the act of buying fish freaked me out. The next day, we went to the fishmonger at the West Hollywood farmers' market, and at the El Royale, she made us a magnificent mahimahi, as I carefully watched. That night we ate on our rooftop, overlooking all of Los Angeles during a beautiful, almost spiritual sunset. She served the fish with steamed vegetables and naturally, a few glasses of white.

---

1 cup panko bread crumbs
2 tablespoons wasabi paste
4 tablespoons mustard powder
½ teaspoon ground ginger
1 teaspoon lime zest (from 1 lime)
4 tablespoons canola oil, plus more if needed
Salt and black pepper to taste
Vegetable oil spray
4 fish fillets (cod, tilapia, mahimahi, or salmon)
¼ cup hoisin sauce

Preheat the oven to 375°F.

Combine the bread crumbs, wasabi, mustard powder, ginger, and lime zest in a medium bowl. Mix until everything is well incorporated. Drizzle in the canola oil and mix again. The crumbs should just barely hold together when squeezed. (Use more oil as necessary.) Season the crumbs to taste with salt and pepper.

Coat a cookie sheet with vegetable oil spray and lay down the fish fillets, allowing space between them so they cook evenly.

Divide the hoisin sauce among the tops of the fish fillets and smooth out for an even, light coating. Top each fillet with the bread-crumb mixture, covering the tops entirely and gently patting it down.

Bake the fillets in the oven for about 15 minutes, or until the center of the fish reaches 145°F. The fish should flake when poked with a fork.

Serve immediately.

Unbridled Chicken Salad

SERVES 4 AS A MAIN, 6 AS A SIDE

I've had a lot of ups and downs with mayonnaise, but I still avoid it out of habit. So, when Paisley and I found this mayo-less chicken salad, we had to run with it. All the way to the roof! The girls at my nonwedding devoured it. So did Moses, the doorman at the El Royale, when we brought him a big bowl. This recipe is adapted from Amanda Hesser's on Food52.com, and it's outstanding.

¼ cup thinly sliced red onion
Salt
4 cups cubed roasted chicken (homemade or store-bought)
3 tablespoons roasted red peppers, thinly sliced
1 cup marinated artichoke hearts, drained thoroughly
¼ cup roughly chopped smoked almonds
1 tablespoon whole-grain mustard, plus more to taste
1 tablespoon sherry vinegar
2 teaspoons chopped fresh thyme
¼ cup extra-virgin olive oil
Freshly ground black pepper
Juice of 1 lemon (2 to 3 tablespoons), or to taste

In a medium bowl, sprinkle the onion with salt and toss to coat. Let sit for 15 minutes, then gently pat it down with a paper towel to drain any liquid. In a large bowl, toss together the onion, chicken, peppers, artichoke hearts, and almonds.

In a small bowl, whisk together the mustard and vinegar, and add the thyme. Gradually whisk in the oil. Season with salt and pepper.

Pour the dressing over the chicken mixture and fold to incorporate. Add lemon juice to taste, starting with half of the juice and adding more if desired. Let sit for 15 minutes.

Taste and adjust the seasonings with salt, pepper, and more lemon juice if needed. Serve.

Cherry Crumble for Those Who Crumble Too Easily

SERVES 6

I have made pies that turn into cobblers, and cobblers that turn into clafoutis, and clafoutis that turn into custard, but this recipe is a full-blown crumble (in my eyes, at least). Cherries are one of my favorite things in life, as is my famous auntie Lizzie, for whom I made this. The crumble is delicious served with vanilla ice cream.

Filling

6 cups tart red cherries, pitted
1¼ cups granulated sugar
4 teaspoons cornstarch

Topping

1 cup all-purpose flour
¼ cup granulated sugar
2 tablespoons packed light brown sugar
1 teaspoon baking powder
½ teaspoon cinnamon
3 tablespoons unsalted butter
1 large egg, beaten
3 tablespoons whole milk

Preheat the oven to 400°F.

For the filling: In a medium saucepan, combine the cherries, the sugar, ¼ cup water, and the cornstarch. Cook over medium heat, stirring until bubbling and thickened.

Pour the filling into an 8-inch baking pan or casserole.

Meanwhile, for the topping: In a large bowl away from the stove, stir together the flour, granulated sugar, brown sugar, baking powder, and cinnamon. Cut in the butter until the mixture is crumbly.

In a small bowl, mix together the egg and the milk. Add the milk mixture to the flour mixture and stir with a fork just until combined.

Drop the dry topping onto the fruit filling 1 tablespoon at a time, almost like big polka dots. Most of the fruit should be covered by the dry mixture, but it shouldn't be smoothed out. Everything will meld together in the oven.

Bake for 25 minutes, until the dish is browned and bubbly. Serve warm or at room temperature.

10.

Shredded

"*Crudités* is such an uptight word, isn't it? It's like, the opposite of me in an appetizer. But that's what I want to order, as long as we call it something else though. Cool?"

I am sitting at the bar of Jean-Georges's exceptionally chic ABC Kitchen, in New York City, and acting batshit crazy.

Three weeks ago, I left Chef. I'm living in my parents' Brooklyn loft, in the same spare, prison-white room I slept in the last time I had a bad breakup, but this time I'm sharing a bed with my sister, who's also nursing a vile broken heart. I refuse to see any of my friends because I'm just too miserable to socialize, and all I want to do is compulsively go to restaurants (alone) and communicate with Chef.

"You're *there* now? Weren't you at Colicchio's place just an hour ago?" he says, checking in on me for the third time today.

"Being at restaurants makes me miss you less."

"I know what will make you miss me less . . . coming home!"

My split from Chef is not at all a clean break. Through e-mails, texts, and calls, we're in nonstop contact. Sometimes we talk as if nothing has happened. "Hey u . . . will I like grilled fish with habanero?" I text. "No, sweetie, 2 spicy for my luv," he responds, immediately. After a drink or two, of course, the messages get increasingly angrier. I tell him he ruined everything; he says I abandoned him and our home. But our nights always end with sad and sincere admissions of guilt. I know I was impulsive about the wedding, refusing to listen, pushing us over the edge. And he deeply regrets the person he turned into during those last few months.

Still, I've made the choice to move on and I am trusting my instincts.

You would think, however, that after leaving my chef fiancé, I'd resent the restaurant world for a while. Not so. All I want to do is explore the "it" spots I've been reading about since leaving New York two years ago. It's as if in transitioning from life with a chef to life alone, the New York restaurant scene is my halfway house. For solace, I turn to French brasseries, hyped noodle shops, dirty-spoon diners, and suspicious shawarma stands. I've become a savvier eater, but I've never been the type to keep a restaurant bucket list until now. As I cope with the collapse of us, *Zagat* is my Zoloft.

Beth and Jill don't even know that I'm back, and I absolutely cannot stomach the pity of my family. More than ever, I refuse to explain myself to anybody. My grief is not for consumption. When my sister asks if I want to walk the Bridge, or get backrubs, or just quietly be near each other, I snap, "Why don't you just worry about yourself!" When Liz at *People* asks if I want some work for extra cash, I ungraciously reply, "I cover food, not gossip."

Instead, I walk for hours a day, restaurant hopping with the displeasure of my own company, finding my way to *New York* magazine's "Best Bloody Mary" and *Eater*'s "Favorite Fish Taco," continuing to blog about my experiences when I can find the energy. I use these lists as arrows, as I have no idea what else to do with myself, or where I belong. Almost every day I roam around Mario Batali's new Italian food mecca, Eataly, disappearing in its thick, fresh fettuccine aisles, rows of vinegar cartons and sardine cans, and bustling eating stations. I can't walk past the *salumi e formaggi* table there without thinking about the mortadella sandwiches I'd make for Chef—and those early memories of us make me smile. But then I remember being fed my engagement cake by my sister, instead of him—and I push away my *mini dolci* in disgust.

At night, I despondently walk to other expensive hot spots, like Keith McNally's Minetta Tavern, where it's dimly lit and saloonlike, and everyone has letterpress business cards and bitters-based appertifs. I sit at the bar and order a Barolo, trying to read my book in the dark, oaky room. Sometimes I'll order a small dish like roasted beets or veal carpaccio, just so I can eat to appear occupied, instead of baiting the looming, close-talking bachelors who apparently can't resist a mysterious lush like myself. A little flirting might be healthy for me, but I can't seem to hold a decent conversation. My mind is so fragmented.

Usually I'm sick of food by dinnertime and because I'm so off balance, my appetite is, again, underwhelming. I'm really going to these restaurants only to be part of something, to catch a wave. I like the sounds—from the clank of the glassware to the gossip at the bar. And the observations—the pulse of couples heading to the sack, or the doom of those heading to divorce. And the restaurant staff! I could eavesdrop on disgruntled bartenders and sexually confused servers for the rest of eternity.

One afternoon back at ABC Kitchen, on the ground floor of ABC Carpet & Home, where I once worked, I see my old boss. He's a dashing Englishman who has been extraordinarily kind and generous to me and my family, even after I inconveniently quit the job just before a huge store event. Furthermore, a few weeks ago, he gave my mother a Moroccan rug for a nice price. Now he's spotted me from across the dining room and is coming over to say hello. I slap down twenty bucks and jet.

I am too tense for human interaction. My fists are clenched and my face is tight. And the most pathetic part is . . . that I know exactly what can make me feel better. A chunky tomato sauce with lots of fresh herbs, or a gingery fish baked in aluminum foil, or a pumpkin pie with a walnut topping, or a chocolate gâteau with strawberries around the border. Any of that would work, theoretically, if made by me.

All my cookbooks and kitchen equipment are stored smack dab in the middle of my parents' loft, with a few Frette bedsheets covering it all up, like a huge, high-thread-count casket. My family, who can find humor in the hardest situations, calls my sheet cake of crap "Moby," because clumped together, its shape reminds them of a whale. They think Moby is a riot; I think it's the most depressing thing I've ever seen. My livelihood is under there—my therapy, my career, and my memories of Chef. Yet I won't lift the sheet. I suppose my self-punishment isn't over yet. It's been a month since I left Los Angeles, and I haven't tied on an apron since.

My parents can see that I'm in a volatile state. They've been in New York for about ten years now, and my mother's career in real estate has been extremely successful. They're still too frugal to hail cabs or go to fancy restaurants; instead they enthusiastically (and quite lucratively) buy and flip country homes with their cash in the kitty. This weekend, they're visiting their latest investment, an antique, post-and-beam barn, in Litchfield, Connecticut, because the plumbing needs work and I need space.

While they're away and my sister is at her office, I stay home with no restaurant excursions on the agenda. My body is extremely jumpy. I initiate a venomous e-mail exchange with Chef, as if for sport. I am the meanest I have ever been. I keep getting dressed and undressed with nowhere to go. I am drinking a Starbucks chai latte, which I can't get down and I don't remember purchasing. On the counter there's a package of chocolate-covered graham crackers that I could have accidentally stolen. I'm dizzy and drooly and wondering if I might die. I think the word to describe me is "manic." I weakly reach for my cell phone.

Asking for help in a direct way is strange territory for me. I don't even know how to assemble the words, but I manage to call my sister at work and ask her if she could please come home, because I really need her. Before I can tell her it's an emergency, she leaves her editorial meeting, hops in a taxi, finds me shivering in a fetal position in the master bedroom, and clothes me in my mother's soft robe. My body has stopped its spasms, but my voice is shaky.

Rachel is a rock when I need her. I tell her I'm losing my mind, and she suggests that I'm just getting sick. We take my temperature and it's 102 degrees, and in Rachel's arms, I submit to the flu. She gives me two Tylenols, draws a tepid bath, and sits with me as I drift in and out of sleep. We decide not to tell my parents, because having the loft to ourselves is probably the best medicine. And I don't tell Chef, because I need to break our vicious cycle before it breaks me.

After two days of agony, I'm starting to feel better. Except now I'm starving. My stomach growls are louder than my sniffles. And all I want is pizza. Rachel puts on her coat to fetch us a pie, but I stop her halfway out the door. "Wait," I scream. "We should make our own."

Because I'm just recovering and she's just crafting her own cooking confidence, we agree to cheat a little on the preparation. Living in Brooklyn, we're surrounded by delicious pizzerias, so we come up with a great idea. We'll "borrow" some dough from the nearest pizza shop, and personalize it with our own sauce, cheese, and toppings. A genius idea, we think. Turns out, it's not such an innovation. Sal and Val from Front Street Pizza hand over the dough and tell Rachel they sell it to customers all the time. She smiles and they throw in a quart of marinara, too. The whole thing comes to four bucks.

Together, we look for Mom's rolling pin. Neither of us have a clue. Crap, we have to call Connecticut. Mom the Virgo tells us precisely where it is and asks permission for her and my dad to come home now. "No! Love you! Bye!" we scream, hanging up. Next, we try rolling out the dough on the counter, but it keeps springing back. It stubbornly won't stretch. So we each grab an end and play tug-of-war, thinning it out just enough till it fills the large, rectangular baking sheet. We pinch the sides over the rim and put it aside. *Phew.*

I caramelize some onions, while Rachel shreds some fresh mozzarella and cheddar. We ladle the sauce, then the cheese, then the onions. We season with salt and fresh pepper. Over in the window boxes, where my mother grows flowers and herbs overlooking the Brooklyn Bridge, we find a handful of basil leaves. Then I sprinkle the whole thing lightly with olive oil. I feel a million times better just having an apron wrapped around my waist and my sister by my side. We slide the pizza in a hot oven, and after twenty minutes, just as I'm about to eat the countertop, our masterpiece is ready. *"Buon appetito!"* I say, digging in. The pizza is amazing. The crust is brown and firm; the cheese is melted evenly and gooey without being greasy. It cuts clean, and the basil is woodsy and unwilted. Sal and Val would be so proud.

I ask Rach if there's anything else fun we can do. "I can show you the guys I'm talking to on Match.com?" she says without any inhibition, knowing I'm no fan of online dating. I'm too drained to be disapproving, however, especially after she just put my pieces back together again. "That sounds perfect," I say. We log in under my sister's "LoveTheBeach" username, clicking on guys named "ChallahbackYo" and "MisterButtsky" and "WillIron4urMom." My general argument against online dating is that when you live in a city like New York, it's so easy to meet people. Why hide behind a computer when you can meet your soul mate on the C train? Also, I've always put a high premium on having a good story to tell—"meet-cute," as they say in Hollywood. Falling in love on the Internet just feels so flat. But tonight, I understand the good fun of it all. Tonight, love is too serious to take seriously.

As we lie in bed, like the little girls we once were, I sense that together, we weathered the storms of our breakups. Scrolling to a guy with the enticing name Benito Bagel, I say, "Let's look at *his* pics!" quickly acclimating to the lingo. I'm under the weather, but I can still sniff out a cute guy. My hunch is right. Benito appears to be handsome, smart, and funny. He's *allegedly* 6'2", a lover of cheap eats, and a self-employed financial consultant. From the name, we decipher that he's probably Jewish and Latin, a flavor combination as alluring to me as apricot and Brie. He also lives not far from us in Brooklyn Heights. I can't find anything bad to say.

"I wonder if he's as hot in real life!" I blurt out.

"Wait!" my sister says in shock. "For you?"

"Yeah, why not."

"Oh my God. Really? Do it, Lys! Do it!"

"The best way to get over somebody is to get under somebody, right?" I smirk. "And besides, I can't keep going to restaurants alone."

From my sister's account, I send an e-mail to Benito Bagel that says, "This is actually LoveTheBeach's sister. . . . I realize you have no reason to believe that I'm not some escaped mental patient or a morbidly obese she-male, but I can assure you I'm neither. I'm a freelance writer and a budding home cook. Write 'us' back if you're interested!"

Before we turn off the computer to go to sleep, my sister has a blinking message from Match.com. It's Benito Bagel! He says he wants to meet me and that he makes a killer paella, which Rachel totally mispronounces. "What the hell is pah-ella?!" I ask her. "Do you mean *paella*?" I say, bursting into hysterical laughter.

"Oh yeah. *What is that again?*"

We laugh so hard that I almost fall off the bed. Once we calm ourselves down—and I remind her that paella is "the yummy dish that's usually mixed with rice, shrimp, and, like, saffron or something"—I tell her that I'll write him back in a few days, but first, I need to find an apartment. "I'm ready," I say, kissing her forehead and rolling over to my side of the flowered, flannel duvet. Something tells me that this week was the last stop on the bus. There is nothing I want more than to let it all go and plant my two feet on the ground. We switch off the lights and I close my eyes. My fever has broken.

Easy Pizza After a Tough Time

SERVES 4

There are endless variations to this recipe, especially if you make your own crust. The evening Rach and I made this pizza was a life-changing night—I was feeling so low and this dish left me so happy and hopeful. Something was in the air . . . and while making this, you'll get the unbelievable smell of caramelized onions and fresh basil in the air, too.

1 ball pizza dough (can be purchased from a pizzeria)
2 tablespoons extra-virgin olive oil, plus more for greasing the pan
¼ cup flour, or enough for dusting the surface
1 red onion (or other vegetables such as mushrooms, bell peppers, tomatoes), thinly sliced
2 to 4 cups tomato sauce, store-bought or from a pizzeria
2 to 3 cups fresh mozzarella (or other cheeses that melt nicely such as fontina or provolone), shredded
Salt and freshly ground pepper to taste
½ cup fresh herbs (such as oregano or basil leaves), loosely packed

Preheat the oven to 425°F.

Grease a nonstick pizza pan, or line a cookie sheet with parchment paper and dust with flour. Roll out the dough with a rolling pin or by hand. (A wine bottle can work well, too.) Transfer the dough to the pan or cookie sheet.

Heat a skillet over medium heat, then add the 2 tablespoons olive oil. Throw in the onion and sauté it until very soft, about 10 minutes. Reduce the heat to low and continue to cook the onion until it turns golden brown, about 20 minutes more. Set aside.

Ladle the tomato sauce over the dough. Spread it evenly with the back of a spoon or brush. Sprinkle the cheese on top of the sauce, leaving about a ½-inch border around the edge of the crust. Scatter the onion on top of the cheese. Season with salt and pepper.

Place the pizza on the middle rack in the oven and bake until the crust is a deep golden brown, about 12 to 17 minutes. Remove from the oven, add the herbs, and let the pizza rest a few minutes.

Serve hot.

11.

Benito Bagel and Other Exotic Things

When I check out apartment 8F in DUMBO, on the same block as my parents', I am so enamored with the kitchen that I am oblivious to the antagonizing noise level.

Somehow I miss the rumble of the subway every eight minutes, and the whoosh of cars and trucks rushing over the Manhattan *and* Brooklyn Bridges. The apartment sits scenically, yet piercingly, smack in the middle of both, which I take as a selling point. The kitchen is so beautiful that I also don't hear the constant catfights and love spats of the street, which in true New York fashion, are belted out loudly enough to penetrate the barely cracked windows on the eighth floor.

I rent the small studio on the spot, knowing that a separate chrome kitchen, large and well lit, with endless open shelving to boot, would be impossible to find again in my price range. The kitchen is almost half the apartment, resulting in minimal space for anything else besides a bed and an oversize farm table (on which I will eat, work, and pile up stacks of newspapers, bills, receipts, and organized chaos). The place also has a tiny Juliet balcony, with just enough room to grow rosemary, thyme, and basil. It's only November, but I already have quite a fragrant vision for spring.

On move-in day, my family dismantles the Moby pile and hauls everything to 8F. As soon as I walk into my new pad, which I've already decorated in my head down to the peach-scented bathroom spray, I am taken aback by even more noise than I anticipated. In addition to everything else, there is so much construction going on outside that you can't walk out the front door without covering your ears and giving the finger. The outdoor anarchy is set to last half a year, says a sympathetic neighbor, and incidentally, it starts at six o'clock in the morning every day of the week. "You can sleep late when you're dead!" My ever-optimistic mother winks. *Ughhh.*

I continue to unpack my things and try to ignore the ruckus, busily setting up my Cuisinart food processor, All-Clad stock pot, boho dishes and Kmart coffeemaker; unrolling my shag rug; and dusting off my pineapple-shaped chandelier—the only material possessions I brought back from C Street. My new mattress arrives in the afternoon and I make the bed with crisp, white sheets and perfectly feathered pillows. Beth brings over fancy-smelling soaps from one of the luxury brands she does the PR for, and I blissfully line them along the edges of my porcelain tub (another perk that offsets the earache). My dad orders a large pizza from Sal and Val. My mom buys an orchid at Costco, where she's also invested in a lifetime supply of Mom-things like tampons and rice pilaf. And my sister sneaks out of work with bejeweled candlesticks and Richard Avedon photography books from the "giveaway table."

As night falls, I kick everyone out so I can play my music softly and really make apartment 8F my own. I am exhausted from all the lifting and bending, yet apprehensive about falling asleep with all the clamor. "Pretend you're hearing the ocean," says my mother, on her way out. Assuming I'll be up all night, I grab a pile of cookbooks. I can't even get through Gwyneth

Paltrow's pantry essentials before I pass out. From under the subway, in one of Brooklyn's loudest nooks, I sleep like a baby. Without having to quiet all the inner noise, the outside noise is no problem.

Hello, responsibility; good-bye, restaurants, I say to myself, after having put down the first and last month's rent, plus the sucker punch of a security deposit. My bank account is almost empty, meaning not only do I have to seriously simmer down on my restaurant binge, but also it's critical that I focus on my freelance work, too. Benito Bagel and I have even been e-mailing a little, but since I'm tenaciously pitching ideas and reconnecting with editors all day, and covering events all night (and still nursing a broken heart), I'm in no rush for our rendezvous. Though I know it will happen sooner than later.

The most exciting assignments I get come from *New York* magazine's food blog, *Grub Street*. I initiated the relationship by asking to cover a private event at Barneys on Madison Avenue to celebrate their holiday window display, featuring some of New York's most iconic chefs. I hoped that my first food assignment at my favorite magazine would be a little less daunting against the backdrop of my favorite store. And I was right. That night, I delivered ten fresh food stories to *Grub Street,* three of which they published the next day: Anthony Bourdain recommending me his favorite food memoirs; Mario Batali describing how to roast a Thanksgiving turkey in a pizza oven; and Bobby Flay confessing that he keeps only vodka and ice cream in his freezer. Ultimately, I make less money that night than what I spend in the shoe department, but it results in a steady, and priceless, stream of assignments from the food editors at the magazine. *Happy holidays to me.*

Back in DUMBO, I work on maximizing my minuscule Brooklyn apartment. I go to ABC Carpet & Home and apologize to my former boss for rudely running away from him weeks earlier. He gives me a big hug and an even bigger discount on a birdcagelike lamp. I refresh Craigslist every five minutes, finding sweet deals on Saarinen tulip chairs and a Scandinavian sideboard to store my quirky dishware and mismatched mugs, which are indeed collecting dirt, but crying out for their comeback. My mom and I go Dumpster diving, roaming the Brooklyn Heights promenade, where she once scored an oriental rug worth $20,000, along with two abandoned Oscar Awards. ("Divorce!" said the doorman, winking.)

My most highly anticipated day comes a week after moving in, when I finally have time to drive to the iconic, foodie fairyland called Fairway. I am so giddy you would think I was heading to the south of France, but really it's just the south of Brooklyn. Fairway is a giant warehouse with its most dramatic location in Red Hook, overlooking the harbor and evoking the feeling of both Alcatraz and an open-air European market. It's a labyrinth of lush produce, cheeses, and chocolates, with aisles of domestic and imported *everything*.

I spend three hours there, grazing the rows of dried pasta, exotic beans, and excessive candy bins, dragging my happy feet from semolina flours to grapeseed oils, exuberantly discussing the definition of "unctuous" with the cheerful cheesemonger, who introduces me to Spanish Mahon when I ask for something impressive but not too expensive. He also suggests I purchase some chestnut honey for my next cheese plate, and I obediently add the jar to my cart.

In the end, I leave with most of the same foods I've always lived on as an adult: Greek yogurt, moderately flavored (and priced) cheese, dark chocolate, black licorice, crisp apples, plump avocados, whole carrots, smoked almonds, dried apricots, earthy breads, long pasta, and fizzy water. The upgraded version of me adds some expensive olive oil, coarse sea salt, lots of fresh herbs, a rack of lamb, and a bouquet of winter white daisies.

As soon as I get home, I sit at my computer with a huge chunk of chèvre melted on a thick slice of grainy bread, and I e-mail Benito Bagel (who's asked me to call him Benjy). "Let's meet up tonight."

We agree to have our first date at a local dive bar, which is equal distance from both our apartments. I have an hour to get ready when it occurs to me that I desperately need a new "single chick" look. For the past few months back on the East Coast, I've worn dark skinny jeans with a beat-up T-shirt and a tight leather jacket. My shoes are either dirty Converse sneakers or bedraggled ballet flats. I wear no jewelry except for Shelley's long, gold, twinkling necklace. *Vogue* might classify my style as New York bitch. Maybe this isn't the right message for a date.

Straight from the shower, I scurry down the street to my sister's closet. No one is home. I quickly snag a soft, white peasant shirt that she bought a few years ago in Italy, and squeeze myself into a pair of her light blue jeans with a slight bell-bottom flair. I swap my sneakers for her alligator-skin wedges, and I bangle up my right wrist with a dozen wiry bracelets. Pulling up my hair all messy and morning-after, I've transformed myself from pissed-off to pretty. It's cold in mid-November, so I reluctantly take a nubby peacoat from the closet and duck out the front door. *Let's do this.*

I've never been nervous for first dates and this one is no different, even though it *is* my first one in a while. Excitedly, I walk to Henry St. Ale House, where I'm blown in the door by the wind. I immediately notice Benjy. He's *very* good looking, with a big head of floppy, light brown hair, beautiful olive skin, and a cool corduroy blazer. I quickly ditch the unflattering coat and say hello. We kiss on the cheek, but before I even sit down, I excuse myself to the ladies' room. My eyes are watering badly from the wind, and my mascara has run. When I come back to the bar, I overexplain the fact that I'm "totally not crying." He says I can calm down, but nicely.

I order a beer and urge myself to shut up about the tears already. He's a mellow guy, who preempts the conversation by saying that the reason he subscribes to online dating is because he thinks he might be a little socially awkward. He also says that he's looking for a serious relationship because he's "very lonely." It's endearing to meet someone who puts it all out there up front, and who isn't embarrassed to admit that being alone can be rough. I've always gravitated to open people like myself, but I am not sure how to respond to his utter lack of ego. So I shift the conversation to the ultimate neutralizer: food.

Much more of an eccentric creature than I am, Benjy is on a mission to try every roller coaster in the country to combat a childhood fear, he collects fading photography from weddings of the 1950s, and he considers himself New York's most eminent coleslaw aficionado—oh, and he is also an expert on the underground food scene. I've never heard of *any* of the cheap and chic dives he swears by. A true nonconformist, almost to the point of being a buzzkill, he couldn't care less about my secret phone number for all of Keith McNally's restaurants, or that Emeril Lagasse once fed me banana cream pie on national television, or how many people follow me and my blog on Twitter. But that's okay. This odd duck is attractive and intriguing.

I would be lying to myself if I didn't acknowledge the one thing about Benito Bagel that really blows my mind: he is Chef's raging opposite. Where Chef was luminous, Benjy is dimly lit. He's appalled by anything involving consumerism or celebrity, without an iota of interest in being popular, or even well liked, by anyone other than himself. And because he works from home and isn't all that engaged by his career choice in "helping the rich get richer," Benjy has *a lot* of free time on his hands. Even though I don't feel love at first sight, I'm pleased about spending time with such a fundamentally different type of man.

A few days after our first date, I go home with my family to one of my aunts' houses in Massachusetts for Thanksgiving. Benjy leaves me a message wishing all the Shelaskys a happy holiday. I am moved by his thoughtfulness, which doesn't preclude me from missing Chef, who still calls me almost every day, pleading to get back together every time I apprehensively pick up. Yet he *obviously* forgets to call or write on Thanksgiving. In fact, I wait for Chef to contact me all afternoon, giving my relatives only a fraction of my attention, while worrying if he's okay, asleep, in jail, or just over me.

That night at a bar outside Longmeadow, I meet up with Anzo, Kates, and Court who have all moved to their own nooks of New England and are home visiting family like me. The girls are planning a big fund-raiser in Boston to commemorate ten years since September 11, raise money for the Jean D. Rogér memorial fund, and celebrate her life with as many good people as possible. It's hard to believe it's been that long. My circle of friends is still so transparently wounded by her death.

There's not much I can do to help since I live farthest from Boston geographically, and in another orbit all together from most of our married-with-children classmates, but I mention that maybe Chef will cook for the event, especially if it will help raise money. The girls get a little excited, but I emphasize that there's no guarantee—there were never any guarantees with him, even when we were together.

Of course, the next morning, he calls the second he wakes

up, singing our favorite song into the receiver and suggesting that we watch the season's premiere of one of our TV shows together via the telephone that night, as if we didn't break off our engagement two months ago, as if he didn't forget Thanksgiving, and as if he's done absolutely nothing wrong. The call reflects so much about him—a two-part recipe of love and pain. I tell myself that this is why I need to keep dating decent, if less magnetic, men like Benjy.

Actually, the hour I come back to town, Benjy is waiting to take me to some carpet-stained, second-floor Peruvian restaurant to divvy up skewers of succulent lamb and what I think might be veal hearts. (I tell him I don't want to know.) We gulp down a couple pisco sours, exchange dating catastrophes, and then outside the restaurant, share a funky-tasting, but nonetheless enjoyable, first kiss. No electrical current runs through my veins, but it's fun kissing in the street after eating exotic foods in a city where anything is possible.

The next night, we trek to Flushing to traipse around a "Chinese food" strip mall, spilling over in food stations decorated in hung meat, serving fishy broths, duck buns, mystery dumplings, and various fatally spicy shit. All the forceful smells and sounds are considered paradise to many, but it's an excursion I personally never need to make again. Still, with that being our third date, we go from soy sauce in Queens to sex in Brooklyn.

Almost every other night, we start bouncing around affordable and eclectic spots that are usually a little too down and dirty for me, but absolute nirvana to Benjy. As far as he's concerned, the dodgier, the better. Our bills are *always* under thirty bucks; I am *always* too scared to use the bathroom. Whenever I shiver over a location or a certain cut of meat, he jokingly calls me a diva or a snob. "So be it!" I say, inspecting my alley-cat surroundings. There is always a tinge of hostility between us at these often-delicious shitholes. He quips that I can't call myself a food writer if I don't even have a little interest in trying, for example, hot pockets of lamb placenta. Perhaps he has a point, but it only makes me think about Chef, who thought I was Ernest Hemingway just because I could describe the crunch of a celery stick.

Benjy and I don't see eye to eye on much, but he's an interesting companion, and is opening my eyes to several secret gems. The ultimate treasure he introduces me to is a tiny, BYOB West African hideout called Abistro in the Fort Greene neighborhood of Brooklyn. The food is so incredible, and the place is such a find, that I overlook the four-dollar bottle of white wine he buys around the corner. When we don't finish the bottle (the wine is so sugary that I can barely swallow it), we offer it to the kitchen staff, who peruse the label and pass.

After a few weeks of dating, I've had enough fifty-cent banh mis for one lifetime, and am ready to have Benjy over for a cooked meal. He met my family briefly, when we all bumped into each other on the street, and my mom is definitely encouraging me to see what happens.

"What an interesting guy," she kept repeating.

"Not too weird, Mom?"

"Who wants a dullard?!"

In light of her endorsement, I'm hoping that a full night at home will soften our edges as a new couple, and potentially transcend us into *lovers,* instead of eating buddies who sometimes screw. I'm still not drawn to him the way I have been with others, but perhaps our relationship is that of a slow boil. An intimate night in my lovely, though loud and marginally vibrating, apartment will be good for us.

Frugal as he may be, Benjy has a voracious appetite and an extremely discerning palate. He typically eats slowly and abundantly, sometimes analyzing flavors for hours at a time, gushing over good, balanced bites and brooding over bad ones. I already know he'll approach my meal intellectually and articulately. In other words, my rebound is bound to hate anything I make.

A woman can always count on a roast chicken, as all home cooks know, so I thaw a frozen bird the night before Benjy comes over. I still haven't found my signature method for roasting, and I ask Gael Greene via Twitter which recipe I should use. Who can speak better to food *and* romance? After all, she wrote my favorite food memoir *and* shagged Elvis. I am at her culinary command. She tweets back that I should look up Judy Rodgers's Zuni Café recipe and I loyally follow—even though it's a little more laborious than I'd like!

Making dinner for Benjy in my sexy, industrial kitchen, I am calm and content. We've been dating for about six weeks now, it's officially the dead of winter, and I'm happy to have someone to hibernate with. A slight terror hits when I realize I've screwed up the Zuni chicken before I even start—you're supposed to salt and season it at least one day in advance. Oh well. I think I'll be okay. I'll let it sit, all nice and seasoned, in the fridge for a few hours. The good news is: no trussing! Trussing has always seemed superfluous to me, even though the majority of home cooks would fight me on that.

As the cold morning turns into late afternoon, I take the chicken out of the fridge, pan roasting it exactly per the instructions. Then I roast it inside the oven, with heaps of carrots and potatoes all tucked in like naptime. As night falls, I take the entire dish out and let it rest. It's time for the chicken and vegetables to suck up those juices while I wait for Benjy. Just when I'm about to light a few cucumber-scented candles, I stop myself. The apartment couldn't possibly smell any better.

Right on time, he knocks on my door, bundled up head to toe. I tell him to get comfortable, so he strips down to his long underwear (which doesn't really work for *my* juices). I'm surprised he doesn't bring any wine, but luckily I have an Argentinean Malbec, a red that was recommended by an *Apron Anxiety* reader, and cost a respectable twenty-six smackers.

We both agree that the chicken comes out close to perfect. Benjy points out a few minor things he would have done differently—like trussing, for one, and slipping some lemons into the cavity, but I don't really listen. By now, I've accepted that Benjy is a contrarian.

After dinner, we climb into bed with a bowl of homemade strawberry mousse (luscious and sensual, even if we are not) and bicker, not for the first time, over which movie to watch. Everything I like is too "commoditized" for him, so we agree to watch something with subtitles and I fall asleep being held in my own onion-scented hands. I wonder what Gael Greene would say if she knew the warm Zuni Café chicken led to ice between the sheets.

I'm not sure if I should release Benjy back to the world of Match.com, where many girls would want to marry him tomorrow, or keep working on it. I like how good he is to me—he's dependable, reliable, and always available—which makes me incredibly calm. There is a comforting dreariness to our relationship, in the way of a long walk through an afternoon fog, or a peasant soup on a raw day. So instead of making a rash decision that I might regret, I keep things going, but dial it back a bit. I tell him I need to focus on my writing and that we should only hang out once or twice a week for the rest of the winter.

Really, I'm home alone, playing classical music and making bone-warming dishes like meat and plantain casseroles and caramel apple pies, which I delightfully savage alone in my long fleece nighties. I am more relaxed than I've been in a very long time. Between the ownership of my resplendent kitchen, the drama-free fling, and Beethoven's Fifth, I am officially defused.

As the duration of our casual relationship grows, even though the emotional connection really does not, I have to tell Chef—who's in town for a new monthly TV segment—about Benjy. This brings me no secret satisfaction. We have a somber dinner over soggy nachos and salty margaritas at Pedro's in DUMBO. During our hyperemotional meal, he tries to convince us both that his career doesn't control him anymore, *that everything has changed*. Then he takes a disturbing call from his partners in which he nervously fibs by saying he's on the train, heading home.

"What?" he says, reacting to my dirty stare. "Some cook just quit and everyone is freaking out!"

"Don't you see?" I ask, shaking my head. "All you had to say was, 'I'm with Alyssa, this is important. I will deal with the situation later but I cannot talk right now,' and I'd start believing in us again."

He still doesn't get it.

By the time the partners call again, we agree (for the umpteenth time) that we are *still* atrocious as a couple, but forever unstoppable as friends. It's probably unhealthy for me, and a little unfair to Benjy (who thinks Chef is sealed airtight, *sous vide,* in the past), but no matter how much he drives me crazy, we just can't put each other away. I ask him to keep visiting, and he implores me to end it with Benjy because "I took you to the Greek Islands; he took you to fucking Flushing." We erupt in laughter, as we always do. And share an incredible kiss, as we always have.

"You know, there's nothing I won't do for you," I say, as he gets into a cab.

"Besides moving back to Washington," he adds, closing the car door.

~~~

NEW YEAR'S EVE is a week away. I really just want to cook dinner for my parents, who have spent most of the winter redoing the Litchfield County barn and haven't been around to taste any of my inspired dishes. Assuming everyone will have better plans, I also casually invite Beth and her husband, Tommy; Jill and her new boyfriend, Andrew; and my sister plus her date du jour to my parents' loft. Benjy had mentioned that he was probably going upstate with some college friends that night, so I invite him, too, thinking he'd decline. But everyone immediately RSVPs "Yes!" I am a bit stunned, but quickly wrap my head around cooking for all ten of us. I'll be hosting a smashing dinner party in six days and four hours.

Creating a menu continues to be my great pleasure, but this one needs to be extra special. It's about time I outdo myself. Surfing for ideas on one of my favorite cooking blogs, Food52.com, I come across a lamb meatball recipe featuring pomegranate seeds. The color of a single pomegranate aril, my favorite shade of red and the very reason I wanted a ruby ring, inspires the party's entire concept. I commit to that dish as my main course and find a pasta—a fusilli with toasted pine nuts and feta from the *Nigella Kitchen* cookbook—to accompany it. I'll serve it with a spinach and fig salad. Figs are not in season, but I'm sure some place will have sweet smelling ones.
~~~

Benjy, who I've been a little frosty toward, kindly offers to be my sous-chef. I say sure. I'll also put him in charge of making his signature fresh guacamole, which we'll serve with homemade garlic pita chips. As always, I'll cover the table with dramatic cheeses (definitely a thick slice of Mahon and the chestnut honey beseeched upon me at Fairway), and bushels of baguettes, green grapes, and smoked almonds. For dessert, I'm going to make a walnut–brown sugar torte from the *Chocolate and Zucchini* cookbook, and a three-layer red velvet cake from the *Baked* cookbook. I'll whip up Bobby Flay's vanilla bean crème fraîche, which will go well on both. My mother badgers me for something to contribute, so I tell her, if she must, I'd love a batch of dark chocolate clusters that I often long for, a holiday treat from my childhood. As our cocktail special, I'll serve Nigella's "Filthy Fizz," made with Prosecco and Campari (presumably called that for the tainted pink color of the bubbly, or the subsequent dirty thoughts).

The day before New Year's Eve, I go to Eataly alone to buy ingredients. I obsess over having enough food, so I snag a few boxes of freshly made focaccia at four dollars a pop. My bill is close to three hundred dollars in the end. I remind Benjy to pick up his own guacamole ingredients, since it's his recipe and I don't know which produce are involved. Forever frugal, he seems miffed by this, but I really don't care. With his help, I make the meatballs that night, trusting that like most meaty meals, they'll taste even better the next day. Though I wisely decide to accessorize them with the pomegranate seeds just before we plate.

The morning of New Year's Eve, I wake on edge, kicking Benjy out early so I can bake my desserts in sweatpants and stress in private. My reputation as a hostess is at stake tonight, and even though I consider myself a good home cook by now,

I'm not superhuman. Cooking for all those people at Dara's proved my competence, as far as preparation and presentation are concerned, but this dinner makes me feel a little vulnerable for many other reasons, above and beyond the food. It's going to be a roomful of people who know me well; who know when I'm winning and when I'm wilting. They're going to see how hard I'm trying to be happy, but that, of course, I'm still healing. It's tricky to hide behind food, when the people you're serving know to look past the dinner plate.

I change out of my jeans and dirty T-shirt into a knee-length, indigo slip dress that I bought in Venice Beach over the summer, and head over to my parents'. The doorbell there rings and keeps ringing. It's a delight to see everyone, but the atmosphere quickly becomes a little frantic. My family and friends are loud and hilarious—and it's hard to focus on completing the meal while keeping up with their charismatic stories. Plus my phone keeps vibrating on the granite counter, and I can see out of the corner of my eye that it's Chef's number. I am screening him against all my basic instincts. The meatballs are ready, and the pasta is cooking, and even though Benjy is helping me in the kitchen, I feel torn between giving my attention to him and to my friends, the phone, and the food. "Go catch up with everyone," he says sweetly. "I got this."

So I step away from the kitchen, take a deep, meditative breath, grab a drink, and try to lighten up. Even though I feel like an attractive-enough hostess, Beth, who doesn't have an undermining bone in her body, takes one sip of her Filthy Fizz and whispers to me that she misses the inner glow I had with Chef. Her truthfulness throws me off. We've been extremely close for fifteen years and she doesn't just throw words around.

"Beth," I say sharply, sipping my cocktail and looking her straight in the eye. "You say that because you spent time with us in the beginning, but trust me, Chef didn't make me glow in the end. He made me cry."

Then I remind myself to be a cool and composed hostess like Jennifer Rubell or Gwyneth Paltrow and I confess to her that I'm a little stressed, hence my oversensitivity, that I love her, and we'll talk about everything later.

I excuse myself to the stove, and to Benjy. He's very helpful by nature, a wonderful quality, but tonight I also sense his timidness around all the new people, and I find him seeking extra refuge by the burners. My mom takes my place to keep him company, as I refill everyone's drinks. She really likes him—he's passionate and peculiar, the kind of man she'd lock down for herself (or so she says) if she had to do it all over again. She's even been handing down some antiques from the barn for his hipster-meets-hermit tenement apartment. But really she likes how he's helped me "get over the hump" of another hellish breakup and find my balance back in New York even in his own weird way.

I ask everyone to take their seats at the festive table, which is in the middle of the open loft and looks lush with milk bottles filled with wild flowers, baskets of focaccia bread, piles of toile cloth napkins, white unscented candles, and long, willowy champagne flutes. As Benjy and I plate everyone's dinner, Tommy, Beth's infinitely likable husband of ten years, cracks a joke that has everyone keeled over in laughter. Benjy sprinkles the pomegranate seeds exactly so and whispers into my ear, "I'm sorry I'm not a funnier guy." I put my hands through his great head of hair and give him a long kiss on the lips. "You're perfect just the way you are." *Someone will be so lucky to have him.*

Unlike Dara's dinner party, which was family-style, tonight, Benjy and I do the plating behind the scenes. Thank God, the tones and textures of the collective dishes work as well together in real life as they did in my head. It's a fetching plate of food! Tiny dots of pomegranate kiss the dark and handsome lamb; curlicue fusilli is studded with flecks of pine nuts and chunky white feta; the quietly confident salad tames its counterparts' pulsating sass.

I text a close-up picture of a plate and send it to Shellz, who is skiing in Aspen; to Paisley, who has taken to a tree house; to Liz from *People,* who's hopefully not at the news desk; and to Anzo, Kates, and Court, who I know have struggled with the holidays since Jean's death. I also text Dara, who's getting engaged in a yurt; the C Street neighbors shooting Patron and praising Jesus for childcare; and all the other supportive women I wish I could spoil and surprise tonight.

It takes every bone in my body not to send the pictures to Chef, but considering how off-kilter he's been today (having droned on and on about the unfairness of life in the five messages he's left me), I decide against it. Baiting him would be cruel . . . to both of us.

Before even taking a bite, my family is visibly astounded. They admit they never believed that I could pull off an entire meal, let alone something so elegant. "I hope you eat your words!" I say, smiling. "Literally! Eat!"

This New Year's Eve dinner turns out to be the most delicious meal I ever made. There are second and third helpings, loud moans, and by the end of the meal, every single plate is licked clean. Our brains are soaked in flavor. My friends are stuffed. My sister can't stop smiling. The meatballs were scrumptious small wonders and the pasta was earthy and addictive. The only minor disappointment was the fig salad. I should have listened to my gut; figs just aren't meant to be served midwinter. *Seasonal* is a real thing. But no one really noticed except me (and probably Benjy).

I sneak away to check my BlackBerry and read everyone's reply to the food porn I sent earlier. In the course of our hour-long dinner, I see that I have five more missed calls from Chef and a text that says he's throwing his phone in National Harbor if I don't pick up again. He knows I'm throwing a big dinner party, but he is upset, which makes me upset. I try with everything I have to push my emotions aside. If I fall apart now, it will steal every inch of integrity I put into this monumental meal. And I'm *not* going to let that happen.

It's just before midnight and the fireworks on the Hudson River are starting. My mother and father insist on cleaning up while us "kids" go up to the roof. Drunk and bundled up, overlooking the Brooklyn Bridge, I confess to Beth and Jill that months ago on C Street, I served them banana bread with bugs in it. "You did what?!" cries Jill, a raging germophobe to began with. We are screaming and crying with laughter. My sister is entangled in her new beau, who is hopefully a better kisser than he is a conversationalist. Tommy is taking candid pictures of the bombed Jill and Beth, party-girl poses and pouring champagne into each other's puckered lips. Benjy is quietly keeping me warm.

We have one minute left to go until 2011. Some of my parents' neighbors, also taking advantage of the view from the roof, introduce themselves and extend their chilled bottles of French bubbly and opulent trays of berries and bonbons to us. I raise my glass, in my favorite city, with my closest friends and my well-fed family and toast, "To new beginnings!" Wiping away my runaway tears, dismissively blaming the wind, I release all the tension of the day, and maybe even the year. And then, hoping the sweetness will cut the tang, I add a raspberry to the fizz.

Lamb Meatballs Garnished with Pomegranate Seeds and Resolutions

SERVES 12

If becoming an amazing cook was last year's New Year's resolution, these meatballs made it all come true. I think it's safe to say that this is the most delicious dish I've ever made. The original recipe was inspired by a home cook who submitted a recipe to Food52.com under the screen name "My Man's Belly." I imagined the ruby red speckles of the pomegranate arils and felt an instant connection to the dish. That recipe suggested serving the meatballs on top of orzo, but I served them alongside Nigella's Fusilli with Toasted Pine Nuts and Feta (page 209). You can serve the meatballs freshly made or cooked the day before, but either way, make enough so you have leftovers. I made meatball subs ("grinders" to those of us from Western Massachusetts) for weeks.

For the sauce

4 cups unsweetened pomegranate juice

6 tablespoons packed light brown sugar

3 teaspoons cinnamon

For the meatballs

Olive oil

3 pounds ground lamb

2 medium yellow onions, grated

3 large eggs

1½ cups crushed crackers (I used Carr's poppy and sesame crackers, but any kind is fine)

6 garlic cloves, finely chopped

3 tablespoons fresh rosemary, finely chopped

1½ teaspoons lemon juice, from 1 lemon

1½ teaspoons fennel seed, crushed

1½ teaspoons kosher salt

1 teaspoon freshly ground pepper

Pomegranate arils

Preheat the oven to 450°F.

For the sauce: In a small saucepan, add the pomegranate juice, brown sugar, and cinnamon. Simmer over medium-high heat, reducing the juice to roughly 1 cup. This should take about 20 minutes. When reduced, set the sauce aside.

For the meatballs: Grease the bottom and sides of an 8 × 8-inch baking pan with olive oil and set aside.

Place the ground lamb in a large bowl and add the onion, eggs, crackers, garlic, rosemary, lemon juice, fennel seed, salt, and pepper. Using your hands, mix thoroughly.

Form the meatballs into 1½- to 2-inch balls. Place them in the pan.

Roast the meatballs in the oven for 5 minutes. Remove them and brush on two coats of the pomegranate sauce. Return the meatballs to the oven and roast for an additional 15 minutes, or until they are sizzling and well browned.

Remove the meatballs and let them cool. Before serving, drizzle with the remaining pomegranate sauce and sprinkle with the pomegranate arils.

If making a day in advance, let the meatballs cool completely, then cover and refrigerate. Reheat the meatballs at 350°F and apply the arils as a final touch.

If there are leftovers, the arils can be combined with the meatballs and refrigerated as one dish.

Nigella's Fusilli with Toasted Pine Nuts and Feta

SERVES 12

I first tried this pasta from Nigella Lawson's Nigella Kitchen *(Hyperion, 2010) for purely superficial reasons. Nigella has great style, and she is my kind of woman, a real vixen. So if she revered an earthy pasta with spinach and pine nuts, then surely I would, too. And I did! But watch out: this is the kind of dish you can really gorge on. Once I saw how roasty and fragrant the pine nuts were toasted, I got into the habit of toasting all my nuts, which, drizzled with a little olive oil and some sea salt, are a delicious, warm snack or party food on its own.*

Salt
½ cup pine nuts
4 teaspoons olive oil
2 yellow onions, sliced
2 pounds frozen chopped spinach
4 garlic cloves, finely minced
2 pounds fusilli or penne pasta
16 ounces feta cheese, crumbled
8 tablespoons grated Parmesan cheese, plus more for serving

In a large pot, boil the water for the pasta. Once it comes to a boil, add a fistful of salt to the water.

Toast the pine nuts in a small, dry skillet over medium-low heat for about 5 minutes. Be careful because they will burn easily. Put the toasted nuts in a bowl and set aside to cool.

Heat the olive oil in a large skillet over medium-low heat. Sauté the onions, letting them soften without taking on any color, about 10 minutes.

Give the bag of spinach a few good whacks to break up the pieces. Add the garlic and spinach to the pan. Keep stirring, breaking up any more large chunks of spinach and allowing it to melt.

Meanwhile, cook the pasta according to the package's instructions. When finished, reserve a cup of the pasta water before you drain the pasta.

Add the feta, toasted pine nuts, and some of the pasta water to the spinach mixture, allowing the feta to melt a bit. The sauce will be a bit chunky with the feta. Add the pasta and Parmesan to the sauce, and more pasta water if the sauce seems dry, tossing everything well to combine.

Spoon the pasta into bowls and serve with extra Parmesan at the table, if desired.

Luscious Chocolate Clusters

MAKES 24 CLUSTERS

I have never met a cluster that I wasn't madly, passionately in love with. I'll eat them for breakfast, lunch, dinner, or dessert. These rich, rocky mounds of chocolate bliss originated with my great-great-aunt Edith Pava, whose son, Thurman Pava, became a chocolatier and founded Rosa's Fudge in Massachusetts, now sold all over the country!

One 12-ounce bag semisweet chocolate chips
1½ cups raisins
1½ cups walnuts, roughly chopped

Line a cookie sheet with wax paper.

Melt all the chocolate chips in a double boiler. If you don't have a double boiler, fill a small saucepan with water and bring it to a boil. Reduce it to a simmer and set a heatproof bowl on top of the pot. Proceed with melting the chocolate, stirring frequently, until smooth. Remove from the heat.

While the chocolate is still warm, incorporate the raisins and walnuts.

Take a heaping tablespoon of the chocolate mixture and spoon onto the cookie sheet, leaving 1 inch between the clusters (they'll spread).

Refrigerate for 1 hour or until set. Gently remove the clusters from the cookie sheet and transfer to a plastic bag or tin. Refrigerate until serving.

Filthy Fizz

SERVES 2

This is such an easy, elegant cocktail, and it seems to have an aphrodisiac effect, too. Prepare your inner siren.

Prosecco, chilled
Campari, room temperature
Raspberries, optional

Fill two champagne flutes halfway with Prosecco. Finish them off with a splash or two of Campari. Float a raspberry in each glass for extra style. Let loose, drink up, and have fun.

12.

Market Fresh

No matter how hard I try, after a few months together, my chemistry with Benjy is just not there. In fact, the decrescendo is happening rapidly. We're starting to distinctly annoy each other, or so it seems, and I feel it's time to cut our losses before anyone gets too hurt. So just before Valentine's Day, I ask Benito Bagel to join me at the dive bar where we had our first date.

I try to make the breakup as quick and painless as possible, telling myself that he's just as likely to be done with me. But because I'm nervous, and because I truly respect him, I get myself too worked up and my delivery is off.

"I'm thinking this has gone as far as it can go," I start off, sounding nasty and coldhearted straight out of the gate, instead of tender but direct, which was my intention.

When he looks at me with sheer shock, I dig myself into a deeper hole.

"You know, I'm letting you off the hook. We can just be, like, over."

He abruptly stands up, looking horrified and extremely offended, raising his right hand like a first grader who needs the bathroom, and says, "I would like to go now, please." Before

I can begin to redeem myself, change lanes, actually behave like a compassionate human being, he leaves me stranded in the corner booth sooner than our Blue Moons can arrive. I end up drinking both beers and never hear from him again.

I suppose I thought we both saw the same subtext of our relationship: it wasn't true love—or even trudging in that direction—at least not for me, and perhaps naïvely, I assumed not for him. Looking back, I did drag him along while I tried to rebuild, but at the time I thought I was just giving dating another shot. I'll always be grateful for my sweet stint with Benjy. What I learned from our short time together was how nice it feels to be with someone who is simply kind, honest, and dependable.

On Valentine's Day, just a week after my ungraceful breakup, I take my first spin class at SoulCycle since leaving New York for Washington over two years ago. I'm so excited at the prospect of putting on my spandex and spin shoes that I'm barely mindful of the potentially gloomy holiday. The 7:30 class that usually has a waiting list is close to empty tonight. It's just me and a few other upbeat, well-toned singletons that, as unattached New Yorkers, would rather be productive than pathetic. We all share a collective "Never let 'em see ya sweat" mentality. Well, unless you're about to burn off eight hundred calories in under an hour.

Our teacher's name is Rique, and he's a full-blown sex bomb. In fact, when the lights go down and the music goes up, the first song he plays is "Tonight (I'm Fuckin' You)" by Enrique Iglesias. *And we're off.* The beat is transforming, Rique is turning us all on, and the room is as electric as I had remembered. Even if I'm wearing a sports bra instead of a lace bra, and riding a bike instead of a boyfriend, this intoxicating, unventilated room is the only place I want to be tonight. For forty-five minutes straight, I spin my ass off. I spin like never before. And I spin the last of any feelings I had for Benjy right out of me.

After class, my legs throbbing in the best possible way, I walk a few blocks to Whole Foods in Union Square. At nine o'clock on Valentine's Day, it's prime dinner-reservation hour. Dozens of lovestruck couples are strolling by me—girls in flippy blow-outs and boys in popped, pin-striped collars. I can't help but notice all the roses in hands and sparkles on faces. But I am happy for the lovebirds, eating their prix fixe romantic meals wherever *Yelp* tells them to, and going home to be spanked thanks to Victoria and all her secrets. *Good for them.*

The only action I'm getting tonight is in the apron. It's a great night for a test kitchen under the bridge, so I'm steaming mussels for the first time, if all goes well. I don't even know if I like mussels, to be honest, but everyone keeps saying they're the perfect home-cooked meal for an easy, intimate dinner (should I ever have another worthy candidate). Benjy introduced me to a few new dishes and cuisines, whether I liked them or not, and I'm trying to keep the *food-venturous* momentum going. Mussels aren't exactly alligator schnitzel, of course, but they're not a move in the *wrong* direction. Any recipe that includes the term "debearding" seems unusual enough for me.

As I search for my ingredients, I look around the market at all the single shoppers who tonight will be reading recipes instead of Hallmark cards, and reveling under the light of the refrigerator bulb instead of a candelabra. The Goth girl in front of me will be making a tofu pad Thai, it would appear; the divorced dad is planning a filet mignon for one. I feel the struggle in the air, which I appreciate, and as I create all their stories, I wonder if they have figured out mine. (Then again, have I?) I am proud to stand in the organic aisles with the likes of secret mistresses, chronic commitment phobes, sexually deprived, out of luck, independent and codependent dumpers and dumpees. They might not have suitors, but they have spirit.

In the long checkout line, I'm surprised to see a random food writer friend approaching as I stretch my sore limbs. His reviews can be merciless, and depending on the restaurant, he's either blacklisted or beloved. We became friends several years ago, back in the *Us Weekly* days, long before Bolognese and bouillabaisse were how anyone paid their rent. I tell him I'm experimenting with mussels. He tells me he and his girlfriend are taking a break. He delicately asks what happened in D.C., explaining that no one really understands the story of our breakup. I tell him it's not so black and white, but if it's all off the record, I can try to explain. A minute into my monologue, and six Bridget Joneses before checkout, he interrupts me.

"The problem is, Alyssa," he says with seriousness, "you never caught on to the secret."

"What secret?" I ask, terrified, knowing he's a hawk.

"The secret is that *you* were the special one."

Whoa. In all my conversations about Chef with my best friends, family members, and wise editors, I've never had a more poignant moment. Hovering over my garlic and parsley, wearing fleece and pom-pom socks, alone on Valentine's Day, I feel deeply liberated by his words.

There has always been a part of me that's avoided too much deep self-reflection on the downfall of Chef and me. I can recite all of our fights, all of our issues, and all of the mistakes, from which there would be no return, that he and I *both* made. But I've never been able to identify what was at the core of our ultimate contamination. And here it is, plain and simple: my identity was compromised; the sentiment of being "less than" made me feel ugly and made me act erratically. Yet all along, I was the special one. I see that now; I feel that now. But if only I had known then.

"Lys, there's one more secret," he calls as I walk toward the cashier.

"What is it?" I shout back.

"Those aren't mussels. They're clams."

Ah, crap!

By ten o'clock, I am home preparing an impossibly easy, yet very elegant meal (of *actual* mussels) that takes no more than ten minutes. First I give the little suckers their facials, the "debearding," then they all go into a bath of butter, wine, and garlic. Presto! Dinner is ready, my favorite playlist is singing softly, and I eat my Valentine's Day *moules* quietly and contemplatively. I get into bed and watch a couple of TV shows saved on the DVR. I fall asleep alone, stretched out, well fed, entertained, and enlightened.

~~~

AS WINTER turns to spring, I get busier than ever with cooking, baking, entertaining, dining out, and writing about it all. Some foods like speck (*a speck of what?*) and offal (which I misspelled as *awful* when transcribing an interview) still throw me off, and I am as awkward with chopsticks as I am with, say, doing the moonwalk. Yet I see myself constantly evolving, almost without trying. I now use words like "anise" to categorize the black licorice flavor I love so much in foods like fennel, drinks like ouzo, and of course, candy like Good & Plenty. "Sassafras" describes soft drinks and sweets that remind me of root beer; I say "custard" instead of "pudding," "squid" instead of "calamari,"
~~~

"crème fraîche" instead of "Cool Whip." Sandwiches are no longer sandwiches but tartines, and such tartines often bestow homemade pickled radishes, plum chutney, and the tolerable cousin to my nemesis, mayonnaise, which I can finally spell and pronounce: "aioli." I am turned on by turnips, offended by overcooked eggs, and can finally deliver the word "cockles" without cracking up.

Rapacious vernacular aside, there are many acquired tastes that I don't think I'll ever actually acquire, and I'm not going to pretend otherwise. Sardines make me quiver (and not in the good way), and the avant-garde lard trend is a huge gross-out. Any food too spicy, raw, or fleshlike is not going to happen—search me, you won't find them, no matter what food crime I'm committing. My Jewish-girl aversion to pork, in general, is another massive violation of the gourmet code of behavior. So chances are I'll never be a gangster eater—no pig butt or fish eyeballs for me, please—but I make no apologies and still consider myself largely culinary-spirited. Like most things in life, it doesn't have to be so all-or-nothing.

My home cooking is equally an ongoing experiment. It wouldn't be any fun otherwise. A James Beard Award nominee recently came over to raid my stacks of cookbooks, only to be disillusioned by the slice of homemade whole-wheat bread I proudly fed him (it admittedly resembled the texture of a football). "Are you sure you used the right yeast?" was his gentle feedback. Unfortunately, my beautiful bread-making days seem to have been tied to beginner's luck, because now they all come out wildly unattractive and generally inedible. However, I like to think that if everything were patisserie-perfect, then I'd have less to laugh about.

Whether it's in my skill set or not, there is nothing in the food world that I'm not sweet on learning about. *Nothing*. One of the perks of interviewing great chefs and foodies for *Grub Street* is that I get the chance to ask them anything I want. *Mocha Frappuccino or steeped green tea? Describe your last Taco Bell binge. Do people do drugs in your bathroom? Ever burn toast?* They usually respond well to me. I think it's because, by now, I *get* chefs. I know the glossy daze in their eyes, like a toddler at the tail end of a tantrum, after exiting the all-consuming tunnel of their shift. I know to give them space, five minutes for some, a few hours for others, as they mentally transition from workhorse to human being. And even once they've changed gears into the very cool creatures they intrinsically are, I know that there are still some chefs who can't veer far from restaurant talk, and others who will stop at no intellectual rampage to prove that they *can*. In the end, it's a safe bet that they all just want to talk about bacon, sex, and themselves, anyway.

From the French-trained demigods to the tat'ed badass chicks to the infantile, alcoholic savants, I find myself emulating anything I can shake out of these culinary daredevils with their chipped-at personalities and tremendous talent. Floating in and out of restaurant openings and tasting tables, I extract sound bites, both highbrow and low, that tailor the way I look at food.

The über-purist chef, Michel Bras, from a little village in the French countryside, tells me that one of his favorite treats is an apple core, simply because it is always dismissed with such wasteful disdain. He makes me try one and it gets lodged in my throat, but I totally get his point and now look at broccoli stems and banana peels differently, too. Thomas Keller—the most pleasant and perhaps important chef in the country—admits he can't walk past Reese's Peanut Butter Cups at the grocery store without throwing them in his shopping cart. He's probably just trying to humanize himself, but now I grab them, too, with glory instead of guilt. Grant Achatz, of Chicago's Alinea fame, sings the splendor of a vegan Japanese chef in New York who's "revolutionized the vegetable," so I make a reservation for a table for one, walking away seventy-five dollars poorer but a pea shoot more evolved. Paul Liebrandt of Corton and the documentary *Matter of Taste,* and whose crystal blue eyes make me lose all concentration, argues that Marco Pierre White was the last of the rock star chefs, imploring me to buy *White Heat* right away. Gabrielle Hamilton prescribes Negronis for when life gets rough; Padma Lakshmi prevents hangovers with an "egg in a hole" before bed; and Ruth Reichl finds her Zen in cartons of Szechuan Chinese food while sitting silently on the couch. And so I do as they do. I do as they say. Call me a foodie follower. I've heard worse.

As I explore the likes of Cambodian *num pang* and avocado ice cream, popping into artisanal cheese shops and swanky whisky rooms, I am, by default, meeting a lot of men again. The funny thing is, when I go on dates now, most guys admit they're nervous about making the reservation or ordering the right food in front of me. I try to explain that even though I'm uploading as much culinary information as I can into my brain, I still buy wine based on packaging, shiver at pig hearts, can't stomach oysters, and hesitantly pronounce "pho" and "chicken *paillard*." But they think I'm just trying to be disarming.

In the lobby of the Bowery Hotel, I get cozy with a Jared Leto lookalike who wears eyeliner and smells like a wet dog. When I stop returning his calls, because he's just too out there, he leaves endless voice mails in which he simply chews food into the phone. He calls it gastro-poetry. Enter the once-famous child actor who is now a struggling film producer. I like him a lot, even though my gut says he's hiding something (and trust me, it's *not* residuals). Then he tells me he's going fishing in upstate New York and ends up in rehab. At a coffee shop in Brooklyn, I meet a novelist whose books I've bought, and whom I can't believe is flirting with me. For the next few weeks, we text profoundly and pornographically, but on the night I'm set to see him for an actual date, I come down with a miserable migraine. I cancel via e-mail and ten minutes later he writes back, "No second chances, sweetheart." *Asshole.*

I don't jump into bed with all these new guys, but I'm not knitting them sweaters either. In case of "gentleman callers," my kitchen is always ready. I usually keep an onion, potato, and cumin quiche in the fridge, as well as a berry tart or something simple and sugary that stays fresh for a few days. This way, day or night, sweet or savory, G-rated or X-rated, I always have something to offer.

Against my better judgment and after months of kitchen-rat restraint, I even go on a blind date with another well-known chef named Alexi. It takes weeks before I agree to meet him, but after three close friends vouch for his solid character, I pop my head into his restaurant, wearing sunglasses and a hat, and notice him peacefully reading the *New York Times* and sipping a coffee. There's no chaos, iPhone, publicist, or posse reverberating around him. I intuitively like his disposition, and tell our mutual friends to move forward with the matchmaking.

Alexi and I meet up on the first warm evening of spring, a Monday, his only night off, and sit outside for wine and a few flatbread pizzas. He looks like an Italian immigrant straight from Ellis Island, with translucent white skin, raven black hair, and a five o'clock shadow that could make a grown woman cry. He's incredibly composed, much more intelligent than most of the sexy things I'm drawn to, and seriously committed to his critically adored cuisine. We have a wonderful conversation about the future of the New York City food scene, share a smoky carafe of red wine, and after kissing good night on a SoHo street corner, I get on the subway, hoping he asks me out again. "Alexi *is* yummy," I text our mutual friend.

We spend a few more Mondays together. They each pass in a woozy haze, always consisting of one impossible restaurant reservation, two killer orgasms, and a three-o'clock-in-the-morning cab ride home with a smile on my face and thong in my clutch.

I don't dare ask for more of his time. He likes that I know the drill—that I'm not expecting a date every Saturday night, that I don't pester him for midweek dinners, movies, or spontaneous picnics in the park. Fortunately for him (less fortunately for me), I've been the other woman to a restaurant before.

On our fifth Monday, Alexi asks me to join him at a downtown, carnivorous hot spot. As we catch up on our week while holding hands across the table, I amaze myself at how I can actually keep up with most of his culinary musings. Had we met even a few weeks earlier, many of his interests would be way over my head. Pondering the menu, I mention that I won't eat anything involving bone marrow or sweetbreads. "You know I'm still a culinary prude," I say, hoping to sound cute rather than uncultured. In the same breath, I order the tripe. When the waiter walks away, Alexi says, "I'm shocked that you like tripe!" My answer? "Really, why? I love fish."

When the dish comes, I know that I've embarrassed myself. The following day, I go to Eataly and ask the butcher what the hell I had forced myself to swallow. "Cow tummy," he says with a grin.

The next week, Alexi changes things up a bit, and arranges for us to see a movie at a downtown film festival, suggesting that afterward we hit the opening night for the most talked-about restaurant of the year. What a hot date, and my editors at *Grub Street* will be so impressed! I shop all day long for the right outfit to wear on such a fabulous night, and end up buying a short, silky nude-colored dress from a high-end boutique in my neighborhood. It's a bit provocative, but I've been working out so much at SoulCycle that I want to show off my legs. The salesperson whispers that she just sold the same dress to Maggie Gyllenhaal, my fashion hero, and this closes the deal without further dread over the price tag. A few hours later, I throw on scarlet red Louboutins and dry my hair to look long and wind-blown. Spring is in bloom and so am I.

The movie is unremarkable, but sitting so close to Alexi compensates for it all. Truthfully, I am wary about any real future together—food is not just his career, it's his absolute airstream—yet I adore him and can say for sure that my inner fire is ablaze. The film ends around midnight, and even though I'm starving, all I want to do is skip dinner and slip out of our clothes. I hint at this, but he's obviously excited about seeing his friend's new restaurant. "Don't you worry." He winks. "Our night is just beginning."

On the cab ride over, he mentions that we're not dining alone, which I never even thought to ask about. We'll be sitting with foodie royalty: a handful of elite chefs, restaurateurs, journalists, and sommeliers. "You know, like, *ehhhveryone*," he says. Oh great, here we go with the obnoxious *ehhhveryone* . . . again.

I think he's trying to impress me, knowing I'm growing my career in food writing and trying to infuse my world with as many knowledgeable people as possible, but he's got it all wrong. This social structure is anathema to me. I have no interest in being on display as some popular chef's arm candy. Not anymore, at least. But soon enough, we're heading straight into the eye of the storm—the hard-core, cliquey, New York food "industry" scene.

I quickly reassure myself how far I've come. I think of all the meals I made at the El Royale, my New Year's Eve feast, the endless grazing days at Eataly, the big-ticket interviews for my *Grub Street* byline, and the victorious Valentine's Day *moules*. I even arm myself with an opening line, something fun I just learned from the popular food blogger Restaurant Girl: "Did you know tiramisu was originally called 'a prostitute's pick-me-up' because of all the sugar and caffeine?" *I'll be okay.*

We pull up to the restaurant just past midnight and I'm shocked at the mobs of people inside and out. "Can you feel the energy?" Alexi asks, paying the cab driver with a crisp bill. To be honest, I feel like puking. Hand in hand, with him leading the way, we make our way through the front door, past the crowds and to the corner VIP booth, which is spilling over with culinary somebodies, the same not-so-friendly faces that made me uncomfortable at food festivals with Chef.

My dress has no place in this anti-glam crowd, where almost everyone has chosen a life of food over everything else, especially fashion. It looks like I've tried way too hard, but there's nothing I can do. *I was supposed to be on a hot date . . . what do they want from me?* When we get to the coveted corner table, it's packed tight, and a few courses have already been served. I take the crammed seating as a blessing and hope that we can leave, maybe make some naked paninis at my place and be private. But my date asks everyone to move over for me: "You all know Alyssa, right?" He's being pulled in a million different directions and wants me to be comfortable while he checks out the industrial equipment and reconnects with a decade of kitchen pals.

I wiggle myself into the table, accidentally flashing my underwear to the crowd. "Oops! At least I'm wearing some!" I tease. No one laughs but me. Everyone is looking down, clinging to their iPhones, frenetically tweeting about meat pies and plywood. "When did tweeting become the new chain-smoking?" I joke to the sommelier to my left. "Well, I think we all have a responsibility to share these high-level culinary experiences," she replies, dead seriously. *Oh, okay.*

I try to remember that *I'm the special one,* but right now, I'm also the starving one, and I know I won't find any inner glory until I'm nourished. I don't care if it's a Michelin-star chef or Mister Fucking Softee, someone needs to feed me. There's nothing on the table except some critically acclaimed cornbread, which a pastry chef and a food publicist are analyzing like it's the secret to immortality. I grab the basket and pound two pieces.

It's noisy and everyone is talking over me. Satiated at long last, I try to join another conversation, one about wineries in Tuscany . . . or is it Tuscans in wineries? I can't really hear. I awkwardly interrupt and say that I'm vying for a press trip to Siena. No one looks up. At least with celebrities, they *pretend* to care. There's some back and forth banter about a legendary restaurateur's farm in Martha's Vineyard. I actually know who they're talking about, so I announce that I'm from Massachusetts and that my friend had her wedding right across the street from his property. An older woman responds, "Speaking of, Alyssa, I'm confused. Which chef are you with now?"

A year ago, I would have been too fragile to withstand a comment like that. But I take her crassness as jealousy and let it slide. Although her herb-encrusted dagger *does* stop me from trying to fit in with everyone—not because I feel bullied or bitter, but because I'm bored to death.

Before the plates of "ironic" fried chicken arrive, close to one o'clock in the morning, I discreetly tell Alexi, who has finally come back to the table, that I have a big day tomorrow and need to head home. I twist myself out of the booth and wave good-bye to the gourmands. He follows me outside, encouraging me to stay and apologizing for leaving me alone for so long. While changing out of my Louboutins and into the ballet flats I wisely stashed in my bag, I tell him not to worry, and I truly mean it. I am not mad at all. This scene is his home and he's killed himself to get here. But for now, I'm cool with just writing about it.

As I walk away, through the streets of the Village, looking for fresh air and maybe a falafel, I am oddly unfazed by the experience of being ignored or insulted by the foodie mafia. I will always meet people who don't like me, or don't *get* me, who think I'm dressed like a high-class hooker or raised by wolves. But as all the women I've ever admired would say, "At least you're interesting enough that someone gives a shit." Which reminds me: There will always be people who think I'm not interesting enough at all.

Just down the block, I see a crowd of people in Washington Square Park. Even though it's late, and the park can be a rough-and-tumble environment at night, I sense some good music and the reporter in me sails over. As I get closer, I hear "Sittin' on the dock of the bay . . ." It's one of my favorites. So I walk faster. I make my way through a crowd of forty or so, and see that in the middle of everything, there's an old, soulful black man on the guitar, a weirdo white guy with an Afro and ripped overalls on the drums, and a gypsy-faced, songbird couple who are either rockers from the seventies or escapees from an asylum (or both).

Together they're all jamming to a mixture of folk and funk,

and it's fabulous. I join the circle of yuppies, vagabonds, street-cart vendors, prostitutes, and perfect couples, and we're all loudly singing along, "Sittin' on the dock of bay, watching the tide roll away . . . !" When someone starts Smokey Robinson's "My Girl," an NYPD officer with ruddy cheeks and a big belly taps me on the shoulder and twirls me around and around, and for some reason, I think of Jean and I sing even louder. The crazy songfest is the most uplifting New York moment I've ever experienced, and suddenly, I am belting out "Here Comes the Sun," by the Beatles, and sobbing. Forget the dinners, Twitters, Bellinis, bylines, and boys. *This* is life.

Eventually, I drag myself away. It's almost three o'clock in the morning, and the moment couldn't possibly get better. The entire cab ride home, quietly humming Bruce Springsteen's "Thunder Road," because that's what was being played when I left, I can't stop wondering if these highly emotional experiences find me, or if I find them.

Lying in bed, I decide to stop seeing Alexi romantically, at least for now. He is not the warm washcloth on my face that I require from a relationship. And I think that part of me, maybe, believed that being with him provided a chance to prove that I *could* endure life with a chef. A second act. Because deep down, there will always be a sense that I failed so miserably the first time. But I have to grow up. If it's redemption that I'm looking for, that's something I need to resolve from within. And should I decide that I *do* want such a sweet and vicious life, thumping in narcissism, sleeplessness, and unspeakably good sex, I already know the white-smocked schmuck I want to live it with.

The next day my mother e-mails me, wanting a full recap on the date, as she always does: "So? How was it? Whatcha eat?"

I write back: "Mom, I ate the bear."

Gentleman Caller's Onion and Cumin Quiche

SERVES 8

Quiche sounds a lot more complicated than it is—it's really just two parts: the crust and the filling. You can buy premade crust, but it feels so good knowing you made the entire thing from scratch. This recipe is adapted from Chocolate and Zucchini *(Broadway Books, 2007). I follow the crust instructions religiously but sometimes experiment with other cheeses, or throw in potatoes or asparagus, depending on what's fresh at the market. It's delicious for breakfast, lunch, and dinner, or for entertaining* special *company. The filling can be made a day in advance, or you can make the whole quiche a day ahead, then reheat it for 15 minutes in a 350°F oven to revive the crispiness of the crust.*

Crust

1⅓ cups all-purpose flour, sifted, plus more for working the dough
½ teaspoon fine sea salt
8 tablespoons (1 stick) chilled unsalted butter, diced
1 large egg
Ice water
1 teaspoon olive oil

Onion and cumin filling

1 tablespoon extra-virgin olive oil
6 medium (2 pounds) yellow onions, thinly sliced
½ teaspoon fine sea salt
3 large eggs
¾ cup light cream
¼ teaspoon freshly ground pepper
2 teaspoons whole cumin seeds
1½ cups (5 ounces) freshly grated Comté (Gruyère is a good substitute)

For the crust: If working with a food processor: Combine the flour, salt, and butter and process on low for about 10 seconds, until the mixture resembles coarse meal. Add the egg and mix again for a few seconds, until the dough forms a ball. If the dough is a little dry, add ice water, 1 teaspoon at a time, and process in short pulses until the dough just comes together.

If working by hand: Sift the flour into a medium mixing bowl. Add the salt and butter to the flour and rub the mixture with the tips of your fingers or a wire pastry blender until the mixture resembles coarse meal. Beat the egg lightly in a small bowl. Form a well in the center of the flour mixture, add the egg, and blend it in gently with a fork. When most of the egg is incorporated, knead gently until the dough comes together. If it is a little dry, add ice water, 1 teaspoon at a time, until the dough forms a ball. Avoid overworking the dough.

Turn out the dough on a lightly floured work surface and gather into a slightly flattened ball without kneading. Wrap the dough tightly in plastic and refrigerate for 30 minutes and up to a day (or freeze up to one month).

Sprinkle flour lightly on a clean work surface and on a rolling pin, then place the dough on the surface. Roll the pin over the dough two or three times with moderate pressure. Rotate the dough clockwise by a quarter of a turn, and roll the pin over it two or three times. Repeat these steps until you get a circle large enough to line a 10-inch ceramic quiche or pie pan, sprinkling the work surface and the rolling pin with a little more flour if the dough begins to stick.

Refrigerate the dough in its disk-like shape, wrapped in plastic wrap, for 20 minutes. Meanwhile, grease the quiche or pie pan with the oil and preheat the oven to 350°F. When the dough is chilled, transfer it to the pan, prick all over with a fork, and press on the sides with your fingers so the dough will adhere to the pan. Bake for 7 minutes, or until lightly golden. Remove from the oven (leaving the heat on) and set aside.

For the filling: Once your crust is ready, heat the oil in a large skillet over medium heat. Add the onions, sprinkle with

¼ teaspoon salt, and stir. Reduce the heat to low, cover, and cook for 30 minutes, stirring from time to time, until the onions are soft and translucent.

Remove the lid, raise the heat to medium high, and cook for another 5 minutes, stirring regularly, until most of the liquid has evaporated. (This step can be done 1 day in advance if cooled, covered, and stored in the fridge.) Set aside.

In a medium mixing bowl, whisk together the eggs and cream. Season with the remaining ¼ teaspoon salt, the pepper, and the cumin seeds. Fold in the cheese and cooked onions, and pour the mixture into the crust.

Bake for 35 minutes, or until the top is golden and the center is still slightly jiggly. Turn off the heat and leave the quiche in the closed oven for 10 minutes, or until the filling is set. Serve warm.

Springtime Tart

SERVES 8

Just like the Gentleman Caller's Onion and Cumin Quiche, this recipe, from the same Chocolate and Zucchini *cookbook, is deceptively easy and versatile. I started making this tart in the early months of spring, so I prepared it with gorgeous strawberries, but the strawberries can be replaced with raspberries in the summer, figs in the fall, or even pineapple in the winter. The crust, of course, is perfect year-round. Tarts make great breakfasts, light lunches, or pretty desserts; they're in the precious category that I like to call "the interchangeable calorie."*

Crust

- ⅓ cup sugar
- 1 cup plus 2 tablespoons all-purpose flour
- ¼ teaspoon sea salt
- 7 tablespoons (3½ ounces) chilled unsalted butter, diced, plus a pat to grease the pan
- 1 to 2 tablespoons cold milk

Filling

- 1 large egg
- 1 teaspoon pure vanilla extract
- 2 tablespoons sugar
- 2 tablespoons cornstarch
- ½ cup milk
- 4 cups fresh strawberries (about 2 pints)

For the crust: Grease a 10-inch tart pan with butter.

If working with a food processor: Combine the sugar, flour, and salt in the processor. Add the butter and process in short pulses, until the mixture resembles coarse meal. Add 1 tablespoon of milk and process again, in short pulses, until the milk is absorbed.

If working by hand: In a medium mixing bowl, combine the

sugar, flour, and salt. Add the butter and rub it into the dry ingredients with the tips of your fingers until the mixture resembles coarse meal. Add a tablespoon of milk and blend it in, handling the dough as lightly as you can.

The dough should still be crumbly, but it should clump if you gently squeeze a handful. If it doesn't, add a little more milk, teaspoon by teaspoon, and blend again, still working lightly, until it reaches the desired consistency.

Pour the mixture into the prepared tart pan and use the back of a tablespoon to spread it evenly over the bottom. Using your fingers and the heels of your hands, press down on the dough to form a thin layer, covering the surface of the pan and creating a rim all around. Don't worry if the dough feels a little dry—this is normal. Cover with plastic wrap and refrigerate for 30 minutes, or up to 1 day.

Preheat the oven to 350°F. Start the filling and then bake the pastry for 12 to 14 minutes, until golden, keeping an eye on it. Remove from the oven and let cool.

For the filling: In a medium bowl, whisk together the egg, vanilla, and sugar. Whisk in the cornstarch and set aside.

In a medium saucepan, bring the milk to a simmer over medium heat. As soon as the milk simmers, pour it into the egg mixture, whisk vigorously until blended, and pour the mixture back into the saucepan. Return the saucepan to low heat, and whisk for 30 seconds as it thickens. Spoon the milk mixture into the prepared pastry, level the surface with a spoon, and let cool completely on the counter, about 1 hour.

Rinse the strawberries, pat them dry, and hull them. Cut the strawberries lengthwise in half. Arrange the fruit on the tart in a circular pattern, starting from the center. Serve immediately, or cover with plastic wrap and store in the refrigerater. Bring to room temperature before serving.

13.

A Harmless Weekend in Washington

Laura, one of my dear neighbors on C Street, is throwing a birthday bash for her one-year-old son, Baxter. The little guy was born a few months early and has had a rough year.

I miss my old neighbors, especially the kids, and I'd like to be there to celebrate the B-Man's excellent progress. The last time they all saw me, a little over eight months ago, I was a bedraggled, bony mess, with mascara dripping down to my clavicles and a dozen garbage bags filled with cooling racks, photo albums, and dirty jeans. I vividly remember the neighborhood kids' sad faces as I packed up the Jeep, kissed them good-bye, and explained that Miss Alyssa was moving away, that there would be no more milk and cookies on our stoop, and to please take care of Mister Chef if they see him around.

These are much sunnier days.

Chef encourages me to make the trip down to see the big, groovy loft he rented shortly after we broke up. He also keeps promising me that he now has more time to be a functional human and wants me to see the positive changes he's made to his work hours and overall well-being. *Same old,* but it's nice to know that we're both happy and centered in our individual lives. While my career is keeping me exhilaratingly busy, his seems to be slowing down just enough for him to finally take inventory of all the changes he's experienced and all the choices he's made, both good and bad. He's spending a great deal of time mentoring inner-city kids and cooking with terminally ill children. His charity work has become more important to him than any partners or publicists. It's pure, and sincere, and I'm proud of him.

Our affection for each other has hardly diminished; we've just found a way to live with the fact that we might always be crazy in love, but unable to be happy together. Given this clear message from me, I know he's consoled himself (so to speak) with a few flings, and he's aware of my dalliances, too. It's neither of our favorite topics, but because we talk a few times a day, about everything from my delicious discoveries to the things we wish we could do over from our past, it's impossible to hold anything back.

I'm not sure how much time I'll want to spend there, so I purchase a one-way ride on the bus, warning my family and friends that if they have an opinion, they better keep it to themselves. Anyway, we're not getting back together. *If* I saw that in the past few months Chef had magically turned into the kind of guy who made me certain that we could handle real life, and that we'd always put each other first without a strand of doubt or insecurity, *maybe* I'd come to town with a more romantic point of view.

But after last night, no. On the phone, I reminded him about the upcoming fund-raiser in Boston in honor of Jean on the ten-year anniversary of 9/11, which he originally said he'd "most likely" attend to cook at, be supportive of, or whatever worked best for me and my friends from home. It's in a few weeks, but now he's wiggling out of it, mentioning something about being double-booked . . . a prior work commitment that he can't get out of now. It's an honest mistake (as it always is), but it's nearly impossible to manage my disappointment when his actions affect the people who matter the most to me.

"I'll never be that guy who's always right there next to you, Lys," he said at the end of the call. "You have to accept it already."

"Yup," I say, in that stale tone.

"Will you still come see me tomorrow?"

"Yup," I say, hanging up, coldly.

I wake up willing to let go of the Boston situation, because he really did seem in a bind and he *was* forthcoming about it. And shame on me for thinking he'd come through in the first place. I fill a duffel bag with T-shirts and jeans and clean out my junk drawer, grabbing swag for the kids—a faux-gold necklace I got at Fashion Week that reads "FABULOUS," and a rainbow lollipop shaped like Lady Liberty. I pack up my laptop and Gabrielle Hamilton's newly published memoir and rush out the door. Halfway down the hallway, running impossibly late, I turn around and grab the nude minidress from my closet. No one appreciates my legs more than Chef.

My dad rides the F train with me to the bus stop at Penn Station. He says he's heading in that direction anyway, but I know that's not really the case. While I've downplayed the trip to everyone including myself, he wants to send me off on behalf of my family with love and support. He hands me an envelope as I rush off and warmly says, "Buy Chef a coffee on me." My parents, who have the gift of seeing the good in everyone, accepted him for who he is long ago.

I wait until I'm on the bus before I open the envelope. Inside, I find a twenty-dollar bill and a little piece of paper with a quote in my mother's messy handwriting that reads: "Life is about not knowing, having to change, taking the moment and making the best of it . . . Delicious ambiguity." She *loves* this Gilda Radner quote. It helps me relax. Delicious ambiguity, indeed. I fold up the note and put it in my wallet.

When I get to D.C., I find out that Baxter's birthday party has been cancelled. He's come down with a bad cold and can't be around people. Because I had reserved the whole day to spend with C Street, I still walk there from the bus stop. My other neighbors want to catch up, with or without the cake and clowns.

As my feet touch the Capitol Hill sidewalk, I feel overwhelmed being back. This city and the streets leading up to our old house take me through a journey of extreme emotions: our house-hunting and anticipation of moving in together, the isolation I felt during the early days, the deliverance of marching toward Eastern Market to make my first home-cooked meals, and the long walks looking for answers when our emotional warfare made it too hard to think straight. Washington is where I thought we'd have it all, but then decided it couldn't be. Was I wrong about both?

When I turn the corner and see our pretty brownstone, a lump grows in my throat. I am transported back to the day I pulled up, almost three years ago, with butterflies in my stomach and joy in my eyes, barely turning off the car before Chef swooped me off my feet and carried me through the front door. I ran around the house, with my hands flung in the air and my legs practically off the ground, screaming like a maniac, "This is ours?! This is *ours*?!" The scene plays in my head like an old projected movie—gritty, old-fashioned, full of depth. So many happy memories rush to my mind as my chest pounds just thinking of Chef.

But then I see that new tenants have cleared out our garden, which makes me feel suddenly queasy. All the flourishing herbs

I once helplessly turned to when cooking scared me so much; the brotherhood of bold yellow and deep orange tomato plants, which we'd water early in the morning and late at night with such vigilance; and the red and green peppers, so crunchy and easy to care for. Here was a testimony to all of Chef's hard work and industriousness and all of my daily devotion, just ripped up, washed away, and replaced with shitty dirt, dead leaves, and cigarette butts.

Our electric green bike is gone, and I remember that Chef told me someone stole it from our front lawn after I moved out. He was so sad that day. A Subaru hatchback with an Obama bobblehead on the dashboard has replaced our beautiful, bird-crapped, and busted-up Jeep that was cluttered with discarded sunglasses, broken flip-flops, emergency picnic blankets, and grocery bags of barbecue potato chips and semisweet chocolate chips. (The poor car even croaked a few weeks back.)

No matter how hard I look, the divine spark no longer exists on the corner of the nation's capital, where two kids in love once shared all their dinners and all their thoughts, who slept in the same interwoven position every night and woke up to bad coffee and rushed kisses every morning. I'm frozen as I stare at the house. Our home was really all we had. As if the soul of the brownstone could read my lips, I quietly whisper, "I'm so sorry I left you." *Why am I doing this to myself?*

Before I get too overwrought with emotion, Maeve and Ronan see me from their big bay window. I can hear them from across the street: "Miss Alyssa is here! Miss Alyssa is here!" So I pull myself together and walk ahead. The moment Joe and Allison open the door, the kids are cheering, and then soon they're crawling up and down me, clinging to my every limb. Allison apologizes, but I tell her it's exactly what I need. First things first, they want to know what I've brought them. So I pull out the "FABULOUS" necklace and put it on Maeve, who's now four. "What does 'fabulous' mean?" she asks Allison. "It means 'Miss Alyssa,'" she says, smiling at me. I've got one child on my shoulders and another in my arms, and I'd keep it like that forever if I could. They want to know, "Where's Mister Chef? Where's Mister Chef?" Joe, Allison, and I say together, "Working!" We all laugh.

I spend the day hopping from door to door to all my old neighbors, telling everyone about my latest interview adventures. They want every little detail—who's nice, who's normal, who's anorexic, who's an alcoholic, and who's doing whom. Allison and Joe urge me to get on the Howard Stern show (our mutual guilty pleasure) and I tell them that his wife spins at Soul Cycle. Laura and Mike are vying for a C Street cooking show. And Kathe and Jody are of course convinced Oprah's new TV network needs a little *Apron Anxiety.* They all read my blog and closely follow my hot dates and ups and downs, and sitting in their presence, I feel like no one could believe in me more.

At the end of the long day, I put three houses of young children to bed, and Allison drives me ten blocks away to Chef's new place, which sits inside a big converted warehouse on H Street, the hipster section of Capitol Hill. He's at a hockey game with huge investors—an event he couldn't get out of and told me about weeks ago. Knowing I'd arrive before him, he's hidden a key for me under the building's doormat. I can tell that Allison thinks he's being inhospitable—all the women on the block have witnessed us at our absolute worst and are instinctively protective of my feelings—but letting myself in the door doesn't bother me. I'm not his to pamper; he's not mine to judge.

Once inside the main entrance, I find the door to his loft is unlocked, naturally. My ex, the eternal free spirit. Slowly entering, I cannot believe my eyes. It's the coolest apartment

I've ever seen, including Christopher Wagner's. The ceilings are seventeen feet high, the kitchen is stupendous and elevated like a concert stage, the pipes are raw, the windows are endless, and half the walls are covered in chalkboards. The bathroom boasts a colossal claw-foot tub, along with a urinal and a bidet—and craziest of all, it has no door. A small part of me takes pleasure in knowing that the girls he brings home will have to publicly wipe themselves. Or worse.

I drop my bags and study his blackboards. Within the fifty-foot circumference of chicken scratch, graffiti art, and tic-tac-toe, the first thing I notice is the small contingency of girly drawings of hearts and lips, with names like "Kari" and "Cassidy" written in round, bubbly purple cursive. Ugh. I never liked girls with that kind of teenybopper penmanship. *Whatever.* I see other notes from his family and friends, gangster lyrics from old-school hip-hop songs, a scoreboard for upcoming Ultimate Fighting Championship matches, some inside jokes that I don't understand, and a to-do list:

Pickles
Plan safari to South Africa
Toilet paper
Good Morning America segment
Find wallet
Watch *Whale Wars*

Laughing out loud, all I can think about is how damn adorable he can be. The strangeness of the situation is temporarily stunted by my everlasting crush on him, despite all that we've been through.

I love it.

Nothing changes.

However . . .

There is no room for me on that blackboard.

I make myself a cup of tea to calm the nerves that have snuck up on me with that last revelation. Just as I have made my own friends, and pushed ahead on my own path, so has he. But his new life is literally spelled out here. It's something I wasn't prepared for, even in rainbow chalk. Enhancing the *in-your-face* experience, seeing our possessions from C Street inside these new, unfamiliar digs is rattling. Every dresser, bar stool, oil painting, and pillowcase once echoed of such hope. I had shopped and agonized over every little design detail that now girls who dot their "i's" with hearts get to enjoy. I remind myself, over and over, that it's just stuff.

The silence of the empty loft intertwined with all these awakenings makes me feel more vulnerable than I ever expected, so I take out my computer and play the National to calm down. I'd happily lose myself in the kitchen if he had anything in his fridge but cider beer (*since when does he drink that?*). I text Chef that I'm sort of freaking out. He texts back, "Take a bath, Lyssie. Be home soon."

There are no soaps or suds, so I soak myself in scorching hot and clear bathwater, listening to my music, and reminding myself that I am grounded and poised, that I'm the special one, and that I've come too far to fall apart now. When he walks in the door at ten o'clock, exactly when he said he would, I am fresh out of the bath. My hair is wet and brushed and I'm wearing a pair of fuzzy, green sweatpants that we always used to fight for at night.

"You're here! My love is here! My Lys is here!" he says lifting me up in his arms and spinning me around. He inhales the scent of my just-scrubbed-and-lotioned body, like it's his secret field of lavender, the way he would every night back when things were nice. He looks handsome as always, my guy. A little rounder in the stomach, a little harder in the eyes, but he's gorgeous, as he always has been. If only we could freeze-frame this moment! Chef makes sure to tell me that he rented the loft knowing how much I'd love the bathtub. "Yeah, yeah," I say. "Go erase those stupid girls' names."

It's just before midnight, and we are both in need of food.

"How do you have *nothing* to eat?"

"Because you always took care of that for me."

"I did?" I know I'm fishing, but it feels so good to hear.

We make our old trip to 7-Eleven, walking just a few blocks away, down the streetlamp-lit Maryland Avenue, holding hands, and I fill him in on the C Street gossip from the day. At the store, I grab a loaf of Wonder Bread, a stick of butter, and some sliced American cheese; he gathers a pint of coffee ice cream and a six-pack of Coke. "Voilà, the celebrity chef and the food writer," I say, as he kisses my cheek at the checkout counter. He looks so happy. We both do. The Ethiopian cashier says it's lovely to see us again.

We stay up till four o'clock, lying on the couch, talking, kissing, and watching our favorite TV shows. Just before I allow myself too much happiness, I bring up Boston. A small part of me thinks he might have recalibrated things so that he could, in fact, make the trip with me, but that didn't happen. Before anything erupts, we wisely switch gears. We watch the first few episodes of the new season of *American Idol,* rewinding and playing back our favorite high points of the performances. We eat several rounds of grilled-cheese sandwiches, taking turns at the stove. He tells me for the hundredth time that the secret is to cook them longer, but over lower heat. "Oui, Chef," I say. "But in the future, I prefer to work with Comté more than Kraft Singles, okay?"

Sometime around six o'clock in the morning, I fall asleep on his lap, and when I wake up around noon, we're both in his bed. His alarm, his phone, and his e-mails are going off, and if he doesn't get his ass to work for the lunch rush, I know that soon the doorbell will be ringing, too. I remember this. When he gets out of his under-a-minute shower, I blast that song "Jai Ho" from *Slumdog Millionaire* and make him dance until his towel falls off. We crack up laughing. With all the fighting, I had forgotten about our magnificent morning dance parties. The best memories had dissolved first.

He gets dressed against the clock, forgoing the toothbrush, and admits that he feels bad that he'll be gone all day. He doesn't have to explain himself. Not anymore. Before he bolts, he asks if he should make us a dinner reservation at one of D.C.'s new restaurants. I know he means well, and that he's striving to be on his best behavior, but I also know that in all likelihood, he'll get too busy to book us a table, or won't make it out on time. I don't want to be disappointed, or for him to feel like he's failed us. That part of our story has played itself out.

"No, sweetie," I say. "I'll cook."

When he leaves for work, I make a pot of coffee and dive right into his cookbooks. I remember touching them for the first time with such trepidation. Now, it's like seeing old friends. I contemplate knocking his socks off. Maybe I'll try a whole fish? A French onion soup? Some braised oxtail? My mother's brisket? And for dessert, all modesty aside, I'm capable of anything! A three-layer fondant cake? Homemade cannolis? As I busily mix and match recipes, I crack the windows for some fresh air. A neighbor next door is practicing the violin and it sounds so pretty. Standing in my bra and underwear, I look outside and to the sky. It's the end of May and already quite muggy out. It feels like a thunderstorm is buffering in the air. I stretch out on the olive green rug (which once took me six weeks to find) and notice that the loft could use some calla lilies. And then I hear the sudden pitter-patter on the window ledge and realize exactly what I need to make: Rainy Day Rigatoni, from our Greece trip. *Bellissimo.* I know this recipe by heart, probably because it lives there.

As I prepare to fetch my ingredients, I decide to take the dish a little further, to show some new moves, with a fresh topping of sheepshead ricotta cheese that I'll mix with olive oil and sprigs of mint. If I make enough, we can first put it on some toasted crostini, drizzled with the superb honey that we smuggled into the United States directly from a "bee lady" in Greece. (The bottle was too sticky to move to New York with me, so Chef has had full custody.) I decide against making my own pasta even though I'm up for the challenge—but why deal with the mess when we have the pasta man at Eastern Market? Tonight is about relaxation. Life, and dinner, must go easy on us.

Chef has a couple Heath Bars on the counter, so for dessert, I devise a plan to make a chocolate Health Bar trifle. It's a brainless concoction, an act of "baking down," but so what? Chef has also had custody of our wide, voluptuous, big-boned glass trifle bowl, and I've missed her.

The menu is perfect: Rainy Day Rigatoni and the Simple Trifle. We'll sit crisscrossed on the couch, sharing one big bowl of pasta, then an even bigger bowl of trifle, our feet entangled, our phones off, and enjoy the remaining back-to-back episodes of *American Idol.* Oh la la.

I take the twenty-minute walk over to Eastern Market through the pretty rows of brownstones and cherry-blossom trees. The rain has pulled back, but it's dark and moody—the weather of dewy skin and frizzy hair. I am wearing one of Chef's sweatshirts over my tank top and shorts—the hood smells like French fries, earth, hustle, and *him*. I pull it to my face and deeply inhale, the way he did with my body straight from the bath last night.

At an old bookstore that I stumble past, I see a framed quote in the window from *Wuthering Heights:* "Whatever our souls are made of, his and mine are the same." I take a picture to remember the words, but then I erase the image from my phone. It's been a long, hard, and painful ride in realizing that love is not enough. Why toy with something that makes me believe that maybe it is? Instead, I keep his broken Boston promise in the forefront of my mind. I would Super Glue it there if I could. *Because that's our truth.*

But damnit, I can't help myself. Shuffling my feet through sticks and petals, I'm drifting in and out of conversations with myself that go something like:

"Just stay."

"Why? To have a few weeks of bliss and then another atrocious breakup?"

"Maybe we're meant to be. . . ."

"You were miserable."

"But all relationships are hard."

"It didn't work before and it won't work now."

When I first moved to D.C., Chef sent me to Eastern Market to buy us some chicken breasts, but as soon as I walked into the souklike room, I was so discombobulated by the food selections that I felt weak and faint, walking home defeated and empty-handed, except for a lemonade I bought from some kid's stand. A sad sight! Almost three years and dozens of trips to the market later, being among the creameries and potato sacks is second nature.

I swiftly purchase my ingredients from the pasta man, the cheesemonger, the butcher, and the Chinese produce lady. I gather little bundles of rosemary, oregano, and thyme. I tell her that I recently read in a book that according to Chinese superstition, cutting your noodles symbolizes cutting your life span. She nods her head and throws in a parsnip. I ask if she happens to have sage, and she throws that in, too. Walking home with my market bag, I stop by a local bakery to buy some brownies for the trifle, and I try to stop talking to myself. Instead, I vow to stay in the moment and enjoy making us dinner. *Because there will come a day when he won't be mine to feed.*

After unloading the groceries and prepping the sauce, I go through all the e-mails I've ignored over the past two days. (I am in the moment, but the moment *is* 2011.)

New York magazine has a full-time job opening at *Grub Street* that they want to discuss. I'm sure they're only informing me of this as some type of courtesy, knowing how much I love freelancing for them. But there's no way they'd *really* consider me. Would they?

A local news channel is looking to interview some food bloggers about the state of the Manhattan restaurant scene. "Stagnant or spectacular? You tell us," writes the producer.

Liz at *People* wants to take me to a private Robert Pattinson premiere party: "Let's dress up and drink champagne, chérie."

A friend had submitted my name to attend a press trip through the Italian countryside, exploring the wineries and farmlands of Siena, Tuscany. Finally, a confirmation note that I'm officially in!

My sister met a doctor. My mother found *A Streetcar Named Desire* for a quarter. My father dropped off mail and stuck some banana bread in my freezer.

Alexi is wondering what I'm doing on Monday night.

And the best news of all: Beth is pregnant. They decided to try on New Year's Eve. "We left your party filled with so much love, that we decided it was time!"

I write to everyone promising to be back in New York soon. Then I book a return ticket for tomorrow.

Turning off my e-mail, I tie on the apron and crank up "Rolling in the Deep" by Adele. It's my new favorite song and I put it on repeat. Chopping my onions and eggplant, I dice to the beat. En route to the olive oil, I find a rhythm to my step. Tearing off the rosemary and thyme, I'm making up the lyrics and belting out the words. Reaching for the crushed tomatoes, I stick out my ass and swirl my hips. Flipping on the stove top, I shimmy my shoulders and swing my head. I am cooking without a recipe, singing without the words, and dancing badly by myself.

As the sauce simmers, I throw together the trifle, layering the brownies, Cool Whip, crumbled-up Heath Bar, and sliced strawberries. It's so processed and wrong . . . yet right! I cover the top with a paper napkin and stick the fat lady in the fridge.

Just like the old days, Chef texts me a "15-minute warning," though, surprisingly, it's only 8:00 p.m. But I'm ready when he is. The sauce has been cooking for several hours; the salted water for the rigatoni is boiling. The apartment smells like the best trattoria in Europe. There's no table to set because that's never been our style, but I light a few candles and scatter them around all our old stuff, and on our sophisticated centerpiece, otherwise known as a flat-screen television.

All I have to do now is take off my apron, which hasn't really prevented me from splattering sauce everywhere, including on my earlobes. Sure, it's a simple pasta, and he's no longer my fiancé, and by this time tomorrow I'll be back in New York City, but as I ruffle through what's left of my clean clothes, I just *have* to put on the nude minidress.

When a wide-eyed Chef opens the door to his apartment, he doesn't know what to breathe in first. He excitedly peeks at the sauce, and then under my dress. It never took much to wow him. I tell him to get comfy and prepare *Idol* as I plate our dinner. First the rigatoni, then the sauce, then the ricotta, and then the mint. The smell! The nostalgia! It's exactly the effect that food should have. We dim the lights and dig in. We both take seconds and thirds, swallowing huge forkfuls, and wiping each other's faces.

Then we make tea and turn our attention to the trifle. It's so naughty and so divine, and of course, we both end up with it smeared all over our faces.

If this night were a snapshot of our real life together, I would never have left the next day. I would have stayed in that sexy loft with my scruffy chef until we were both a hundred years old.

But after a while, you learn that just because you can curl up on a couch, share a bowl of perfection, watch some Ryan Seacrest, and feel nothing but primal love and lust, it doesn't mean love will endure when real life enters your domain.

You learn that life is bigger than a splendid kitchen, and a claw-foot bathtub, and a concert violinist playing Tchaikovsky next door. Although that is quite wonderful, I have to say.

You learn that happiness is yours to find, whether it's through a nonwedding on a borrowed rooftop or a sing-along with wackos in Washington Square Park.

And even if you'll never understand why anyone would want bacon in their ice cream or vinegar on their watermelon, you learn that you can still pull up a chair to the food universe, because there's really room for everyone. Even if you order gnarly chicken curry at a glittery French café.

You learn that there's nothing bad about feeling safe and there's everything good about inner stillness; and above all, just because you're an extraordinary person who deserves extraordinary love, it can't come at the expense of everything else that makes you whole.

The next day, Chef's alarm goes off at the crack of dawn. He is flying somewhere for a TV shoot and the car is picking him up at 5:30. I pretend to be asleep, ignoring him while he rushes to get dressed. We do not need another hard good-bye. He kisses my forehead and whispers, "You don't have to go back to New York, Lyssie, my love." I playfully pull the sheets over my head, mumbling that it's way too early and to leave me alone. Then I cry quietly into the mattress. He knows to exit before we both come undone.

When he's gone, I fall in and out of sleep for a few more hours. Around eleven o'clock, I get out of bed and start cleaning up a little. I shake the crumbs off my apron, wash our dirty dishes from last night, and pile up the cookbooks. All of these seemingly inconsequential kitchen-related objects have so much meaning. They remind me of where I've been and where I'm going.

My culinary journey has, of course, turned into so much more than a love story. But sometimes I wonder if I'm *still* in the kitchen as a way of keeping my connection to Chef alive. But even if he *is* at the seed of every dish I'll ever make, and cooking *is* my way of feeling close to him without actually being with him, I can live with that. After all, everyone cooks for matters of the heart. We're all in the kitchen because it fulfills a longing inside, whether it's for grace, survival, a renewed sense of self, or just the thrill of it all—these are the stories that get us there, keep us there, or sometimes take us away. But without the people who have moved us, pushed us, left us, maybe even hurt us, then really, it's only food.

I call a car service to pick me up at noon, and just before it arrives, I take a piece of chalk to the blackboard and make him a new to-do list:

Buy bubble bath
Eat leftovers
Dance daily
Love hard
Lock your front door

The taxi is beeping. My bags are packed. I gaze back at this glorious space with all his chef coats and parking tickets and remains of *us*. I float to the kitchen, to the wooden spoon I once held like a convict and the cake plate I'd bring to our stoop. And then I grab the brown paper bag with the fresh rosemary, oregano, thyme, and sage, and the hoodie that smells like pommes frites, and I go home to *everyone*.

Rainy Day Rigatoni

SERVES 6

It drives me crazy when chefs say things during food demos like, "This dish is made with love." That doesn't help beginner cooks like me at all, and it just sounds fake. However, this pasta, adapted from Giulia Melucci's book I Loved, I Lost, I Made Spaghetti *(Grand Central Publishing, 2009),* truly is *made with love. At least for me. Chef and I both make Rainy Day Rigatoni in our respective homes now, and we always call and text pictures in the process. I hope we can do that forever. On a less melodramatic note, this sauce works well with any pasta and is delicious hot or cold. Even though the ricotta cheese topping isn't essential to the meal's success, it's worth making just to have in the fridge for the next day—or to serve as an appetizer with grilled bread and a drizzle of honey.*

Ricotta topping

2 cups sheep's-milk ricotta
1 cup whole milk
1 teaspoon fine sea salt
1 teaspoon coarse sea salt
1 teaspoon coarsely ground black pepper
1 teaspoon fresh thyme leaves
1 tablespoon dried oregano, on the branch if possible
2 to 3 tablespoons extra-virgin olive oil

Rigatoni

3 tablespoons extra-virgin olive oil, plus more for finishing
½ medium yellow onion, chopped
Pinch of hot pepper flakes
1 large eggplant, unpeeled, cut into ½-inch cubes
2 teaspoons salt, plus more for the pasta water
One 28-ounce can crushed tomatoes
¼ cup red wine
1 tablespoon sugar

1 pound rigatoni

1 cup fresh basil leaves, torn

Grated Parmigiano-Reggiano for garnish

To make the ricotta topping: Beat the ricotta and milk together in the bowl of a stand mixer fitted with the paddle attachment (or in a medium mixing bowl with a whisk) until the mixture is light and fluffy. Add the fine sea salt and mix well.

Place the mixture in a serving bowl. Generously sprinkle the coarse salt, pepper, thyme, and oregano over the top. Drizzle with oil and refrigerate.

To make the rigatoni: Heat the oil in a large skillet over medium heat. Add the onion and pepper flakes and sauté until the onion is almost translucent. Add the eggplant and 1 teaspoon of salt and cook for 20 minutes, allowing the eggplant to get a little brown, moving it around with a spoon. Then add the tomatoes, wine, sugar, and the remaining 1 teaspoon of salt. Stir often. Cook for 50 to 60 minutes, until the eggplant is very soft.

Bring a large pot of water to boil, throw in a handful of salt (about 3 tablespoons), and cook the rigatoni according to the package instructions. Drain the pasta, then return it to its pot. Add the sauce from the skillet into the pot, on top of the pasta, mixing everything together. Add a dash of oil, and most of the torn basil leaves. Ladle into bowls and garnish with the remaining basil leaves and Parmigiano-Reggiano. Top it off with a scoop of the ricotta topping. Serve hot.

Enjoy the moment.

The Simple Trifle

SERVES 10 TO 12

This trifle might be embarrassingly easy to assemble, and filled with culinary taboos, but to me, it's a portrait of opulence. The angelic white Cool Whip against the blasphemous candy bars? Screw the rules! Of course, you can make everything from scratch, but don't beat yourself up if there's no time, or if your hungry ex-lover is coming home soon and life is difficult enough. Sometimes you just have to do the best you can with what you have. Which is, of course, better than doing nothing at all.

- 1 batch cooled Supernatural Brownies for Breakups and Breakdowns (page 134), or brownies from 1 box prepared mix (per package instructions)
- chocolate pudding from 1 box prepared mix (per package directions)
- 1½ (8-ounce) tubs of Cool Whip
- 5 Heath Bars, crushed, 1 reserved for topping
- 1 carton fresh raspberries, washed and patted dry

Break up the brownies into small pieces.

In a large trifle bowl or clear glass serving bowl, make a layer with one-third of the brownie crumbles. Create another layer with one-third of the pudding mixture, then a third layer with one-third of the Heath Bar bits. Top with a generous layer of Cool Whip. Dot the Cool Whip with one-third of the raspberries. Repeat the layers twice and top with the remaining Heath Bar crumbles and raspberries, if any are left (or save one raspberry for the center).

Basically, just get everything in there; it might not be perfect, but it will be beautiful.

Epilogue

Back when my friend Anzo acted as my "agent," negotiating deals with horny high-school lacrosse players on the topic of seeing (but "no touching!") the architecture of my upper body, as we parked our parents' station wagons on dark cul de sacs and damp swamplands, she always ended the night by saying that when I became "a famous New York writer" she was going to buy me my first black leather jacket.

Fifteen years later, when I show up in Boston for the fundraiser to celebrate Jean's life, a day after accepting a full-time job as the "New York Editor" for *New York* magazine's *Grub Street,* she has the jacket waiting for me wrapped, naturally, in a patchwork of soft-core porn. The note reads, "You were never too cool for us, but *always* too cool for Ruby Tuesday's. Congrats on the dream job!!!"

That night, about fifty people from high school show up at Lord Bryant Marengo's Saloon, a quirky old bar and grill, gleaming with framed photographs of Jean, from the day she was born to her twenty-fourth, and last, birthday. Kates and Court have assembled incredible collages of our childhood memories, too, everyone so young and hopeful. We're all in our thirties now, and I think I am the only woman in the room who's not pregnant, in between pregnancies, or anything even close. But despite the baby bumps, husband drama, and mortgage migraines, or utter lack thereof, it's really like nothing has changed. I feel every bit as close to the magical people in that room as I did on the day we graduated from high school in 1995 (when naturally, I went naked under my graduation robe—just like my mother did twenty years prior).

When everyone has arrived, and the hugging and life debriefing mellows out, Kates—who married her high-school sweetheart, became one of Boston's best nurses, and has two extraordinarily delicious young daughters—thanks everyone for coming. She asks us to raise our glasses, which no one from my big-hearted hometown will ever struggle to do, and begins, "Someone once said that friendship doubles our joy and divides our grief. . . ." And so begins our night of extreme love and sorrow.

We laugh, drink, catch up, and cry, and laugh, drink, catch up, and cry some more. No one in the room knows or cares about the restaurants I've been going to, or the celebrity chefs I've cooked with, or that my new job is probably the best thing to ever happen to my professional identity. They just want to make sure I'm happy. "Not all the time, but definitely most of the time," I say, telling the absolute truth.

It's a hard night to begin with, and in a perfect world, Chef or someone else I love as much as I do him would be there to charm my friends, refresh our drinks, and wipe away my tears. But then again, if life was fair, we wouldn't be there in the first place, softly touching Punky Rogér's 9/11 memorial pin instead of her plush Donna Karan cashmere.

Eventually Kates turns our attention to a slide show, set to

"Son of a Preacher Man" and "Forever Young" and all the other songs we used to blast over and over on the radio while cruising around town, so innocent and immortal. Jean's pretty face flashes in each image, and it's heartbreaking, but we also have to laugh. I had the bushiest eyebrows and the most wannabe-bohemian wardrobe. My friends, too, were ridiculously dressed, with blotchy pink faces and ladybug turtlenecks. How outrageously overconfident we were for small-town teenagers who loved our parents, passing notes and chasing boys.

But I don't see just us. I see inside us. I see a frisky fifteen-year-old in a polyester halter-top who always knew that an antiseptic future was out of the question and couldn't wait to take a gamble on the universe. The girl I see in me? God, she would delight in knowing that in twenty years, she'd still be a little different from everyone else in the room; that her life would be lush with great love and footloose affairs; that at some point she would live, *live abundantly,* in the hills and frills of Hollywood and under the bright sparks of the Brooklyn Bridge. If teenage-me knew that one day she'd look pain in the face, fame in the eye, and that her circle of friends would be as good and loyal as mine, she'd probably toss her hair, put on her Walkman, and say, "Well, obviously."

But what would *she* make of my new life as an epicure? She'd definitely think it was cool that I conquered something so uncomfortable, especially since I'm a better version of myself because of it. But she wouldn't pay too much attention to my tales of Manchego and marzipan, because, as she might say: *The problem with food is that it gets eaten; it goes away. What you're left with when it's gone is so much more interesting.* Then she'd probably switch the subject to the only thing she'd really care about: Mom, Dad, and Rach. And I'd tell her, "They're all happy and healthy," and that our signature dish is still laughter, extra well done.

The slide show flickers to an image of Jean, sitting with her boom box under a weeping willow tree in her big backyard. The whole room stares, *still* in awe of her carefree effervescence. She was only herself. I make eye contact with Anzo, and through her tears, she gives me a wink. Kates and Court are standing, but barely, close to their own handkerchief-clutching moms, who are Punky's girlfriends, and two of my favorite people. The rest of us are holding hands, rubbing backs, taking care. And I think how the women in my life, in this room, in my family, and up in heaven are my symphony, my Riviera, my black, pearly caviar, and I worship them.

When the slide show ends, just after midnight, our eyes are burning and our stomachs are grumbling from six hours of alcohol with only a few trays of soggy sliders festering under heat lamps. Much of the crowd has gone home, including the Rogérs, who had to leave early for a very good reason: their son and daughter-in-law are about to give birth to a little girl, whom they are naming Jean Rogér. "You give your folks and little Rach our love, okay?" Punky says, holding my face and kissing my forehead, on her way out. "And find yourself a nice guy already, goddamnit."

About ten of us remain at the party. I tell Kates to replay the fifteen-minute slide show, which I already know my sappy, sloshed friends will want to watch again and again. Then I slip away to a twenty-four-hour grocery store down the street.

As quickly as I can, I crisscross through the aisles. It really doesn't matter what I make or how I make it, as long as it tastes good. I grab a few hearty loaves of bread studded with sunflower kernels and poppy seeds, some extra-crunchy peanut butter, and a pretty jar of raspberry jam—the color of rubies. I then toss into my basket a few bags of tortilla chips, mangos, onions, avocados, lime, and mint—just enough ingredients for a fresh mango salsa. For something sweet, I decide on vanilla ice cream, some dark chocolate morsels, and a bag of frozen blueberries that I'll quickly heat up for a compote topping. On my way out, I see that Devil Dogs are on sale.

Running back to the party with my brown paper bags, in my black leather jacket, I glide past the projector, which is repeating the slide show yet again, and into the saloon's vacant kitchen. I hurriedly put my blueberries on the stove top, with equal parts sugar and water, and heat things up, stirring often, watching for the berries to burst into their zany juices.

On the side, I peel, pit, and cut the mango into totally incongruent cubes. I dice my avocado even more disobediently, taking a moment to admire its wonderfully ripe and retro chartreuse shade. I chop the yellow onion eagerly and unmeticulously, careful to keep my fingertips. When it starts to sting my eyes so badly that I can't see straight, I shove half a loaf of bread in my mouth and keep it there, an old wives' tale that Chef once taught me and I never actually tried. It works! With wet, drooly sesame seeds sliding down my chin, simultaneously laughing and gagging, I finish the onions, whisk the salsa ingredients together, and add some lime juice and salt. And voilà.

Cleaning myself up, I move on. I pour the bags of chips into a streaked, silver punch bowl, swirl together our disheveled PB&J sandwiches (which could never masquerade as tartines), and scoop the dripping generic ice cream, splashed in cheapo chocolate, into beer mugs and cognac glasses. The blueberry compote is ready, and I serve it alongside in a flower vase with a ladle.

There are no crystal fleur-de-lis dangling from the stems of my glassware, no artisanal honey drizzled into the nonorganic peanut butter, no edible dandelions garnishing the clunky salsa, no high art in the Tostitos. The meal is messy, crazy, uncouth, and full of more meaning than anything I have ever made.

And then, I feed my friends.

ACKNOWLEDGMENTS

When I was six years old, I wrote a three-paragraph memoir, ending with the following promise to myself, *"One day, I'm gonna move to Greenitch Vilage and be a wrighter."*

Soon thereafter, my parents and sister became my first editors for the scribbled stories in turquoise crayons that we mailed to the *New York Times* for fun. Then others, for real. All along, my aunts, uncles, and cousins made me feel beautiful, important, and writerly, as I grew from a kid to a teenager to a thirty-something. A million thank-yous to all of them. Especially to my mother's mom, Dorothy Pava. No one has a family as loving as mine.

But eventually, I had to bring in the big guns.

My eternal gratitude goes to Pilar Queen at McCormick & Williams, who, while inhaling macaroni and cheese at City Bakery, said that I had a book in me and then became my agent and confidante. If it were up to me, I'd consult with you before every first kiss, sit-up, and midnight snack.

Also, to the great David McCormick, who graciously let me talk his ear off before his first cup of coffee. Sorry I'm so loopy around you—extremely dignified people just have that effect on me.

I owe so much to Emily Takoudes, my editor, who kindly and generously guided me through mountains of self-doubt and tough times without ever losing her patience. I've thoroughly enjoyed being your most unprofessional author, telling you way too much information, and stalking you as an editor and friend for life. Not to mention the bragging rights included!

Angelin Borsics, thank you so much for all the warm encouragement and spot-on edits. And to Emily's assistant, Hilary Sims, bless your heart for tying up so many loose ends. How lucky was I to have you both?

To all my friends from Longmeadow, New York, D.C., and L.A., you can finally stop saying, "You need to write a book about this shit." I live for you guys; I mean it. Shelley gets first dibs on who should play her in the movie though.

A huge thanks to Alan Sytsma at *Grub Street* for giving me a shot, even after I told him that the *real me* would rather eat dinner on a picnic blanket than at Per Se. And to my former colleagues at the various magazines, thanks for letting me stick around for all of the glamour and none of the grit. Especially Liz McNeil, who has provided me with work and wisdom at the best and worst of times.

Rachel Shelasky, my exquisite sister, gets a second shout-out because she's also a professional research editor and helped me enormously with nitpicky details that would have otherwise ruined my life. Rach, I love you so much.

To all the men I have loved hard or liked briefly, don't be mad; I made you all sound really hot.

And to Chef, whose heart is of the purest kind: You helped me more than *anyone* with the *Apron Anxiety* blog and book. Thank you forever and ever. Now finish up those potato chips; this is the final page.